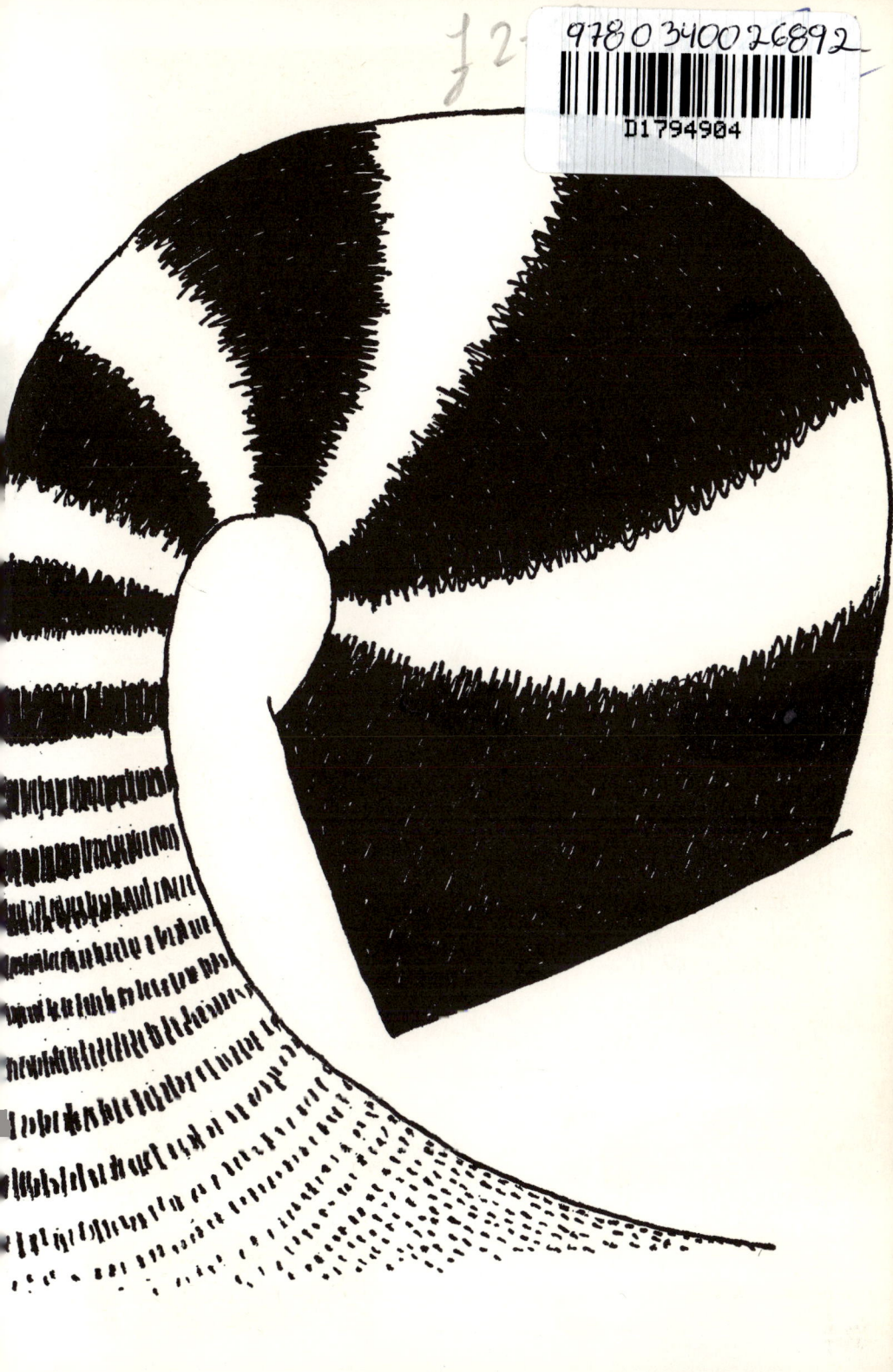

GOOD,
GOD AND MAN

By the same author:

Travel and general books:

    THEY DIDN'T MEAN TO KILL
    LET'S LOOK AT AMERICA
    ROUND THE WORLD IN 465 DAYS
    OPTIMISTS IN AFRICA

Mystery stories including those about Roger West, Gideon, The Toff, The Baron, Dr. Palfrey, Dr. Cellini and Patrick Dawlish.

GOOD, GOD AND MAN

An Outline of the Philosophy of
SELF-ISM

by

JOHN CREASEY

with illustrations by
Martin Creasey

HODDER AND STOUGHTON

"It might be a good idea during this Christmas season to remind ourselves about the nature of Men . . . and Man. Men are sometimes cruel, but Man is kind. Men are sometimes greedy, but Man is generous. Men are mortal, but Man is immortal. And I believe along with Faulkner that Man will do more than survive, he will prevail."

(ADLAI STEVENSON,
Christmas Week telecast 1962)

CONTENTS

ACKNOWLEDGMENTS

IN THE writing and preparation of this book many people helped, some already friends, others whom I knew – at first – only casually.

I am grateful indeed to them all.

To Olga Stringfellow I owe more than I can possibly say. She sparked so many ideas and nourished them out of the rare quality of her mind. Quick to see exactly what I was striving to say, she helped me time and time again to greater lucidity and pointed out countless implications which I had not perceived but which had real significance. Perhaps the greatest help she gave was in her absolute belief in the theme and her whole-hearted dedication to it.

Robin Denniston, my editor, encouraged me greatly, perhaps most of all by believing that a writer in one sphere could and should be encouraged to write in another. Professor J. H. Fremlin read the whole book and gave me a penetrating analysis which was invaluable in revision, while Leo Harris read and probed unceasingly on points of logic, fact and detail. And Lynette Howis helped from first to last with the single-minded devotion and untiring energy with which she works on book after book.

I would also like to thank the following: Gibbs Proprietaries Ltd. for permission to quote from their publication about the making of toothpaste; the *New York Times* for permission to quote the open letter to President Johnson; to the *Daily Mail* for permission to quote from several articles; and to the *Week-end Telegraph* for permission to quote the article *The Slumless City* by Ian Ball.

If ever I needed final proof of my dependence on the help and goodwill of others, writing *Good, God and Man* provided it absolutely.

JOHN CREASEY

Chapter 1

IDEALISM AND REALISM

How much effective influence have moral philosophy and ethical systems had on human behaviour over the centuries?

In seeking to answer this question through the years, I have been deeply and increasingly disturbed by the conclusions forced remorselessly upon me. The religious philosophies, although mostly so good in themselves, are nearly all inconsistent with one another, while most are unhappily split by sects and internal doctrinal differences. Is it even remotely possible, I ask myself, for any existing religion to satisfy all mankind as the world is today, when there are nearly as many different religion-based codes of behaviour as there are religions?

The non-religious philosophies appear to suffer from much the same kind of restrictive barrier. Although the great philosophers, from Aristotle to Bertrand Russell, have searched their minds and spoken them – some obscurely, some lucidly – it has usually been to pronounce upon the society or mankind of their own day, or to challenge or even refute some other, earlier philosopher. There has been no successful revolutionary philosophy in the way that there have been revolutions in political, social, industrial and religious affairs. Philosophies explain or attempt to explain things as they are, attempt even to explain why they are, but none has ever been able to satisfy man's yearning to know with certainty what ought to be; to be told unequivocally and with lucid simplicity how he must behave if he aspires to a full and happy life.

Yet we know that man is in desperate want – indeed, in fundamental need – of such a code of behaviour, and is forever searching for it.

Some of the most profound philosophical pronouncements have been understood *only* by fellow philosophers or students of philosophy, and I wonder uneasily how much has been intelligible to the man in the street, particularly to any who lack a classical education. A considerable degree of advanced academic education is often needed if one is even partly to comprehend the normal parlance of philosophers and sages, intellectuals and scholars.

11

Good, God and Man

It seems to me that comparatively few do fully understand this language and, consequently, comparatively few of us even begin to understand what the philosophers are saying. Whether or not they themselves always know what they mean, there is certainly considerable discrepancy and misunderstanding between them. Bertrand Russell is particularly passionate in defending their right to change of view and attitude, arguing that a mind which will not change is a mind which cannot (or does not) grow.

Obviously, there is much wisdom in this, but in philosophy, as in every aspect of living, there surely must be some unchanging fundamentals on which all arguments and philosophies can be based. No single fundamental appears to be common to all philosophies, however, for as soon as one philosophy is widely accepted, another can be quoted to refute it. Certainly no one has yet presented mankind with an infallible code of behaviour which will assuredly help *all* men of *all* races, nationalities, religions, social levels and stages of development, to live more happily.

The influence of philosophers on ordinary people – on Everyman – has, so far, been through distillation of thought. The deliberations and the conclusions of scholars and intellectuals, all of whom so clearly have the good of man and the search for truth at heart, have impregnated the minds of those who understand at least a part of what they say and who then distil a small proportion, which seeps through to the untutored or semi-tutored masses. Very little is *clearly* understood, however, even by the disciples of philosophers, hence we have a variety of interpretations, each in itself difficult to understand. It is hardly surprising that by the time confused and conflicting interpretations reach the man in the street, he can seldom have either a clear or a true understanding.

In spite of this, philosophers have always been able to, and still do, exert a great influence on life and thinking, even though offering little direct guidance (and benefit) to man in his day-to-day activities.

The first philosopher to condemn war was Socrates, and millions of ordinary people have followed him, yet war is still accepted by many in modern society as a cure for ills. Other philosophers throughout the centuries have doubtless between them examined and pronounced upon every aspect of human behaviour with equal sincerity. Yet can any be said to have actually offered us a guide for living? And is there any serious doubt that the greatest value of the communication of ideas –

of thought, of philosophical findings and beliefs: of all knowledge – is in its contribution to the long-term happiness of mankind?

A mother, *feeling* in anguish the loss of a son, is not comforted because centuries ago some philosopher thought that war should be outlawed, or because others think so today. Condemnation without constructive alternative is virtually worthless. The need has always been for a code of living acceptable to all men, which would render war unthinkable to any; yet we have had to wait for the coming of wars which no one can win, to see the tide begin to turn against war.

The main influences which have led to reforms have sprung from the emotions of grief and fear, not from cool, philosophical appraisal. I have an uneasy feeling that philosophers, like doctors, are influenced mostly by the ills of mankind as they exist, instead of the life or health of man as it should be. In medicine, however, there is a great deal of research into how health can be improved; in philosophy, there appears to be little research into how *life* can be improved. There may, as in the case of Bertrand Russell's latter-day anti-war writing and campaigning, be a passionate desire to end war, one of man's greatest afflictions. But has he really had any significant influence on affairs? And if he hasn't, could it be because he has not really approached it in the right way? What is needed, surely, is not a philosopher's attack on a particular evil but philosophical guidance on how to live so that *all* evil will wither and die.

Many will no doubt argue that only trained theologians, evangelists and religious leaders are really qualified to give us a guide to daily living. Most religious leaders certainly think this, and appear passionately to believe their own to be the only true and right way. Yet if the centuries in which religions have been born, flourished, died or become moribund can provide one unchallengeable lesson, it is surely that despite the missionary fervour of the Moslem and the Christian, despite the single-minded objectivity of the Buddhist and the tolerance of the Confucianist, no religion *has* offered the answer to every problem even of its own believers. And *no* religion has, or is ever likely to have, the answer to all the spiritual – let alone all the material – problems of *all* people *everywhere*.

The deeds, dogma, attitudes and thinking of certain Christian sects or groups, appal adherents of other Christian sects. The Inquisition and the Reformation have both passed into history without solving a single problem for the Christian Church or

13

for the world at large. Indeed, both movements created problems and schisms which have weakened Christianity to this day.

Undeniably, many human beings need religion desperately and are greatly helped by their differing beliefs – yet as undeniably one man's religion is often another man's heresy. Do we need any further proof that in religion as the world knows it today, there is *no* common guide to behaviour for all people, *no* clear road to mutual understanding – and in fact no basis for either? Do not religious faiths often encourage their own adherents in misunderstanding or disapproval, or even active dislike and intolerance of other faiths? Religious wars apart, what Buddhist ever helped a Christian to prove the truth of Christianity? What Christian ever helped a Mohammedan to believe in Mohammedanism? True, there is a lessening of religious divisions today, but barriers of prejudice and misunderstanding exist everywhere – and on them, religious intolerance thrives. Whether "cold" or "hot", all forms of religious or racial intolerance harm mankind.

Given an excuse, a surprising number of religious people still fight about their beliefs, too. The fundamental differences between Moslem and Hindu are potentially as dangerous today as they were four hundred years ago. Those between Roman Catholics and Buddhists are all too tragically obvious in Vietnam.

If a single Omnipotent Being *has* created a code of human behaviour which man must observe if he is to achieve fulfilment – happiness for all – there is certainly no sign that He has yet vouchsafed to any *one* religion enough of it to meet the needs of all mankind. Priests may argue that He has made some of the rules clear to different races through a variety of religions, but many of those rules appear to cancel one another out: Christ turning the other cheek and Mohammed carrying the Koran and the sword, is a simple, vivid example. The Christian belief that a man may rightly have only one wife and the Mohammedan belief that a man may rightly have four, carry this conflict into the fundamental human relationship between man and woman.

I am convinced of the need for religious beliefs and the good born of them, but no longer feel even hopeful that, as we understand them today, any one of them has the answer to humanity's basic problems – how to be happy, how to be good. Yet I am convinced that there *is* an answer. Probably religious leaders have done more in one way than most philosophers, for at least they have separately preached and taught in terms which ordinary people can understand. However, the babel of their combined teaching is loud and confusing, and despite all of it, we still live in a war-torn world in which fear rules, disaster threatens and the problem of feeding all who are hungry remains unsolved. Yet more and more are born to need feeding every day, every minute, every second.

Cynics believe that there is and can be no answer to these problems. They believe that mankind will eventually destroy itself, simply because human beings have not learned how to behave towards one another – how to be *good* towards one another.

I do not share this cynicism – which I believe is born of fear. It seems to be related closely to an older, deeper cynicism, evinced over the centuries by the philosophical mentors and religious leaders of man. Philosophers will explain, or explain away, man's behaviour. Religious leaders will allow – indeed, exhort – their erring flock to placate their one or their several gods so that they may be forgiven their sins. "Confession" in the Roman Catholic sense seems to me to be only one aspect of this readiness to compromise between good and evil.

This compromise has many aspects and many names. It is known as "forgiveness". It is known as "redemption". It is known as "being washed by the Blood of the Lamb". It is known as "making allowances for human failure, human nature being what it is". It is conceding that "the spirit is willing but the flesh is weak". In each of these, there is a modicum of truth. But while there is confusion between what *is* good and what *is* evil, between what is a "major" sin and what a "minor", between what words or deeds or attitudes are approved or condemned by different religions, there can be no clear-cut basic code; no law of human behaviour, which enables and encourages man to respond to his own instincts.

We are exhorted to do good – and the instinctive reaction of the human being *is* to do good, to be kind – but this reaction is often stifled or discouraged by fear that if one follows the instinct, one will injure oneself.

We are, at heart, all good Samaritans. We are also aware of the thieves waiting in the shadows, men – of the same mortal clay as ourselves – who may attack us if we stop to render help. These "thieves in the shadows" may be said to spread over every sphere of human life. It is fear that we ourselves will not have enough for tomorrow's needs, which inhibits us from giving as much as we safely could today. Fear in the United States, in

15

parts of Africa and alas in England, that the Negro, the Indian, the Pakistani or Chinese will take away from the prosperity of the European races creates thick barriers of prejudice, intolerance and ill-will. Fear, in Africa, that the European will continue to dominate the indigenous African creates revolt and riot and resentment. Wherever such fears are removed – as, at the time of writing, in Kenya – the barriers are lowered, and tolerance and understanding grow.

So it seems to me that the instinctive goodness in man is suffocated by the conditions of society, and that philosophies, whether humanist or religious, have failed to show us how to rid ourselves of these conditions. What is needed is a way of life in which all men can release their instinctive goodness without fear that kindness and generosity will redound to the disadvantage of themselves or their families.

We need to find a way of releasing the goodness in man.

The form of release must take into account the fact that what seems wrong to some people may seem right to others, since human beings are not and will never be cast in exactly the same mould. Yet the quality of goodness *is* in all men; it *has* only to be released.

All my life I have been writing about crime. (For the pedantic: I began at the age of ten.) Crime, of course, is the aspect of sin, or evil, which most obviously injures society and against which society protects itself by laws. Latterly, these laws have been approved and sometimes conceived by the mass of the people. This is true of societies at all levels, from bush natives of Central Africa to the most highly cultivated communities, the centres of which shift from time to time from one capital city, or one nation, to another. (Once, it was Athens; for a longer period, Rome. The Egyptians, the Babylonians, the Turks and the Persians, the Chinese and the Russians, the French and the Germans, the Spaniards and the Italians, the English and the Americans, have all believed themselves to possess the Mecca of culture and accomplishment, of law and of power.)

To break the law of any nation is a crime. But as the laws of nations vary, what is a crime in one country is not necessarily one in another. True, the centuries have bequeathed us some crimes that are basic to all (or at least to most) peoples, but it is still possible to break the law in one American State by buying a bottle of whisky, yet take two steps into a bordering state and buy a bottle of the same whisky with the law's blessing. In most cities a motorist may park a car in one street and break the law; park it around the corner and be innocent. It is not so much what we do but when, where and why we do it, which makes the crime.

There are, however, certain acts which are criminal in all countries – murder, theft, blackmail, fraud, forgery, kidnapping, smuggling and drug-trafficking prominent among them.

Western countries in particular have acquired a common understanding of these and many other forms of crime, and make laws to punish criminals. Consequently we have the law-makers and upholders opposing the law-breakers. It follows that if one rubs shoulders with crime, an aspect of evil, one must inevitably rub shoulders with the law, an aspect of good. Evidently it is not possible to learn much about the one, without learning something of the other.

This was borne in upon me in my early writing days, although I was not fully aware of it; perhaps not aware at all, in a moral sense. Over the years, however, I have become fascinated by human behaviour; by the good as well as the bad in man, by its causes as well as its effects, by what happens to people when they commit crimes, and why it happens. The writing of over four hundred and fifty books, mostly based on crime in a wide variety of aspects, has inevitably made me learn a great deal about the wickedness of man, and his weaknesses; the goodness of man, and his strength. It has taught me that a man who makes his living from crime – by breaking the law – may be an extremely kind husband and father and an understanding and generous friend.

True, the habitual law-breaker who mixes only with hardened criminals may become brutalised, but I have no doubt at all that the basic capacity for goodness is in every human being, whether he upholds or breaks society's laws. Indisputably, the criminal is as subject to the emotional influences of life as is the policeman. The way a man earns his living has little to do with the way he falls in love; or the way he makes love.

Further, the years and my profession have taught me that what is one man's good *can* be another man's evil.

This is the most absorbing conundrum on earth. It is the stuff of which philosophies – and philosophers – are made. Because long before any baby born first draws breath, one thing is certain: it will be identical with no other human being on earth. From fingerprints to footprints, brain-cells to blood-cells, while it will bear many similarities, it will yet have some unmistakable and easily identifiable differences. Wherever it is born, into whatever social, racial or national sphere, under whatever star and in whatever circumstances, it will look on life differently from every other person who ever breathed. And it will see good and evil differently.

I like truisms, simply because they express simple truths succinctly. It is a truism that every boy born in the United States might one day sit in the White House as President. Similarly, any child born into this world might be another Christ, another Mohammed, another Pasteur, another Shakespeare, another Hitler; but will much more likely be just another human being, with no outstanding gifts but with all the human capacity for love, hate, hunger, thirst, greed and generosity; possessed of all the human characteristics, qualities and needs, yet so very different from every other human being.

The needs are basic. The quite primitive Indians of the Mato Grosso in Brazil, the freakishly tall Dinkas of Africa, the factory workers of Cincinnati, the miners of South Wales, the Fellows at Oxford and Cambridge, the scientific prodigies of the nuclear age, the astronauts of East and West – everyone, everywhere, has the same physical needs. Their bodies must have the right kind of basic food, for instance, and cannot thrive without it. Everyone knows this. Yet it is by no means as generally realised that our minds and our hearts – what we think with and what we feel with – also need a basic food, which very few seem to get. Consequently, as the years pass, most of us become dissatisfied with some aspect of living, vaguely and sometimes angrily aware that life could be vastly better.

We yearn for something we do not have, often uncertain whether even our hunger is material, mental, or spiritual. This yearning, and the inevitable seeking born of it, possibly offers the most significant pointer to what is missing in life. Some are concerned with the need of improvement, or fulfilment, only for themselves; others (surprisingly many others) care deeply that life should be improved for all mankind. There can be no doubt, however, that sooner or later, the great majority settle for less than they at some time dreamed of having; they come to accept as unchangeable a situation which leaves them dissatisfied and discontented throughout much of their daily lives. In short, they settle for second best – second best for themselves, their families, their friends, their country, even for the world.

To me, this is mankind's greatest sin. It is both shocking and dreadful that so many of us sit back and accept a state of unhappiness and disillusion, and do practically nothing to *try* to help even our children to avoid the same fate. We simply say resignedly: "It's life," and teach them to expect it. If we can behave like this to ourselves and to our own children, small wonder there are so many dissatisfied and discontented nations; small wonder people of different races can hate each other. We behave almost as if we hate ourselves.

It may be fear, or even hunger, or perhaps simply temperament or lack of opportunity, which causes so many human beings to give up trying; and by not trying, to condemn themselves to what is in fact no more than a subsistence level of living. They are in effect confining themselves to a dimly comprehended half-world, at times of sheer misery, at others of near-happiness – but in either state, accompanied by a sense of unfulfilment. If "Hell is a point at which one cannot forgive oneself," then surely purgatory begins at the point where one settles for less than the best of which one is capable.

We start living in purgatory the moment we give up hope of a better, happier life. The ease with which we give up is surely the reason why man has never found the Golden Fleece, never seen his dreamed-of Shangri-La, never found the elixir of happiness, never had enough good to go round.

I am increasingly convinced that the fundamental cause of human unhappiness, the state of mind which leads to the social and economic evils of the world and eventually to war, is that man has given up trying to find the source of his innate goodness and to draw from it. Indeed, he has failed to recognise this innate goodness for what it is, and consequently has no reason to want to go on doing more and more good. Yet an inexhaustible supply of goodness is essential if the conditions of happiness are to be created for all mankind. It is one thing to forgive or be forgiven for failure and sin (or evil); it is much the same thing to make allowances for human weaknesses; it is quite another to give up hope of a sufficiency of goodness, and believe one must settle for less than the best in *any* aspect of living.

It is often demonstrably untrue that we need settle for less than the best. Surprisingly often, men in need or in danger have discovered in themselves far greater ability, resourcefulness and courage than they suspected they possessed. All human progress, at whatever stage in history, has been made possible only because one man or a group of men could call upon qualities in themselves by which they and others have been stimulated to tremendous heights of endeavour and achievement.

Lord Shaftesbury could call upon such qualities, so could Abraham Lincoln and Winston Churchill, to name but three

Good, God and Man

who have stood head and shoulders above their fellow men and
inspired them to astonishing achievement.

All great men of science and all great explorers work and live
on the assumption that "The difficult must be done at once,
the impossible may take a little longer." This familiar paradox
is not altogether the joke it is accepted to be; it is almost a
truism.

All outstanding men, then, whether knowingly or not, have
always rejected the greatest evil known to man. They have
refused, that is, to submit to the belief that there is a limit to
what man can achieve.

In their separate ways, Machiavelli and Hitler set out to
achieve what to others appeared to be impossible. Both were
utterly ruthless, just as both were inspired by a vision. Both
rejected ethics and moralities which had long been accepted by
men of goodness; but few have fought for goodness with the
passion, tenacity and dedication with which these two fought
for what was inherently bad. Each sought power without ap-
pearing even to suspect that its greatest rewards can only lie in
using it to its greatest advantage: the good of all mankind.

Power for power's sake is exciting, but no one has yet seen
the attainment of total goodness as a tremendously exciting way
of life. *Yet it is.* And moreover, it is within the reach of any
generation, even of today's. Universal happiness, Utopia, has
been seen as a distant miracle which, if it ever comes at all, will
come by slow evolution, not by revolution. Goodness is very
often regarded as dull; evil as exciting. That is why one evil
deed will capture newspaper headlines while one good deed
might achieve a paragraph.

Thus, on a "publicity" level, values have been turned upside
down.

The most exciting thing in the world, surely, is happiness. Is
there anything in life so exhilarating, so absorbing, as the happiness of being in love? Isn't this the clearest indication of the
state of well-being, euphoria, exaltation, which true happiness
can bring? Isn't it demonstrably worth striving for with all
one's might? Isn't it proven beyond doubt that money and
material things – the realisation of ambition, the gaining of
position and honours – do not of themselves bring happiness?

Of course it is proven; and the philosophers have told us so
over and over again. Yet I can find no philosophy and no
religion which has shown how exciting the pursuit of goodness
can be; how exhilarating is the search, the chase, for *attainable*
happiness.

20

Idealism and Realism

Surely the lesson which follows is that happiness is born out of goodness; that we need to find and have access to an illimitable store of goodness before we can find universal happiness. The goodness must come first.

What do we know of goodness, and its source? We know, of course, that it is generated in and by man. Whether God put it there in the beginning is inescapably a matter of opinion; of belief. It cannot be questioned that man himself can be good or bad; can choose to *do* good or bad; can find goodness in himself or inspire it in fellow human beings. The only accessible reservoir of goodness known to man, then, is in man himself. Yet despite this, it has become a commonplace to believe that man must settle for that second-best: for what is colloquially called "realism". And realism, in this widely accepted sense, falls far short of the greatest spiritual quality recognisable by and available to all men – that is, awareness of the ideal, and a longing for it.

Mankind must accept and live by the belief that nothing but the best is good enough in any sphere of human activity; only then will idealism and realism be recognised as identical twins. And when that time comes, the world will have made its biggest single stride towards universal happiness. Every man *can* live by this belief, once he realises that it asks from him only the best of which he is capable: *the best he can give* – to himself, to his wife, children, family, friends, community, nation and the world.

The cynics will scoff, no doubt, but the gravest threat to widespread acceptance of this belief once it is properly propounded, will come from people filled with honest doubt. All their lives – in their work, home, school and religion – they have been taught that idealism is a dreamy, head-in-the-clouds, pie-in-the-sky philosophy; thus to them the very suggestion that the ideal can result from down-to-earth, day-by-day behaviour will at first seem absurd. People have been so drilled into believing that they will be forgiven for sin, that they have come to regard sin, and in consequence, forgiveness, as their birthright. Yet I have never heard or read of any man who denies that in an ideal world, man would be without sin: without evil, hate, greed, bitterness, selfishness.

The great question is, can we make our world ideal?

The answer is: yes – once we reconcile realism with idealism.

Lest there be any doubt about the truth of this answer, let us consider idealism and realism in relation to world food (see also Chapter 7).

21

Good, God and Man

The "realist" may believe that famine or hunger in some parts of the world is inevitable; some may even think it necessary, particularly if the people of a hostile nation are starving. But no one considers it a "good" in the sense of an "ideal" thing.

There are, say the "realists", insuperable difficulties in the way of feeding everyone: difficulties of growing sufficient food, of distributing it, of being paid for it. Except for a few charitable groups and the World Food Organisation, which has woefully little support from the well-fed nations, few people appear to think it worth trying to achieve the ideal of ensuring that everyone in the world *will* be fed. It is also considered "realistic" and inevitable that grain and meat surpluses are thrown away or burned, and harvests artificially restricted.

"People" are sorry and their hearts are touched whenever they are compelled to think about others being short of food, but it does not seem to occur to them that famine anywhere in the world affects their own standard of living. Just how it does so, however, is very easily shown.

The starving or the undernourished do poor-quality work, perhaps resort to petty thievery, or become sick and listless because they have too little to do; and, as they cannot enjoy this enforced leisure, they gradually become dissatisfied. Their buying power falls, so fewer goods can be bought from abroad: consequently the supplier nation either sells less or sells at uneconomic prices, demonstrably affecting its own economy and the buying power – the prosperity – of its own people. This alone presents a grave enough picture, but there is far, far worse.

In poverty-stricken countries, dissatisfaction with conditions inevitably leads to political unrest. Wars like that in Vietnam are a consequence; had the Vietnamese been prosperous and well-fed there would surely have been no Viet Cong uprising, no reason for the United States to feel any threat to its own security – no need for war.

There are revolts and uprisings everywhere, some short-lived, some disruptive over a long period. The direct and indirect consequences of all of these things *to the West*, as well as to Eastern countries bordering the hungry nations, are always grave and often extremely dangerous. The so-called "realistic" approach holds these things to be inevitable.

But consider the "idealistic" approach.

If the hungry are fed, they will work with greater energy, earn more, spend more – buy more. And a well-fed nation is

22

Idealism and Realism

the least likely to start an aggressive war. (The seeds of the Second World War lay in the desperate conditions in Germany between 1918 and 1933, when a mad genius took over.) Agricultural machinery producers, steel manufacturers and countless other allied trades and industries all reap benefit from that distant well-fed land. Those responsible for packaging, distributing, shipping by air, sea, road and rail – all feel the benefit; so, obviously, do *all* the people employed in these industries.

Aren't these things *real* enough? Aren't they what we should be striving for? Isn't it the finest and yet the most sensible form of "realism" to strive for the ideal of "good for all"? And isn't there only one possible way to get the best out of life for everybody – that is, to aim for the ideal, for *plenty* in every sphere of human activity?

I believe that the need to achieve this ideal places the gravest *responsibility* not only on mankind in general but also on man as an individual. Which brings us to one of the most commonly misunderstood facts of human life: the nature as well as the significance of responsibility.

Accepting "responsibility" is not as difficult as it is often made out to be. Before we consider this claim, however, one fact must be clearly established: the only man who can strive for the ideal (the best) in himself *is* himself. Others may help, but only he can find the answer, whether it be seen as a material, an intellectual, a spiritual or an emotional ideal. Only he can find, use and develop to the full the qualities inherent in himself.

Political systems and religious guidance may help him in society, but only man himself can do his *personal* best by the society in which he lives, and so improve it. Each improvement he makes, however trifling, contributes towards the general good, and so towards the ideal society. The more who see and understand this, the sooner the ideal will come, but it can be approached only by each man for himself – even though millions may be moving towards it at the same time.

Chapter 2

THE SIMPLICITY OF RESPONSIBILITY

EVERYONE knows it is right, or good, to accept and carry out one's responsibilities, but they are often seen and understood only as burdensome. Goodness, in this respect, has also become something vaguely undesirable, or at least unpalatable, something to be avoided. The relationship between goodness as a dull and uninspiring thing and "responsibility" as a burdensome thing, has obscured the instinctive, inherent nature of goodness and the benefits which derive from it. Before man can hope to see goodness in its true guise, he must first see responsibilities for what they are, not for what he has long considered them to be.

The ominous note first sounds in the youthful ear at school. "Ah, wait until *you* are old enough to be responsible for . . ." And whatever subject is under discussion, the word will always carry an implication of burden, of the good fortune of youth in not having to face up to the hard facts of life. This note, causing apprehension and gloom, continues through life almost without ceasing. It is always the serious-minded people – the headmasters, ministers of religion, judges, politicians and suchlike – who talk about responsibility, and they often encompass it with such an aura of obligation and unpalatable duty that the very word becomes anathema. The implicit suggestion is that "responsibility" is always something to be carried out solely for others' benefit, seldom if ever for one's own. Self-sacrifice only is implied, never any suggestion of privilege, or of something which may well yield a reward of pleasure or satisfaction. If the certainty of reward were established in the young mind, there would be far less reluctance to do what one should.

It is one thing to talk of carrying out responsibilities, however; quite another to define them. Are certain responsibilities common to all men, for instance? Or is each one intensely personal? Is the ability to carry out responsibilities within the capacity of each individual, or is each dependent on others to help him? The answer to this last question is surely that both are true, although it is fundamental that just as no human being

24

can see, touch, taste, hear, feel, love or think for anyone but himself, only the individual himself can carry out his own responsibilities.

Yet many responsibilities are common to all men. All must eat, for instance. This is a primary personal responsibility. If one fails to carry it out for oneself, then one pays for the failure. A man who does not feed himself will starve or fall sick; may even die as a result. The person who fails himself always *suffers* himself; he is also likely to make others suffer, too.

If one fails to carry out legal responsibility – for instance, to one's children, one's neighbour or the State – the law may prescribe punishment. But over a vast range of responsibilities common to man, the law has no control; and of these man all too often has only a vague awareness.

Here again, it is immaterial whether or not the source of responsibilities (as the source of good) is in God. It is *man* who must carry out these responsibilities, and obviously he cannot do so until he knows what they are. If the premise in the first chapter is valid, the first ethical responsibility common to all is to give of one's genuine best, whatever one is doing. This is something which every individual can undertake, young, middle-aged or old, whether he be millionaire or pauper, Olympic athlete or cripple, schoolchild or teacher.

Responsibilities can be such simple actions as brushing one's teeth or shaving, dressing oneself, or driving one's car – or even frying an egg. A great many of them give positive pleasure, while others, though not pleasant in themselves, have pleasing and beneficial after-effects.

Today so many people are disillusioned and cynical that comparatively few will exert themselves to carry out some of their more obvious responsibilities to themselves, while all but legal responsibilities to society (or even to family) are sometimes not even attempted. Some individuals will shoulder more than their share but they are too few in number to make any material difference to the general community or to the world. Moreover, if a man takes on too much responsibility in his own family or his own society, he is not only over-burdening himself and so heading for breakdown or failure but also robbing others of their right to carry out their own responsibilities and weakening their ability to do so when left to their own resources.

One of the greatest needs, of course, is to demonstrate just why the fulfilment of one's personal responsibilities should be so important to others as well as to oneself. It is also important to emphasise that, although in some specific and exceptional instances it may be necessary to make a special effort costly in time, money or bodily wear and tear, for the most part the effort needed for the carrying out of one's normal responsibilities is very small; and the rewards, in satisfaction and sense of fulfilment, are very great.

No man, obviously, can ever do or give more than the best that is in him, although, as we have seen, he may often be surprised by his own capacity. Any attempt to drive him beyond the limit of that capacity would only make him crack. Great leaders learn to judge the capacity of the men who serve them and try not to drive them beyond it except under great duress, such as forcing a man to fight to the death for the sake of victory or the safety of others.

In daily life, however, the likelihood of being driven to breaking point by one's responsibilities is comparatively small. One simply has to carry out whatever one has to do *as well as one can at that particular moment.* No more; no less. This is as true of sleeping as it is of eating. If one allows too little time for sleep, one becomes physically depleted. If one eats too fast, one gets indigestion; here is further proof that *all* failures to do what one is doing to the best of one's ability, lead to some form of harm. A combination of circumstances which prevents one from carrying out such responsibilities as working, sleeping or eating, can drive one to breaking point; but a man in normal health can always do what he must in his daily life.

The housewife in the kitchen, the physicist in the laboratory, the pilot in his cockpit, the fisherman in his trawler, the schoolboy in his class, the miner down his shaft, the driver of a bus or train, the hairdresser and the tailor, the shopgirl and the department store manager, the dustman and the draughtsman, the hall porter and the chef, the artist and the writer – all can carry out their responsibilities simply by putting their very best into everything they do. If they do less than their best, whether by wittingly shirking or short-cutting on responsibilities, or whether prevented by circumstances from carrying them out, then harm to the individual and to the community always results.

Although this is not always apparent, it is simply the failure of certain ordinary individuals to do their ordinary jobs *properly* which jams the gears of human relationships and leads eventually to economic chaos, national upheavals, and all too often, to war. The failure may well be due to hunger, illness, selfishness, intolerance, ignorance or a dozen other factors. Society must create the conditions in which none of these can thrive: only then shall we be within reach of the Golden Age.

The Simplicity of Responsibility

No doubt all this will be regarded as an over-simplification, but it is not. Most human problems must initially be reduced to the simplest terms, before we can understand and therefore cope with them. This fact has been obscured by centuries of dogma, tradition, convention and habit.

Each of these has its rightful place, of course: all religions must have dogma, just as all nations must have pride in tradition. Such things are wrong only when they obscure the simple and comparatively easy-to-live-by rules of ethical behaviour. (While the words "ethical" and "moral" indicate what is good in human conduct, I have come to understand each as having its own quite distinctive and specific meaning. So for the purpose of this book, ethical behaviour is simply *what* one should do, while morality is simply *why* one should do it.)

Is it easy to learn "what one should do"? To be certain what is the good and right thing to do, in all circumstances?

I believe that man does know, instinctively. But this instinctive or inherent knowledge has been so obscured by environmental training that every individual could benefit by a few minutes' effort at listing his own simple, daily responsibilities. One might begin with such obvious responsibilities as cleaning one's teeth every morning. Yet is anything so easy as cleaning one's teeth actually worth special mention? If one fails to do it occasionally, is it so very important?

In posing this very question to myself, as you will see in the next chapter, I came upon some impressive and bewildering facts. And the pursuit of this single theme alone demonstrated beyond doubt how important and potentially dangerous is *every* failure, however minor, to the individual, the family, the neighbourhood, the city, the nation and the world.

Take, for example, a car-driver at the wheel. He may well be highly competent, may have driven hundreds of thousands of miles without a single mishap. But he may also be tired, preoccupied, annoyed, angry; he may have been drinking; he may simply have allowed his attention to lapse for one split second. If in that split second he fails to do what he is doing properly (that is, fails to carry out his ordinary responsibility), he is quite, likely to:

   (i) kill or injure himself;
  (ii) kill or injure others;
 (iii) damage his car;
 (iv) damage other people's cars;
  (v) damage the highway or property close to the highway;

(vi) frighten other drivers into making errors of judgment
and so prevent them from driving properly, thus setting
up a chain-reaction of accidents . . .

Whereas if he drives as he should (that is, accepts his responsibility), he will get both pleasure and satisfaction out of it.
Is *this* an over-simplification?

In Great Britain, seven thousand people die on the roads and
over three hundred thousand people are injured *every year*, at
an estimated financial cost of £500 million. No one can
measure the cost in pain and grief. In the United States of
America, fifty thousand people are killed and over three million
injured on the roads each year at an estimated cost of $15,000
million – yes, fifteen thousand million dollars; here again, no
one can measure the pain and grief these tragedies cause.

At least as much death, injury and damage befoul the roads
of the rest of the world, and *the whole horrendous total is made up of
individual accidents, all with rare exceptions caused by one person failing
to do his simple job properly in one split second of time.*

One by one, the deaths, the maiming, the cost in money, pain
and grief, build up to the terrifying total. *One by one.* If everyone on every day used the roads properly, and if everyone
involved in the making of cars and roads did their job properly,
there would be very few road accidents indeed.

That is how vital, even simple and obvious, responsibilities
are.

For an even more vivid example, consider a mechanic at
Cape Kennedy, when Gemini 6 was being prepared for launching. He left a tiny plastic cover on a valve, sent a shiver of alarm
through the nation (and much of the world) and also came close
to causing the failure of the space-craft's launching, the failure
of the rendezvous in space – and the death of two astronauts.
He might conceivably have delayed a landing on the moon by
months if not years, and caused a fantastic waste of money.

That is how important one man's responsibility can be. The
most trivial-seeming failure even of omission can lead to the
most serious results. This is life. And the sum total of all our
failures to do what we should (to do what is good), is the sum
total of the whole world's plight.

One of the facts which astonishes and in moments of gloom
appals, is that all of this is so transparently obvious. It has been
said with greater or lesser emphasis for three thousand years and
is a commonplace in Western society – *but the theory and importance of it is never taught in schools*. Certain specific responsibilities

28

The Simplicity of Responsibility

are taught, but seldom, if ever, the general principle. Nor do philosophers appear to teach it. There seems to be a belief that a human being grows into accepting responsibility, learning about it in the way that boys and girls were believed to "grow" into learning about sex without being taught.

In fact, the enormous benefits of accepting simple daily responsibilities, and also the deadly consequences of failing to accept and carry them out, dawn very slowly on the human race. Some people are instinctively and others are environmentally made aware of them, but few know why they are essential to a full life, and countless millions are utterly oblivious.

It is common knowledge that the simplest of lessons are best learned when young, such as one's A.B.C., elementary arithmetic and early reading. These can never be learned so easily at a later stage, and until they are learned, one cannot progress to more difficult subjects. But, like the ease, simplicity, pleasure and importance of carrying out one's responsibilities, they *can* be learned later in life. Indeed the A.B.C. of responsibility *must* be learned, if we are to save the world from the disasters which so often threaten. A moment of inattention like that which could have wrecked Gemini 6, could explode a nuclear warhead. In another sphere, the failure of mankind to carry out its group responsibilities could contribute towards a population explosion so terrifying that peace and plenty would become impossible.

And people, like road accidents, are created one by one.

There is no shadow of doubt that in order to cure all the ills of mankind, in order to get the best out of life, in order to do most good to all people, we must know what our responsibilities are. Man's ills can be cured – or better still, prevented. And today's social, economic and political ills will respond to treatment just as smallpox, poliomyelitis, rabies and countless other diseases have done. All we need to know is the real cause of the ills. We have the cure in advance: the acceptance by all men of the responsibility of giving the best that is in them to whatever task they are doing.

It will probably be said that no man can maintain the self-discipline necessary to carry out all his responsibilities all the time. But this is not only defeatist, it is also an illusion. As we shall see, rest and relaxation are responsibilities and are absolutely essential if one is to be at one's best, physically and mentally, whenever necessary. It may also be said that one often *forgets* what one should do, and that even when one remembers, there simply isn't time. In the approaching age of

29

increasing leisure and shorter working hours, *time* is going to be much less important. As for memory: it is surprising how much one remembers whenever it is to one's advantage! – how good one can be when the benefit to oneself is plain to see.

The simple truth is that we *can* always give of our best, although sometimes we need help. Often this help will come from others doing *their* best. As often, it will come from within ourselves, from growing awareness of the fact that if we are to get the best *out* of life, we must put our best *into* it and that we can only do this by carrying out our responsibilities.

Which brings us once more to the all-important question – what *are* our responsibilities?

Chapter 3

WHAT ARE RESPONSIBILITIES ?

In general, responsibilities are those things we should or need do in the course of our daily life. They are intensely personal, and it cannot be said too often that no individual can undertake a single one for any other person. On the other hand, how we carry them out affects countless other people, and each of us is affected in turn by the manner in which countless other people carry out their responsibilities to *themselves*.

If they fail to do such a simple thing as that, they are hardly likely to carry out their responsibilities to others.

C. S. Lewis, the theologian who wrote so much common sense about Christianity in his lucid yet erudite, sophisticated yet homely way, once said that "If all the people in the world had violent toothache, each man could feel only the ache in his own tooth." Obviously this is true, yet the *effect* of one man's toothache can be felt by a multitude of others. It was this which made me pay so much attention to a simple daily task that most people surely take for granted. Because it is so simple, so common to most people in the West, I am going to examine the whole mammoth business of "dental care". I can think of no more vivid example of the importance and magnitude of carrying out a responsibility to oneself, and one which at first thought seems hardly worthy of comment.

We know that manufacturers of toothpaste spend fortunes explaining the consequences of failing to clean one's teeth. Obviously their advertising agents, publicity men and newspaper, commercial radio and television space salesmen are all affected, but who would dream how much they are affected?

In 1964 the American *Drug Trade News* estimated that $44,511,000 was spent on advertising dental products and dentistry, and that *374,640 persons* were employed by the major manufacturers who produce dentifrice. Just dentifrice! In addition to these, there were the people working in the manufacture of dental instruments; the packers and distributors, carriers (shippers) and retailers; the suppliers of raw materials and of packaging. Almost unbelievably, *millions of people* are involved, directly or indirectly, in looking after teeth and gums.

31

True, not all of these are affected deeply by the occasional failure of a few people. When one studies the statistics, however, one must be astounded, if not appalled, by the fact that a large proportion of this enormous expense is commercially justified (that is, profitable) simply to persuade, cajole and almost to bribe individuals to do what no single one of us should ever need telling to do.

I wrote to the General Dental Council of Great Britain and the American Dental Association to learn more about the simple matter of attending the teeth and mouths of two nations with very high standards of living. The simple way to present the estimates they gave me is by table:

	1964	
	Great Britain	*U.S.A.*
Number of Dentists	16,878	97,000
Number of Dental Technicians and Assistants	not known	118,200
Number of Dental Receptionists	,,	25,100
Number of Technicians in Commercial Laboratories	,,	25,000
Number of Patients	15,341,319	78,069,000
Cost of Dental Treatment	£57,598,000	$2,900,000,000*
Loss of Working Time through Dental Treatment	6,000,000 hrs.	21,277,000 (days of restricted activity)
Amount Spent on Oral Hygiene Products	£35,000,000	$517,980,000†

* Say £1,000,000,000. † Say £190,000,000.

In spite of this enormous industry, the great impact of advertising and the comprehensive nature of the National Health Service in Great Britain, one simple failure by an individual may cause incalculable harm. The morning one "forgets" may be the morning when a food particle lodges between two teeth and starts decay in a tooth or pyorrhoea in the gums – which in turn can lead to pain, extractions, the spoiling of appetite and enjoyment of food, poor health and inevitably loss of time at work – a fraction of those millions of lost working hours – and so contribute to the loss of production, income, profit, trade and last but by no means least, the loss of temper. The strain on human relationships due to lack of care over one person's mouth may well be incalculable.

The daily acceptance by everyone of this simple responsibility can make sure that none of these things are due to neglect.

What Are Responsibilities?

Here is a kind of Family Tree in relation to cleaning teeth:

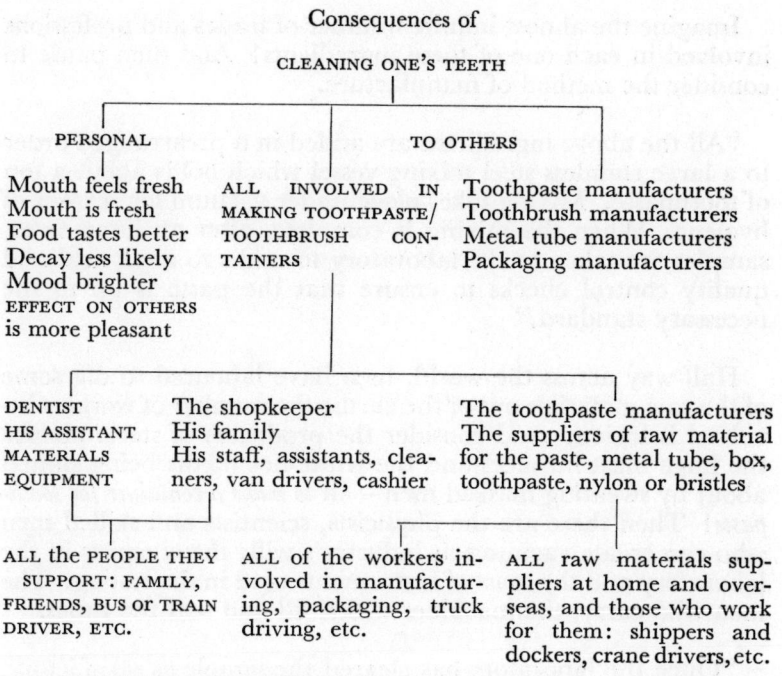

Consequences of

CLEANING ONE'S TEETH

PERSONAL		TO OTHERS
Mouth feels fresh	ALL INVOLVED IN	Toothpaste manufacturers
Mouth is fresh	MAKING TOOTHPASTE/	Toothbrush manufacturers
Food tastes better	TOOTHBRUSH CON-	Metal tube manufacturers
Decay less likely	TAINERS	Packaging manufacturers
Mood brighter		
EFFECT ON OTHERS		
is more pleasant		

DENTIST	The shopkeeper	The toothpaste manufacturers
HIS ASSISTANT	His family	The suppliers of raw material
MATERIALS	His staff, assistants, clea-	for the paste, metal tube, box,
EQUIPMENT	ners, van drivers, cashier	toothpaste, nylon or bristles

ALL the PEOPLE THEY SUPPORT: FAMILY, FRIENDS, BUS or TRAIN DRIVER, ETC.	ALL of the workers involved in manufacturing, packaging, truck driving, etc.	ALL raw materials suppliers at home and overseas, and those who work for them: shippers and dockers, crane drivers, etc.

Now one might think this much ado about nothing, but consider the ingredients, the raw materials, of toothpaste and the hosts of people associated with them.

"First there are the *abrasive solids*, to remove scale and dirt, and to polish and clean the teeth; *vehicle/humectant*, to provide a suitable non-drying solution in which the other ingredients are dispersed; *gum*, to act as a binding agent to other ingredients and enable the manufacturer to control the viscosity or 'stiffness' of the paste; *detergent or soap*, to assist cleaning and dispersion of the paste, retain mouth/food debris in suspension and provide foam; *preservative*, to prevent or inhibit bacterial activity, *germicides*, to attack and break down mouth bacteria; *flavour*, to provide a pleasant taste in use, impart freshness to the mouth, and make the paste pleasant and easy to use; and sometimes even *colour*, to support an advertising message, provide

C

visible evidence of one or more special ingredients such as hexachlorophene."

Imagine the almost infinite number of trades and professions involved in each one of these ingredients! And then pause to consider the method of manufacture.

"All the above ingredients are added in a prearranged order to a large stainless steel mixing vessel which holds about a ton of toothpaste. Mixing takes place under vacuum for reasons of hygiene. When the mixing is complete, after an hour or so, samples are taken to the laboratory to undergo analytical and quality control checks to ensure that the paste is up to the necessary standard."

Half-way across the world, men have laboured to dig some of the raw materials out of the earth; the number of workers involved is legion. And consider the producers of steel: picture the huge blast furnaces and the white-hot ingots being shifted about by sweating masked men – all *to make a container for toothpaste*! Then there are the physicists, scientists and skilled men who can create vacuums at industry's will; the chemists in the laboratory and the mass of instruments used in the testing. The men who carry, the machines which fill and seal the tubes.

"Once the laboratory has cleared the sample as satisfactory, the paste is blown from the mixer under high pressure into large stainless steel storage vessels. These vessels are transported when required to special filling points which are situated above the high speed automatic machines.

"The toothpaste is then blown under pressure into the filling machines and filled into tubes through the bottom end on a high speed rotating platform. This tube-filling machine receives tubes from a feed chute, fills them to an accurate predetermined weight, seals or crimps them at the bottom, and then packs them into cartons before finally putting them on to a conveyor belt for final packing into large outer cases of wood or cardboard or of metal."

If we take a closer look we can see even more vividly the diversity of men and materials and skills involved.

"*Abrasive solids* are usually calcium carbonate (chalk) or dicalcium phosphate. Calcium carbonate is one of the most

34

chemically stable, common and widely dispersed of naturally occurring materials. To obtain the purity required for toothpaste, it is first dissolved in acid, then neutralised and precipitated as a very pure substance. Calcium phosphate is obtained from naturally occurring raw materials and has alternative uses in medicine and dentistry.

"*Vehicle/humectant* is usually water and glycerine. Glycerine is obtained as a by-product in the manufacture of soap and is colourless with a sweet taste. It has alternative uses in medicine, pharmacy, perfumery and, of all things, explosives.

"*Gum* is either synthetic or from animal extracts in the same way as glues.

"*Detergent* is normally a compound similar to sodium lauryl sulphate which is used in detergent powders for washing clothes, etc.

"*Toothbrush handles* are generally made from a material known as cellulose acetate, usually in the form of cotton, which is treated with acetic acid, commonly found in dilute form in vinegar. The cellulose acetate is a white powder and is mixed with liquids known as plasticisers to make the clear transparent material as we know it. The purpose of plasticisers is to make the cellulose acetate tough and transparent, and produce a compound that can be processed by injection and moulding machinery.

"Some cheaper quality toothbrushes are made from another plastic material called polystyrene. Polystyrene is made from raw materials originating in coal tar and the cracking of oils. Polystyrene is less tough than cellulose acetate and is lower in price.

"Various types of packaging are in use for toothbrushes, probably the commonest being a straightforward carton, which of course can have many variants relative to its size and method of construction, whether it shows the contents, or partly, or not at all. Graphic design work can completely change the identity of the toothbrush carton type pack.

"Various forms of moulded pack are used, and this particular method can embrace anything from a simple tube in glass or plastic to a well-designed re-use container.

"*Board of Trade figures for the whole of 1965 show the estimated U.K. tooth/denture brush manufacture to be in excess of 44,000,000 brushes.*"

The mind reels at contemplation of the variety and number of people involved directly and indirectly, and each *one* must do his job properly if the paste is to be of the best possible quality and so do the utmost good. If he does a bad job, *he* might get the faulty tube or the dangerous speck of bacteria or gritty dust or any one of the minute foreign bodies which can contaminate the paste.

This is the essence of responsibility, the interdependence of all individuals and the fact that *any* man who fails to do what he should, is as likely as anyone else to suffer from *his own* neglect.

It is worth considering briefly the consequences of *not* cleaning one's teeth, not taking advantage of this mammoth industry, the skill and knowledge poured into the little tubes and the colourful brushes used by millions of people, day in, day out.

These consequences can depend on local circumstances, the natural condition of the teeth and the minerals in the water one drinks. But in general, the effect of neglect is almost certain to be bad.

Consequences of
NOT CLEANING ONE'S TEETH
|
Mouth tacky and unpleasant
FOOD TASTES less GOOD
DECAY almost certain
PAIN AND DISCOMFORT INEVITABLE

Visit to Dentist (who has plenty of unavoidable work to do) TOOTH OUT DENTURES TIME OFF WORK (OR PLEASURE)	Impatience with others can lead to quarrels, accidents, general failure to carry out responsibilities

Less work for all directly involved Less profit Less money for research Less money for investment	Less work for all indirectly involved, including miners, and labourers thousands of miles away Less profit Less money for research Less money for investment

Two aspects of this Tooth Family Tree might be easy to over-look. The first is that the consequence of *not* cleaning will affect individuals in every stratum of society. The risks of ill-effects in the higher income and higher literacy groups may be less than in the lower, but no group is immune. The second respect, as we have already seen, is that the consequences of, say, a sudden stab of pain at a crucial moment or a week of gruelling discomfort from pain and the drugs taken to ease it, *can* be of major significance.

It can affect a car-driver at a moment of emergency, thus causing grave danger.

It can affect a schoolchild or a student during the course of a vital examination.

It can affect a scientist at a time of important research.

It can affect an artist and prolong the anguish of creation, perhaps stifle creation itself.

It can affect a politician at a moment of decision, a soldier in time of battle, a footballer at the moment of opportunity, a cricketer about to make a catch, a golfer at the point of a decisive putt. It can destroy the pleasures of eating and drinking, disrupt all peace of mind, and seriously affect one's general health long after the tooth is out and the pain is gone.

In this age of commercial advertising it is easy to overlook the truth in much that is claimed for products which are aids to cleanliness and hygiene. It is easy to overlook, also, the fact that some manufacturers make claims far in excess of the benefits from their products, while others appear to make far too big a margin of profit. Yet these products usually contain a basic quality which helps personal hygiene, and so personal health, and so the general health of a community.

Whoever first said "cleanliness is next to godliness" was right indeed. I need hardly list the countless ways in which an individual's need for cleanliness can affect his daily life and the lives of others, but it may be salutary to list the more basic forms of cleanliness – each necessary to health, each making life pleasanter, each having some aesthetic and so psychological significance:

   (i) Personal cleanliness.
  (ii) Cleanliness in the home.
 (iii) Cleanliness in the streets.
 (iv) Cleanliness in rivers and reservoirs.
  (v) Cleanliness in factories.
 (vi) Cleanliness in retail shops.
 (vii) Cleanliness in public places.
(viii) Cleanliness in all forms of public transport.
 (ix) Cleanliness in theatres, museums and wherever people congregate.
  (x) Cleanliness in the preparation of food.

This last category, of course, is not only of vital importance but is integral to some of the others. Cleanliness in the manufacture of foodstuffs, in (in a chemical sense) agriculture, in the preparation of food in the home and in canteens, cafés and restaurants, is essential if one is to derive the maximum benefit (good) from the food and if one is to avoid the dangers of food poisoning – now comparatively rare in the Western countries, but still disastrously prevalent in some of the underdeveloped countries.

When different categories of public and private living are examined, it is astonishing to find how many simple responsibilities arise from each one. Certainly there are hundreds of separate and distinct actions which should and can be carried out by all people, every day.

An intensive analysis of one's own actions will show each individual how many of these responsibilities he carries out unthinkingly; it will also show many people who pride themselves on being meticulous in their habits, how often they fail.

And every failure harms the individual, the community and society at large; just as every responsibility which is accepted, *even* unconsciously, benefits the individual, the community and society.

As with cleanliness and hygiene, so with every aspect of daily living. It would be quite practical to prepare a "family tree" showing the consequences of failure to carry out any daily task well. Take, for instance, the secretary who, in opening the morning mail, leaves enclosures in an envelope which is thrown away. Or the printer who omits the "r" and so turns "friend" into "fiend". Or the seamstress who leaves a hem unfinished, so that a garment tears when used. Some seem more important than others, but each plays its part and each part has its own valuable place in a happy, well-ordered family, community or nation.

Here is a purely arbitrary list of subjects, one's attitude to which can have an important effect on society:

   (i) Cleanliness in all its aspects.
  (ii) Research into ways of increasing food production.
 (iii) Research into causes of illness.
 (iv) Cooking and the preparation of food.
  (v) The manufacture of consumer goods.
 (vi) The avoidance of waste (of food, materials, etc., and time as well as money).
(vii) Education at all stages.

(viii) Youth.
 (ix) Old Age.
 (x) Crime.
 (xi) The manufacture of machinery and machine parts.
(xii) Study of local problems.
(xiii) Study of international problems.

The list can go on almost *ad infinitum*, and the subjects are as vital to people in underdeveloped countries as to those in Western society, although we in the West have less cause and so less excuse for failing in any of the basic responsibilities involved.

Another equally important list covers the natural behaviour pattern of individuals, such as:

Generosity	Application
Kindliness	Concentration
Friendliness	Dedication
Cheerfulness	Affection
Steadfastness	

To all people, some of these come naturally, to most some come very hard indeed, according to the metabolism, early environment and the genes of the individual. If a man is naturally careful with his possessions, including money, and environment has hardened this to meanness, it is clearly not an easy responsibility for him to be generous. His natural instinct is to be generous only when the impulse seizes him, as at some time or other, over some person or other, it *will*. If impulses come often enough and he receives sufficient reward in warmth and friendliness and appreciation, this particular characteristic in that particular person might change. In the same way, if a man has an affectionate nature, his responsibility is to allow such affection to spread wherever it can, without becoming sentimental or insincere.

A great number of people find it easy to be kind to children; many, to be kind to animals. Others have a streak which makes them indifferent, some even cruel, to both children and animals. The responsibility of such people is to repress the streak of cruelty or unkindness: as they succeed in this, so they will become better liked by family, friends and neighbours, while they themselves will benefit from their own recognition and acceptance of basic responsibility.

There is, of course, group responsibility (shown vividly in

39

Great Britain by the existence of the National Society for the
Prevention of Cruelty to Children and the Royal Society for the
Prevention of Cruelty to Animals) not only to be kind as
individuals but also to try to make sure that no child or animal
suffers cruelty from anyone. For while the suffering of one cat
or dog may be felt only by the victim, if it is tolerated it may
well become so widespread that it could claim great numbers of
victims, and actually corrode society. Anti-semitism has its
roots deep in history, but the cruelty to *one* Jew by *one* of Hitler's
fanatical supporters must have led – single act of cruelty by
single act of cruelty – to the mass extermination and torture
which shamed the world. It was the attitude of mind in single
individuals which infected whole groups and eventually whole
communities, which in turn made possible the conditions
leading to the Second World War.

There would be no limit to progress, just as there would be no
wars, if every individual accepted and carried out all his known
responsibilities all the time, for the acceptance of responsibilities
always leads to good. Somewhere along the line, an individual
who knows better omits to do what he should; or deliberately
misleads others because by so doing he will gain a short-term
self-advantage – and trouble to the community results. The
losses as well as the benefits of responsibilities are cumulative,
and it is the need for all to carry out their responsibilities which
makes the interdependence of man, and of nations, so obvious.
And since only man himself can carry out his responsibilities,
and since he needs to be good in order to do so, we see again
the significance and extreme value of the fact that the fount of
goodness is *in* man. The problem is first to generate a sufficient
supply, and then to draw sufficiently upon it.

No one is free from responsibilities, no one has special dis-
pensation, but the greater the quality of a man's mind and
spirit, the more he can influence others, and so the more harm
he can do by failing to put his best into whatever task is at
hand.

Clearly there would be no great art unless there were dedicated men eager to devote their lives to artistic creation. The
artist's responsibility both to himself and to others is to concentrate on doing the best *he* possibly can. Some will work dis-
mally at a single miserable aspect of art and many will believe
this wrong; it is not wrong if the artist believes in it, because it is
no part of his responsibility simply to please. It *is* his responsibility to use his gift *if he can honestly do so*, to help others to
understand and to enjoy life. And if he *sees* the beauty and the

goodness of life but does not try to show it to others, he fails in his responsibility.

So it is with all people – whatever they do, whoever they are. Unless they use those talents they have to the absolute limits of their own capacity, they cannot do the best they can *for others*; and unless they do the best they can for others, they will not be able to bring out the best *in* those others – and so benefit themselves to the utmost. All ethics and all morality spring from these facts, for the basic ethical requirement *is* the carrying out of one's responsibilities, just as the basic morality *is* the reason why one should.

"Best" may not appear to be specific, and yet instinctively all men do know when they have really given of their very best. They may shirk responsibilities, but if they do they are aware of it. They may grow into the habit of giving short measure to life, and hardly notice their failure, but whether they realise it or not they cannot get full measure out of life unless they put full measure in: because without their full contribution, the total amount available for sharing among everyone is less than it could or should be.

To understand this fully, one has to examine it closely and in detail. As we shall see from the next chapter, it is hardly a new theory, but as far as I can find out the full range and significance of it have not yet been understood. Certainly very few societies have even attempted to carry it out. Those which have, such as the Amish of Pennsylvania in the United States of America, have done so with religious intolerance, or have isolated themselves from communities which do not share their views – whereas it can and will flourish only when men are wholly free from all pressures, all fear and all sense of injustice.

Chapter 4

SELF-ISM – A NEW LOOK AT ETHICS AND MORALITY

"ETHICS and morality" have a sombre-sounding ring, even gloomier perhaps than the word "responsibility". To many people "ethics" has a remote austereness, while "morality" often seems to demand stern self-denial, to be bent on denying the individual his right to a good time. So they increase the sense of gloomy apprehension and aversion caused by misconception of the nature of responsibility. And inevitably they make "good" seem less attractive instead of what it really is, the essence of human happiness, of self.

For the religious person it is usually satisfying to go to church; for the non-believer, if he goes at all, it is a social or family obligation. Similarly, for the actor or stage manager it is an obligation to go to a theatre, whereas for the ordinary theatre-goer it is a pleasure. All of these things may be responsibilities: the enjoyment of pleasure, with the consequent benefits from relaxation and "being taken out of oneself", is as much a responsibility as going to church if one is a believer. Both prepare one better for whatever one has to do in life; neither need be burdensome.

Clearly, only if all men carry out their responsibilities can all men receive their rights (or privileges). It is rather like a "kitty" into which each one of a group puts a specified sum for the common use. If one man puts in less than his agreed share, then everyone gets less than his due – except possibly the man who short-changed the others; but while he may get more *money*-value, he will certainly lose in respect, liking and trust.

The world is a "kitty" into which we all ought to put a certain sum, *our best*. As we have seen, some will have more to give in intellectual capacity, energy, vitality or originality; but these inequalities, being natural to human kind, are perfectly acceptable and just. There is only injustice when the man who could afford, say, to put £100 in the kitty, actually puts in only £50, or when a man who is entitled to take out £50 takes out £100. Whether one puts in too little (less than one can or has

42

promised) or takes out too much, it is a betrayal of one's responsibilities.

As I have said, I believe all men know instinctively when they have done what is right and good, although some individuals find it easy to justify their own failures. Moreover, in the state of the world today, many people *cannot* give as much as they could and would if there were no hunger, no fear of war, no sense of being downtrodden and cheated. These and other causes of human failure to recognise and to give to an individual's capacity will be discussed at length in later chapters. It is enough for the moment to realise that a considerable majority of people can, and know they can, put more than they do into the common pool. What they don't understand is that by not doing so they are, in the long run, cheating themselves.

Some political and religious leaders have been advocating this simple precept for many years, stating and restating that no man should have privilege without responsibility. Thinking people may agree in theory, but practical day-by-day application of the theory is the difficulty. Failure to realise that the individual himself will suffer as much as anyone else through his own shortcomings, has prevented its full acceptance.

There is another, obvious aspect: if any man fails to do his own job properly, he will inevitably prevent someone else from performing his. It is like the ripples spread by a stone tossed into a pond; just as one ripple or wave sets up another, so one failure sets off another. And it is the cumulative effect of all men's failures which creates international tensions, hunger, want and most of the other ills in this world.

If this argument is true, as I believe it to be, what of the converse? What if man carries out all his responsibilities as well as he possibly can? There is as yet no way of proving what would happen, as no group of people (so far as we know) has ever succeeded in doing everything it should.

It is a truism, however, that in all team efforts the team does best only when every member of it pulls his full weight. When individual members fail to do so, from whatever cause, the team's performance falls short of its best; dissatisfaction and friction soon set in and record and reputation go from bad to worse. Similarly, to get the best out of a nation all its people must pull together as a team. To get the best – peace *and* plenty – out of the world, clearly all nations must pull together in the same way. Any nation which stands aside is in exactly the same category as the defaulter in the "kitty", or the football player who gives less than his best because he has not taken the trouble to train properly.

If these arguments are valid, then all social and economic evils would lessen – in precisely the same way as the total of road accidents would all but vanish if everyone used the roads as they should. In international affairs and conflicts of ideology, the average man's influence can only be indirect, through his leaders; but it can be decisive. Can any sane man doubt that the world would be happier without war?

There are plenty who will argue that wars and rumours of wars keep industry busy and people in work; that the profits on arms are much greater than the profits on tools, as indeed they generally are. Yet hundreds of millions of people starve and hundreds of millions more live in conditions of appalling squalor, their standard of living barely at subsistence level, because billions of dollars, pounds, francs, marks, yen – money of every currency in the world – as well as raw materials urgently needed for peaceful purposes, are diverted to the appalling cost – *waste* – of armaments. *Yet there is no need for the makers of arms to suffer as armaments are reduced.* A gradual transition from warheads to farm-machines, from gases and bacteria to fertilisers and air-purifiers, would in the long run make more money and more work, not less; and the merchants of death would then become the merchants of life.

If war reaches its logical conclusion there will be a nuclear conflict and, inevitably, the destruction of civilisation as we know it. There will be no market for weapons then, nor for tools or consumer goods. The truth is indisputable – and soberingly simple: *When a man is killed, a customer dies; while he lives, he buys.* When the makers of armaments begin to realise that, perhaps they will start turning their tanks into combine-harvesters.

The longer it takes for all men to grasp the prime necessity of accepting and carrying out all their responsibilities, the longer we shall have to wait for a world without fear, hunger, want or sickness. But Utopia *will* come. The speed of its coming depends entirely on the speed of man's realisation that he himself must create it, that the sooner every individual member of mankind does his share (no more than his share), the better the world will be.

This attainment of a perfect world through a panacea for all the ills of mankind has been the dream of men of vision since civilisation began. The great poets, the dreamers, the prophets, have talked of and sought after it, but they have seldom tried to show how it might be achieved – except in fiction, which indeed has often pointed a way to the future.

Christ showed us perfection, of course. Many of His followers tried to explain it, too, although the years have patently confused and garbled the simplicity even of His message and the messages of the Old Testament. Nevertheless, a few clear, straightforward injunctions come through. "A man reaps what he sows," St. Paul taught men. Christ said, "Always treat others as you would like them to treat you," and "Love your neighbour as yourself," not "better than", or "before" oneself. "Whatever your hand finds to do, do it with your might," we read in Ecclesiastes. St. Paul also wrote, "All of us are parts of one body."

The first of these is surely the clearest injunction to carry out one's responsibilities to others in order to get the best out of life for oneself. The second and third show equally clearly that one's behaviour to others should be based on the effect of such behaviour on oneself, as much as on the others. The fourth states most lucidly and forthrightly that whatever one does, must be done to the absolute best of one's ability: "*your*" might – not someone else's might – is the standard by which to judge. The fifth says with breathtaking simplicity: All people are dependent upon one another, are interdependent.

Of course, these quotations are familiar household axioms, accepted as wise and good guiding rules for human behaviour. Yet very few even among convinced Christians obey them. Most compromise and ease their consciences by regarding such injunctions as counsels of perfection, the unattainable.

Similar exhortations can be found in most religions.

In Confucianism we read:

"What goes out from thee comes back to thee again." *Mencius*.

"If you love men and they are unfriendly, look into your love; if you rule men and they are unruly look into your wisdom; if you are courteous to them and they do not respond look into your respect. If what you do is vain, always seek within." *Mencius*.

"He shall reap hemp who sows hemp, and beans who sows beans." *Chinese Proverb*.

45

In Mohammedanism:

"Every soul shall be paid what it has merited." *Koran.*

"As you sow you will reap." *Moorish Proverb.*

In Hinduism:

"When an action, good or bad, has been committed, its fruit must of necessity be eaten." *Indian Proverb.*

> "Why hast thou said 'I have sinned so much,
> And God in His mercy has not punished my sins?'
> How many times do I smite thee, and thou knowest not!
> Thou art bound in my chains from head to foot.
> On thy heart is rust on rust collected
> So that thou art blind to divine mysteries.
> When a man is stubborn and follows evil practices,
> He casts dust in the eyes of his discernment."
> *Jalal-uddin Rumi.*

In Buddhism:

"Even an evil-doer sees happiness as long as his evil deed has not ripened; but when his evil deed has ripened, then does he see evil. Even a good man sees evil days as long as his good deed has not ripened; but when his good deed has ripened, then does he see happy days." *Dhammapada.*

"As long as the sin bears no fruit, the fool, he thinks it is honey: but when the sin ripens, then, indeed, he goes down into sorrow." *Dhammapada.*

"What goes out of you comes back to you." *Japanese Proverb.*

"By oneself evil is done, by oneself one suffers; by oneself evil is left undone, by oneself one is purified. Purity and impurity belong to oneself." *Dhammapada.*

"All that we are is the result of what we have thought; it is founded on our thoughts, it is made up of our thoughts. If a man speaks or acts with an evil thought pain follows him as the wheel follows the foot of the ox that draws the carriage, but if a

man speaks or acts with a pure thought, happiness follows him
like a shadow that never leaves him." *Dhammapada.*

And in Sikhism:

"Thy weal or woe are according to thine acts." *Trilochan.*

"As a man soweth so shall he reap; as he earneth so shall he
eat." *Japji.*

In spite of the self-evident truth of these sayings, throughout
history, the search for perfection in conduct and for happiness
has been left to the saints, the mystics, the romantics and the
dreamers. Most hard-headed practical businessmen, the
"realists", seem to have accepted the rule that material or
worldly success and "idealism" are incompatible, instead of
learning the obvious lesson from these prophets. For clearly a
rich man would enjoy his riches far more in a happy world
than he can in a world of misery, want and fear. The axiom that
it is easier for a camel to go through the eye of a needle than
for a rich man to enter the Kingdom of Heaven has done incalculable harm by perpetrating the fallacy that worldly
success and spiritual well-being are necessarily in conflict. In
fact, it is slowly becoming apparent that in each there is a sense
of incompleteness without the other.
  History, however, shows that some visionary politicians have
dreamed of social and political perfection: Franklin D. Roosevelt, with his Four Freedoms; Abraham Lincoln, with his dream
of government *of* the people *by* the people, and *for* the people;
David Lloyd George with his "A fit country for heroes to live
in" – this last once taken very seriously, if now regarded
cynically. But for the most part these idealistic objectives have
become obscured by the urgent and pressing need for policies
to cope with current ills or deal with emergencies. Lincoln no
doubt dreamed of a trouble-free land of brothers of all colours
but he had one of the most bestial, fratricidal wars in history to
fight: this must have clouded the issue, even for him.
  This clouding of issues has always foiled man's quest for
human happiness, his seekings after perfection, his endeavours
to free the world from the evils which plague mankind. The
major, long-term issues have always *been* clouded; short-term
problems have made it almost impossible seriously to consider
them, let alone work towards their attainment. In seeking

47

human happiness, astonishingly few people have managed to "see the wood for the trees".

Yet the wood is there. It must be. If it were not, there would not be so many trees.

Although too few practical men in politics, business, commerce and trade of all kinds, have spared enough time for the quest for perfection (see Chapters 11, 12 and 13), it is not uncommon for idealists among them to leave their money to foundations which themselves have had to cope with short-term problems – foundations such as those created by men like Ford, Nuffield and Rockefeller. It is a wry but true reflection that some were originally conceived as a way of avoiding tax, an avoidance often possible *only* by "doing good". Thus, the good was not done for its own sake; yet the good done by the foundations thus established is incalculable the world over.

There have been industrialists like the Quaker Cadburys in England who have attempted to apply religious precepts to trade and industry so as to create model conditions for their workers through a form of benevolent paternalism. Up to a point they have succeeded, but they have seldom influenced social or industrial life except that under their direct control. They have tried to practise what they preached, but have failed to persuade others in any great number to practise or even to preach the same counsel of industrial perfection.

Gandhi practised what he preached and made countless others believe in his ideals, but these ideals had a negative quality which surely won only the trappings of freedom and increased the danger of economic and social chaos. Moreover, whatever its intent, Gandhi's teaching in fact did comparatively little to mitigate the feud between Moslem and Hindu. Gandhi and other great religious leaders have preached of perfection but have been forced to limit themselves to clearing away only some of the barriers to it.

Yet these dreamers, these idealists, must surely at least have hoped that somewhere in this world there was a single, simple answer to all men's desires, all men's needs and all men's hopes – one comprehensive and fully satisfying solution to the problems, the sicknesses, the fears of mankind. They must surely have dreamed continually of a common denominator existing among all men, making possible a code of conduct which could be accepted and observed by believers in *all* religions, *all* ideologies, *all* political systems, through *all* ages, at *all* stages of social, educational and cultural development. There must

surely have been the conviction deep in the minds of all such
dreamers that this desperately needed panacea must one day
be found.

. . .

I myself am convinced, have been convinced for many years,
that there is such an answer.

I can give no positive reason for my certainty, but such
"innate" convictions are not new to me. In my early youth I
was utterly convinced that I would become a professional
writer. Despite the many obstacles and the ridicule poured on
the very idea, it was not to me a question of "whether" –
simply of "when". Later, when I was established as a professional writer, the move to best-selling seemed as inevitable.
I cannot recall feeling that I deserved to "best-sell", only that
it would eventually happen. And in the event, it did – but not
by the usual channel of meteoric success with one particular
novel; my sales accumulated gradually, book by book.

The finding of a single, simple answer to man's needs seems
equally inevitable to me today. I do not doubt the existence of
that answer, any more than I doubt that I breathe. It will come
step by step – and to me the most exhilarating certainty of all is
that most of the steps have already been taken; that only a few
more are needed before we reach our goal.

. . .

Once this single, all-satisfying answer has been found, it will
almost certainly be realised that many philosophers and
scientists, thinkers and searchers, dreamers and politicians have
long been pointing the way. Instead of being new, the panacea
will be immediately recognisable; even more important, it will
be seen in such a form that no one, from the near simple-minded
to the highest intellectual, will fail to see what he must do so as
to get the best out of life.

Only when a man sees this obligation can he carry it out with
the pride, or self-respect, which is essential to his happiness. To
put his utmost into what he does, however, a man also needs an
incentive – a reason or sense of purpose. The inducement of
material reward or money is now known not to be enough in
itself; but nor is it enough simply to work with all his might
for the sake of the job.

One man, as we know, would find work on an assembly line
unbearably dull, whereas another – given good conditions – will
do it quite happily. Experience has shown that music in the
background, more frequent "rest" or "tea" breaks and a

pleasant atmosphere, will often help him to put his best into his task. But a far greater inducement would be awareness of the fact that the work he is doing day in, day out, is of great importance, because by doing his job well he is not only profiting himself but is also helping the rest of mankind to do theirs – be they his own children, his next-door neighbours, the population of a village, a city or a whole nation.

It needs emphasising that most men will need help in learning and later in carrying out their responsibilities, and that much of this help must come from enlightened home, social and working conditions. This does not, of course, conflict with any philosophy or religion; it is in fact inherent in many of them.

In the days of Aristotle, Socrates and Plato, there was much seeking after truth, regardless of the consequences. Plato disagreed with the religious philosophies of his day. Aristotle rejected much that his Master taught and was adamant in favour of absolutism: the argument that there is only one right course of action for any man in given circumstances, and that whatever else he does is wrong. The romantics then rejected Aristotle's arguments – much more acceptable to man – that one should be moderate in all things, and when in doubt, should take the middle course. Soon, Epicurus argued that religion is not a source of happiness and that men must seek happiness for themselves, without over-indulgence. After him came the Cynics, rejecting the precepts of philosophy and seeking simple goodness; they have a great many followers today. The Stoics had their very different theory – that Divine Law rules the world, including man, who must therefore accept his fate, be it good or bad.

All that this arbitrary summary does is emphasise the differences among the philosophers and also the absence of any common code of behaviour among them; nearly every pronouncement they made was in the most general terms. With Christianity came Christian ethics, based largely on Jewish ethics: no other major development in philosophy appeared until, in the later part of the seventeenth century, Spinoza brought mathematics (presumably the immutability of logic) into the philosophic picture, to enrage Christian and Jew alike. It is deeply significant that he should write:

"After experience had taught one that all the usual surroundings of social life are vain and futile; seeing that none of the objects of my fears contained in themselves anything good or bad except insofar as the mind is affected by them, I finally resolved

50

to inquire whether there might be some real good having power to communicate itself, which would affect the mind singly, to the exclusion of all else; whether in fact there might be anything of which the discovery and the attainment would enable me to enjoy continuous, supreme happiness . . .

"I therefore debated whether it would not be possible to arrive at a new principle, or at any rate at a certainty concerning its existence without changing the conduct and the usual plan of my life; with this end in view I made many efforts *but in vain.*"

But in vain.

Deep in Spinoza's philosophy was fatalism, or predetermination. These same beliefs or assumptions have been inherent in most philosophies. In Bentham's and John Stuart Mill's *Utilitarianism,* however, the argument was that the consequence or result of an action makes the action itself good or bad, and this is almost the reverse of determinism. Kant's view that morality is closely bound up with one's duties and obligations, is close to my own beliefs. Perhaps they have been inherited from him; I am keenly aware that this book contains nothing completely new, although some things take on a deeper significance as the years pass.

All religious and political philosophies laid down certain codes of behaviour, from the Ten Commandments and Christ's parables to the precept which seems to run through Buddhism – to "withdraw from life and live within oneself". There must have been three political philosophies for every religious one, and two religious ones for every non-religious one, but it is impossible to avoid or refute the fact that none has succeeded in showing man (*a*) what to do; (*b*) why he should do it; (*c*) how he should do it; and (*d*) what will happen to him if he does. The religious philosophies, it might be argued, *have* said that if man did as he was told by his spiritual leaders, he would go to heaven, and if he didn't he wouldn't, but none appears to have shown the consequences on this planet of any pattern of behaviour. There have been many promises about the delights of the next world, but these are hardly of practical use and hold much less appeal today than in the days when God was taken for granted and few questioned who or what He was.

It becomes more and more evident that the reasonings and pronouncements of philosophers are usually little more than a series of highly intelligent guesses; and it is sadly true that almost any theory is likely to be ridiculed, if not demolished,

51

before it is very old. But there is a basic truth which cannot be demolished by dialectics or semantics: that if *all* man carried out their responsibilities and put more into life than they do, then *all* men could benefit; for there would be more to take out of life. The key question is whether all men can be *taught* to recognise and to carry out their responsibilities, to find the good within themselves and use it to the full.

One could essay a deeper analysis or a symposium of all the philosophers and their advocates and their decriers, their good aspects and their bad. But students of philosophy would see nothing new except perhaps nuances of interpretation, or else would disagree vigorously with my inferences, while those who do not study philosophy would not know whether I was right or wrong. So except for occasional quotations and acknowledgments, the part played by philosophers in the rest of this book will be implicit rather than stated. But mankind's debt to them is very great indeed, for they have all tried to point the way, some have succeeded significantly, and each has derived some benefit from those who went before.

The belief – a conviction which lacks unchallengeable proof – that all men can and one day will behave so that we live in a Utopia, is, of course, regarded as sheer idealism. But as I have said, because it would self-evidently be the best and happiest possible life for mankind, it seems to me that such idealism is the only true realism; they *are* identical twins.

That there *is* a single answer to mankind's problems, a single philosophy or rule of life or code of behaviour which will enable all people of all races and religions to live together in amity, cannot possibly be proved, however, until *all* men act on one simple belief: the acceptance of all their own primary responsibilities *to themselves*.

Freud, with his *id*, was "discoverer" of a truth which most grandmothers knew before he was born. But he could pass on his "discoveries" to savants and the world, whereas the influence of the wise elders of families is restricted to the members of the families, and perhaps also friends. Such elders have instinctive knowledge of the importance of oneself *to* oneself, but often become hopelessly confused or tongue-tied when they try to explain.

It is safe to assume that Christ preached the single answer, but probable that His disciples failed to grasp its significance – or else failed to pass it on lucidly.

A variation of the Christian "love thy neighbour as thyself" is found in all the major religions except Hinduism. In one way

Hinduism comes as near the truth as any philosophy, in its precept that each Hindu, whatever his caste or station, should behave well in the hope of improving himself in his next re-incarnation. The Shintoists, worshipping their ancestors in such guises as tiny streams, trees and rocks, are also near the truth in one way, for their basic concern is only for themselves. Every individual instinctively feels this self-concern before he feels anything else; it is the life-instinct. Buddhism seems to me further away from the truth, with its philosophy of eventually living within oneself to attain perfect peace in absolute *freedom*, *quite independently* of any other human being, for I am sure man cannot be independent of others. Confucianism perhaps comes nearest of all in principle.

Yet Christians surely come nearest to preaching the importance and significance of *the individual*. What has developed in Christianity may well be a dilution of the truth; perhaps Christ did indeed give the whole answer with "love thy neighbour as thyself" implying that one must (and does) love oneself *first*. Whether this is so or not, the distillation of most Christian, perhaps most religious belief, is surely the adjuration: "Do good for its own sake."

Certainly doing good for its own sake has become part of the *credo* of Western Society, most highly developed perhaps in Great Britain and the United States. The world would be a much poorer place without the "service" or "do-gooding" clubs and associations which have arisen and flourished. Several organisations of these are now world-wide, such as Rotary and Round Table, the Peace Corps, and Voluntary Service Overseas – the first American in origin, the second British. Each of these movements continually exhorts its members to do good for its own sake, to put service above self – and this after all is what the Christian, the Jewish, the Moslem religions are saying all the time.

It rises to a crescendo. *Do good, good, good*, because it is good to do good. Practically all great social reforms have been born out of this philosophy, to which the world owes more than it can ever repay. Yet it remains a fact that the great reforms have come in the face of fierce opposition from people who have opposed goodness for its own sake. It also remains a fact that goodness for its own sake does not draw enough goodness out of all men, through whom it is generated, and cannot, therefore, put enough into the common pool to satisfy man's needs.

Why is there so much active or passive obstruction to good for its own sake?

Good, God and Man

What really happens?

Is it not that the very moment this do-gooding *hurts* us, or calls for a real sacrifice of time or money, the vast majority of us fail to live up to the *credo*? Invariably we have some "reasonable" and to ourselves satisfying justification; we may claim that further sacrifices even for the common good would deprive our own families of hard-won privileges; or would rob our neighbours; or prevent us from putting money aside for a rainy day (or a holiday); or hinder us in doing our work properly; or stop us from playing whatever game or following whatever hobby keeps us physically and mentally fit to meet the rigours of daily life.

In short, when it comes to the crunch we put what we believe to be our own interests first – as indeed we must, because as human beings we are bound to do so; it is both compulsive and instinctive. We stop doing good because we fear that it will harm us. Goodness is in short supply only because man does not yet know what is truly in his own best interests.

Man has been told, taught, trained, to believe that the motivation for doing good must be the service of others: good for its own sake. The simple, fundamental, religious, historical and traditional human mistake is believing that it is *better* to do good for its own (or another's) sake *than for oneself*. That motivation simply does not create enough good to go round: it is imposed on man rather than instinctive. (Helping a neighbour in distress, or a fellow human being in danger, is natural, however – although a great number of people still pass by on the other side; the *active* Good Samaritan is still in the minority because many fear they will suffer in some way if they help a man in need.)

How strong *is* the natural instinct to do good for others? And is there any proof of its existence and how it came? Professor J. H. Fremlin makes what is to me a fascinating comment on this:

"I am, at least very nearly, convinced that one of the major basic steps in producing human beings out of some kind of anthropoid was a slop-over, by mutation or otherwise, of the parental concern for young which had evolved over the previous one hundred million years or so, to cover other adults of the same species. You don't have to give extensive arguments to a mother or father to explain to them why they ought to protect their children, and I believe the same instinct, although undoubtedly weaker, now applies to one's own group. This split of instinctive behaviour, of course, gave numerous improvements in survival value to any groups which possessed it, and the present unfortunate situation, I believe, arises particularly because the instinct is not as strong as it should be. This is why we spend such a lot of time trying to condition our children to increase the probability of acting on this instinct and to reduce the tendency to work on purely selfish instincts."

Certainly observation shows that man can train himself, or shame himself, or be trained, shamed or frightened into strengthening any tendency to do good for its own sake. But with comparatively few exceptions, he simply cannot do anything like *enough* good for the needs of mankind if he is motivated by this objective alone. The stress of emotion or a crisis such as war often stimulates selfless good, but once the crisis is passed the stimulus weakens.

The primary and constant motivation for man, then, is to do good *for himself*. He must see this in its true perspective, not as a selfish instinct that should be sternly discouraged but as a natural, proper and unalterable trait, before he can see good for what it really is – and both generate enough and use it properly.

This urge to do good for himself is a part of man's basic animal instinct for survival. Over the ages, however, circumstances and environment have forced him to survive at the expense of others; so that he has learned to do good for himself even though it means harming others. This is neither natural nor instinctive, but has been an integral part of man's existence for so long and is so ingrained that we have come to regard it as both.

Man has to learn that he can do as much good to himself as he likes, provided it harms no one else.

He has already learned by bitter experience that the selfishness or greed or even thoughtless acquisitiveness of others causes harm to him. It must be equally apparent, once he thinks about it, that whenever he seeks his own (or his family's) good at the expense of others, he hurts those others.

Surely it need only be pointed out to him that any good he may do for himself at their expense can very easily be cancelled out by the harm he suffers from others when *they* look after *their* interests at *his* expense. He *must* then see that it would be infinitely more sensible if both he and they stopped doing harm to each other. One of the basic human fears – that of suffering harm at another's hands – would thus be removed.

This must seem to some too conclusively demonstrable for comment. But man has *always* needed to be taught, or shown, most of those simple truths which are so glaringly obvious once they are seen.

We know from experience that people learn most easily things which "come naturally" to them, things which they enjoy doing. And as we have seen that goodness is instinctive or natural to man once artificial restraints or fears are removed, he will obviously *enjoy* doing good both for his own and for others' sake.

We know – we don't have to prove it, we *know* – that goodness is restricted not by man's ability to do good but by his own degree of willingness. The amount of goodness which can be generated by man is as inexhaustible as thought. We have proved by simple logic that if there is no harm to cancel out the good, then much more goodness will be available for sharing among all, and so each man's share will be greater.

We know – we don't have to prove this either, we *know* – that the amount of good needed to overcome the evils of hunger, sickness, hatred, intolerance, ignorance and fear is virtually infinite. But if we have just proved that the supply of good is inexhaustible (infinite), once we have the right motivation, then we have only to find that motivation, and to waste no good by doing harm, to have all the good we need. The effect of this on man's well-being will at last be incalculable. And in the final analysis we shall see that no man can truly do the very best for himself without *in the process* doing good for others.

Such an argument as this needs a summation; and here perhaps I should say that the summation which follows is also, for me, a personal affirmation.

Doing good for oneself is instinctive to man and every act of good swells the sum total of goodness from which all men benefit. Doing harm (evil) to others is not instinctive to man but each harmful act takes away from the total good and so robs all men – including oneself. When this simple fact is understood it will be recognised as a natural law: when observance of this natural law has become the norm, it will be shown as the true source of human happiness.

I call this natural law SELF-ISM.

In simplest terms, Self-ism is a doctrine based on mankind's essential interdependence, which holds that the interests of all are best served by the active self-interest of each.

Self-ism – a New Look at Ethics and Morality

And for me, Self-ism is demonstrably true, since it follows these other unchallengeable truths:

Only when man has acquired knowledge for himself can he pass knowledge on to others. Only when he has acquired wisdom for himself can he pass wisdom on to others. *So:* only when man has acquired goodness for himself can he pass goodness on to others.

. . .

Self-ism accepts and in fact asserts that man will only be able to generate sufficient goodness for the world's needs if he seeks it, *in the beginning*, in himself and for himself.

. . .

I question this assertion no more than I question the fact that no man can feel, understand, think, reason, hate, love or act for anyone else – any more than he can breathe for anyone else.

This book was once to be called *The Evil that Men Do*, a striking title, at first glance. Soon, however, I realised that the quotation implied acceptance of the attitude towards good and evil inherent in the Bible's "The sins of the fathers shall be visited upon the children unto the third and fourth generation." I have reacted against this latter statement ever since I was old enough to understand its implications, because it seemed so wickedly unfair to the children. Even though it was manifestly true, I always hated it. Over the years, however, the breath-taking corollary grew upon me: the *good* of the fathers shall also be visited upon the children, until the thirtieth and fortieth generation – indeed, forever.

Goodness never dies. Evil may stifle and silence it, but it will live on.

Evil dies, as Nazism died. It is often reincarnated, it is too often incarnate, but – it dies.

The dragon dies; St. George lives for ever in the human heart and mind. If he had allowed the dragon to live, *he* would have lived with guilt and the villagers with fear; so even in legend – that oldest of all methods of teaching right from wrong – the greatest good is shown as springing from the need to do good for oneself. Goodness is like rain on the soil of man's mind; with enough of it, the most marvellous crops will grow.

Given, then, that there is an exhaustible supply, we only need to learn how best to tap goodness. The Christian and the Hindu, the Buddhist and the Moslem, members of all religions and creeds and members of none, all will find different ways to tap the goodness in themselves and in their fellows. There is

57

no religion in the world which forbids a man the right to do good for his own sake, for himself. All that any religion demands is that he should also do good for others.

Now, however, we have to face some inescapable questions. How can the theory be put into practice? How can Self-ism be used to generate the good needed by the whole world? How can we show the all-conquering power of goodness through Self-ism? How can we prove that it has the answers to all the problems of mankind?

First, we can learn its summation:

Doing good for oneself is instinctive to man and every act of good swells the sum total of goodness from which all men benefit. Doing harm (evil) to others is not instinctive to man but each harmful act takes away from the total good and so robs all men – including oneself. When this simple fact is understood it will be recognised as a natural law: when observance of this natural law has become the norm, it will be shown as the true source of human happiness.

Next, we can study in detail the influence of Self-ism on man's bodily health: the following chapter will show how much the health (good) of one man may depend on everyone else carrying out his ordinary daily task well.

After that, we can apply Self-ism to all the manifold needs of mankind.

Chapter 5

IN SICKNESS AND IN HEALTH

So far in this book there has been a great deal of dogmatic assertion as well as theory, and no doubt many will interpret much as either platitudinous or the dreamings of a man with his head in the clouds. So it is necessary to establish the truth of Self-ism's beneficial and indeed benign influence on mankind. If this can be shown beyond reasonable doubt, then even the most sceptical are likely to be persuaded that realism and idealism are in truth inseparable.

Health concerns all people in the same way, because money, position, age and sex have little effect on it. We can all become ill, we are all liable to accidents, wherever we may be, and it makes little difference whether we are incapacitated by natural illness or by accident. The rich man can buy certain services, drugs and treatments more readily than the poor, but he is no less susceptible to colds, influenza, rheumatism and divers other everyday diseases. Moreover, some diseases are wealth diseases: coronaries and high blood pressure occur much more often in the wealthy than in the poor.

Then, too, there is equality in the sexes: both man and woman will be equally miserable in any kind of sickness, not necessarily showing but undoubtedly feeling it in the same way. And a child or adolescent can be as grievously ill as an old person.

Health is influenced by so many factors: food and housing affect it, so the starving or the badly-housed are more liable to certain illnesses than the wealthy and well-fed, but in general health is of equal importance to all, and illness and accident are common to all.

It is habitual to take this for granted, and to take the medical profession for granted, too. It would be reasonable to suppose that half-a-dozen or so people are involved in dealing with a single person's illness; perhaps as many as a dozen in serious cases. Another thing we commonly take for granted is doctors' skill: certainly it becomes glaringly obvious whenever one of them neglects to do his job properly. Such neglect might easily be responsible for the death of his patient, and few things cause such an outcry as an allegation that a doctor has failed in his duty. A nurse who neglects a patient, or a pharmaceutical chemist who makes up a prescription wrongly, are equally blameworthy and equally vulnerable to public censure. However, the task of looking after the sick has urgency and also calls for particular sensitivity, and consequently people with a highly developed sense of vocation and skill are most likely to become doctors, surgeons, pharmacists or nurses. These qualities usually make one alive to the responsibilities of one's work.

Anyone with this kind of skill and sense of vocation will take pride in it, too, and be less likely to take the slightest risk of doing his work badly or indifferently. Certainly, when practising his profession, he is likely to carry out his responsibilities very thoroughly, although in other spheres his standard may fail; after all, a doctor may drive a car as badly or as carelessly as the next man. Similarly, a nurse may be a most considerate person to her patient, yet show baffling lack of consideration to that patient's relatives.

In sickness, however, one is not simply in the hands of a few people, those medical, nursing, pharmaceutical and public health officials directly involved. A sick man is affected by many hundreds of people, and the carelessness or inefficiency of any one of them *could* lead to his death. And it often does, even though the human being guilty of the lapse may never know its consequences.

If he did know, he would be filled with remorse. But if it happens miles – perhaps hundreds of miles – from the place where the stranger died, how can he know?

And if the direct or indirect cause of a human being's death occurred a long time *before* that death – days, weeks, months, even years – how can the guilty one know and feel remorse and so vow never again to do the same wrong?

Obviously, these things are impossible.

The purpose of this chapter is to show conclusively how many individuals may be involved directly or indirectly in circumstances which lead to a man's death. It is to show that if a man is never to harm a fellow human being, he must make absolutely sure that he *never* fails to do properly whatever he is doing. And it is to show that if others do their job properly, he himself will never suffer avoidable sickness or accident.

Imagine that a certain popular and frequently used drug is to be administered to the patient, and suppose that in the preparation of that drug, a chemist makes a mistake – perhaps by failing to sterilise an instrument or a piece of equipment thoroughly. Ninety-nine times out of a hundred nothing will go wrong, but in the hundredth case, the lack of sterilisation may set up a chemical reaction which changes the nature of or adds a lethal constituent to the drug *at the time it is being used on the patient* – perhaps days, possibly months later.

As a result, the patient might die.

It may be said that this is an exceptional and far-fetched example, but such misadventures are not uncommon. The margin of error in blood transfusion is sometimes estimated as one in five thousand deaths from *avoidable* error. The range of error is wide, from simple mis-labelling of bottles to indifferent or incomplete sterilisation of instruments, or to faulty storage. Blood should be kept at a steady four degrees Fahrenheit to be in perfect condition. Such simple errors as leaving a refrigerator door open too long, or taking a supply of blood plasma out of the refrigerator and leaving it standing in room temperature for too long, can increase the bacteria so greatly, that the transfusion may be immediately (and possibly lethally) dangerous. Even the modern method of sterilisation with *six* different processes is liable to human or mechanical error at any one of the six stages.

The victim of a road accident is more likely than most to need a blood transfusion, and so is more prone to the dangers of such transfusions – which adds to the odds already against him. The simple and tragic fact is that practically all the errors are avoidable and would not arise if everyone concerned did his or her own simple, ordinary, quite easy-to-do job competently – such as closing the refrigerator door, or washing out a bottle, or making (and buying) bottles which can be properly cleansed without difficulty.

And all of these things would be much more likely to be done properly if everyone realised the *danger to himself* of failure. It is relating the consequences of failure to oneself which will teach the lesson most thoroughly, because no one is so important to oneself as oneself.

There is at least as great a margin of error in the administering of anaesthetics. In the book *General Anaesthesia* by Philip H. Addison and Peter Baylis, it is stated that:

"The standard of professional knowledge required of the anaesthetist is that prevailing at the time. This was illustrated in an action (Roe *v.* Minister of Health 1954) brought by two patients against a consultant anaesthetist. On the same afternoon the anaesthetist had administered a spinal anaesthetic to both patients. The anaesthetic, which consisted of cinchocaine was put up in glass ampoules which were kept in a glass jar containing a solution of phenol. Following the operation each patient developed a permanent paraplegia from the waist downwards. It was established at the trial that the cinchocaine had become contaminated by the phenol which had entered through cracks in the ampoule which were not visible upon naked-eye inspection. Evidence showed that this was not a risk which was generally appreciated by competent anaesthetists at that time and the anaesthetist was acquitted of negligence in failing to recognise this possible danger.

"Later theories are that in fact minute quantities of detergents were left in syringes.

"In either case some degree of simple carelessness was evident. Either the authorities did not warn the workers of the danger; or the workers – cleaners – did not take sufficient notice."

Another vivid example of the consequences of any kind of error, whether by commission or omission, is shown in this report from *The Times* on September 21st, 1966:*

"The contamination of cylinders of nitrous oxide – 'laughing gas' – made by British Oxygen, of Brentford, could have been due only to a series of extraordinary coincidences, the company said yesterday.

"It said the malfunction that caused the poisoning of the gas had been traced to a day on either side of August 21, a Sunday, and to a period of about two hours.

" 'The poisoning cause seems almost certainly to have been the overheating of a reaction vessel', a statement said. 'It can only have been due to a series of extraordinary coincidences that, following this malfunction, contaminated gas actually reached the cylinders.

" 'The elaborate precautions built into this and similar plant have been effective over 40 years of continuous production. It is impossible to be certain of what happened on this occasion but the most likely train of events is as follows:

" 'The overheating which is not, in itself, normally serious, appears to have coincided with a failure in a subsequent purification process.

" 'Two principal tests for detecting contamination rely on

* The italics in the quotations in this chapter are mine. – J.C.

the visual observance of solutions through which gas is bubbled, which change from colourless to pink if contamination takes place. The reagent through which the gas is bubbled consists of two colourless liquids which are mixed immediately before use and which are effective for at least 24 hours.

" 'Contaminated gas could only have got into the cylinders *if the colour changes were ignored, or if the reagent was incorrectly mixed.*

" 'In the absence of any evidence indicating failure to observe the tests accurately *it seems likely that an operative accidentally mixed two batches of the same liquid instead of taking a measure of each.* If this were done the visual tests would be ineffective without those observing them knowing that anything was wrong.

" 'It is clear that by a further coincidence the cylinders selected for a regular random sampling test contained uncontaminated gas, although many of those in that particular batch must have been contaminated.

" 'An electronic instrument which was used for a supplementary test *has been functioning erratically.*

" 'Although such a chain of coincidences is without precedent, *additional safeguards are being introduced.*

" 'As soon as the suspected contamination became known distribution of the production was halted and the plant thoroughly checked.'

"The company said last night that as part of the additional safeguards the random sample test was to be trebled to about 15 out of 100 ready-for-use cylinders; an additional bubble test for observing contamination visually would be put in the final stage immediately before the gas went into the cylinders; and a routine would be adopted to ensure that the reagent that was mixed for the test was correct."

About the same time the following report appeared in the *Daily Mail* on a very different subject.

"The deaths of five hospital patients are believed to have been caused *by a mix-up in the administration* of gas.

"It is thought that they were given nitrous oxide – laughing gas – instead of oxygen.

"A full report on the deaths at Edinburgh Royal Infirmary, has been sent to Mr. Angus MacLeod, the city's Procurator Fiscal.

"The dead patients were all from the same department and

63

had just undergone operations. Oxygen is used for reviving patients after surgery.

"A senior doctor at the infirmary said last night: 'I have not heard anything about this, *but it is possible such a thing could happen. The wrong cylinder could be coupled to the wrong pipe.*'

"The deaths are believed to have occurred several weeks ago. *Immediately afterwards, arrangements for the administration of gas and anaesthetics were tightened up.*"

And in the *Daily Telegraph* this report appeared in September 1966:

POLIO MEN WIN CASE

Drug Firm to Pay $140,000.00

"Two men who claimed that they had contracted poliomyelitis from taking the Sabin oral vaccine were awarded a total of $140,000.00 (£50,000) yesterday by a San Francisco jury. The damages are to be paid by Charles Pfizer, the drug manufacturers.

"The men are Mr. Richard Grinnell, 62, president of a steel products company, and Mr. Carlos Benedetti, 36, who has been unemployed for several months. *The company denied allegations that the vaccine taken in 1962, had contained impurities.*"

Each of these examples show the inescapable interdependence of people, an interdependence which is often unsuspected by most of those involved. The significance of interdependence is third only to the fact that the human being, seeing everything through his own eyes, is a Self-ist, and to the fact that he must become aware of the significance and importance, to himself as well as to others, of recognising and carrying out his responsibilities.

The range of responsibility in health is enormous. We have spent a little time considering how it affects doctors and nurses, and how it affects the health of patients and their chances of survival. Just as important in its way is the responsibility of the dustman. Bernard Levin puts this succinctly under the title of "The Affluent Society" in the *Daily Mail*, October 1966:

"The total annual consumption of copies of morning, evening and Sunday papers (in Great Britain) is roughly *nine thousand million,* and if we add in the total of local weekly newspapers, and also the thousands of magazines, the total number of periodical publications read in Britain in a year is clearly far more than 10,000,000,000.

"Assuming as I do that it is all thrown away after reading, except for my bit, it presents a formidable problem in the way of disposal. And, of course, waste paper forms only a small proportion of the total of refuse pouring out every second from the countless vents of our society into its gaping cloacas.

"Food, wrapping and packing materials, tins and bottles, detergent swill, used razor-blades and cosmetic products – it all goes to swell a continuous tide of dross which must amount to several cubic *miles* a year.

"*The collection and disposal of all this is not particularly well organised and every now and again it breaks down entirely in some unfortunate borough.*   But the fact that the system works at all – indeed, that it exists – seems to me a kind of miracle.

"*More to the point, it seems to me to emphasise the extraordinary frailty of our civilisation, the desperately thin ice on which we tiptoe.*

"For imagine what would happen if the machine stopped, if for a month – even for a week – no refuse was collected, none disposed of.

"Our way of living, in any meaningfully organised sense, would stagger to a halt, choked beyond clearing by rubbish piled as high as mountains all around us.

"This is not, of course, a disingenuous plea for the un-attainable peter-simple life. The corollaries of prosperity are specialisation and organisation, and if we want to share the hand-to-mouth existence of Calcutta, we must also adopt its standard of living.

"*All I say is that we had better beware. One of these days the dustmen may come in out of the rain for good.*"

A man who is aware of the Self-ism which motivates him and its significance to himself and others will surely realise that it is essential to do his best in everything he does, for he will be aware that any shortcoming on his part may injure someone else or deprive him of something he has a perfect right to expect from society. And we have seen that it follows that anyone else's failure may, just as easily, injure or deprive *him*. This is surely what St. Paul meant when he said: "Speak every man truth (do good by) with his neighbour: for we are members one of another."

Human interdependence *is* inescapable. No one can opt out. This becomes vividly apparent if we examine the causes and consequences of a road accident in which a man is badly injured. I have always been particularly aware of the part road accidents play in modern society and how vividly they so often show failure to do what one should for oneself and by one's neighbour, and for that reason have selected an imaginary example which shows:

(i) How many different people can be involved directly or indirectly, in a man's grave illness (injury) and possible death.
(ii) How many people can directly or indirectly influence what happens to that man when he is nearest death.
(iii) How many people can contribute directly or indirectly towards his recovery, if he should pass the crisis.
(iv) How many people are affected by the accident even though they bore no kind of responsibility before, during, or after it occurred.

Instead of a long, elaborately detailed chapter, an illustration is easier to follow than close print and close reasoning. Not only does it show the chain of events at a glance but it also shows exactly how one can be involved oneself. And in this particular example of what happens in a modern civilised community, virtually everyone becomes involved.

Not only is everyone involved but it is also unarguably true that *any single one of those involved could have been the victim* – and might become a victim at almost any moment.

The example involves a man on an operating table in a big metropolitan hospital. An hour before he arrived at the hospital he was fit and well, without any inkling or premonition of danger. Now – he might die.

If he should die, his wife, his children, his friends, will grieve. If he should die, his potential contribution to society will die with him. The cost of his death to society will be very great indeed; in fact, incalculable.

The number of individuals involved is incalculable, too. They include:

(i) All the people whose actions did lead or could have led directly towards the accident.
(ii) All the people whose actions did or could have contributed *in*directly towards the accident.
(iii) All the people who helped directly at the scene of the accident, or to bring the patient to hospital.

(iv) All the doctors, surgeons, nurses and medical staff who helped directly in the operation.

(v) All the hospital staff, maintenance men, etc., who helped indirectly in the operation.

(vi) All the suppliers, manufacturers and distributors of drugs, instruments and equipment used for the patient.

(vii) All who contribute directly to the patient's aftercare.

Added to these, are all the factors which affect the patient's prospects of recovery, and all the factors which affected the patient's vulnerability to the accident and its consequences.

Now it is self-evident that if any one of the host of people involved in these things does his job badly, this man might die. Everything *has* to be done properly if he is to be assured of the best possible chance of survival.

Moreover, a second glance at the illustration will show that the victim might have been anyone of those involved – or anyone of us.

So everything that happens to society and its individual members depends ultimately on how each individual does his job – including oneself.

There are exceptions to this rule. An earthquake, a typhoon, a tidal wave or some sickness not yet curable by man, is not generally regarded as our responsibility. Yet perhaps in a way it is. If we had spent more time and money on research against disease and natural disasters and less on the weapons of war, we might have conquered more diseases and protected more cities against tidal waves or even against earthquakes. We took the risk of concentrating on war – and created the horror of atomic radiation.

The man on the operating table also took a risk with his life.

Of course, this is a particularly graphic and grave example. There could be countless others, showing how many lives we touch even by our simplest action, and how many people unknown to us affect our lives by theirs.

Some unpalatable facts will become apparent when we contemplate these things.

In a world in which such diseases as rickets, river blindness, tuberculosis, beri-beri, yaws, diphtheria, smallpox and many others can be cured or prevented by the expenditure of comparatively little money, hundreds of millions of human beings still suffer from them, and many die.

In a world in which it is a commonplace to spend a hundred million pounds on some piece of military equipment, or a space probe, a few privately organised groups of public-spirited people have to beg for funds to aid in their research on a cure for such diseases as cancer, rheumatoid arthritis, coronary thrombosis, leukemia, and even the common cold. The nature of our society in the past has not only encouraged, it has virtually demanded that a few outstanding individuals, dedicated to doing good for its own sake, should cajole or persuade or shame others into doing a little such good – *for charity*. The resultant good, invaluable though it has been and still is, simply isn't anywhere near enough to solve the problem.

Any one of us, any member of any government or any nation, might die from one of these illnesses, or its consequences. So when nations refuse or fail to give the comparatively trifling sums needed for medical research, they put their citizens – as we put ourselves – in danger from diseases, and extend the period during which such diseases will be a scourge on mankind.

And "disease" includes the many emotional and psychological sicknesses which attack modern society. These sicknesses exist very largely because of our *denial of self*. It is one thing not to get all we *want*; for what purpose would be left to us if we had that? It is another not to get all we *need*, for what we need is essential to us.

The habit of exerting unnecessary self-denial is a major cause of psychological illness. Either we give up what we need and the strain of the effort makes us ill, or we take what we need and because we have been taught that we should have denied ourselves, we develop a guilt complex. This creates inhibitions which cause neurotic or psychotic conditions often believed to be pathological. Once we can rid *ourselves* of psychological sicknesses, we might be pleasantly surprised to discover how free mankind can be from mental illness; and even truly pathological sickness may well respond more and more to drugs and treatment.

To live happily, we *must* live in health. The acceptance by all people of their responsibilities will take us towards the day when illness will be banished. Thus the philosophy of Self-ism shows not only how and why man should *and can* draw upon inexhaustible supplies of goodness, but also how its principles can be applied to man's primary problem, that of ensuring good health.

Until all of us do so, sickness will lie upon mankind.

Until all of us do so, we shall continue to spend fantastic sums of money to alleviate suffering *which need not exist*. All the time, money, skill and energy spent in unnecessary surgical and medical care could and should be devoted to unavoidable diseases, and, beyond that, to the greater human needs. There is deep satisfaction in easing pain, even more in saving life. There would be still more and deeper satisfaction in helping to bring into being a world of human happiness.

But a man cannot give happiness to others unless he is happy himself and he cannot be happy unless he has good health.

All the people who could be in some way involved in somebody's being on an operating table after a road accident.

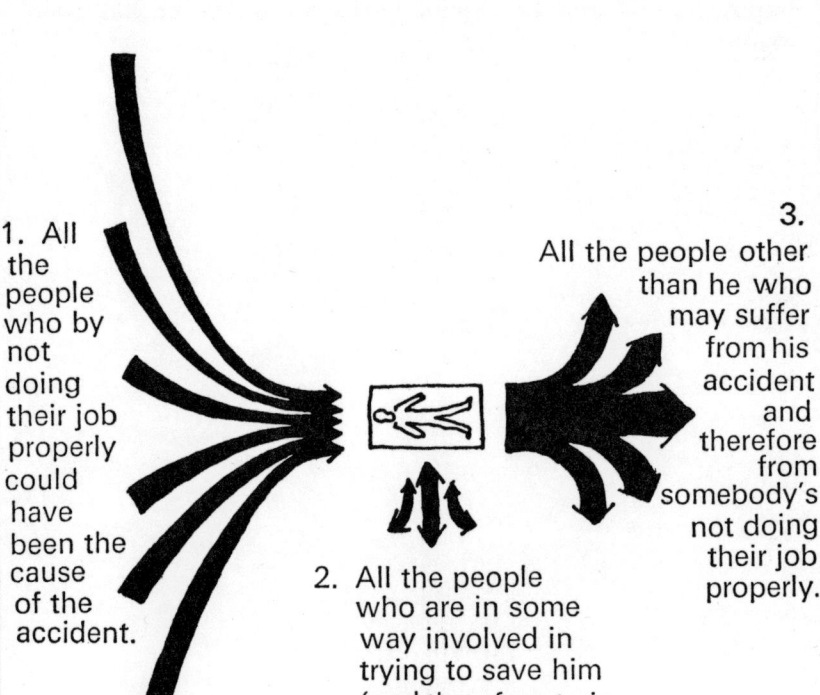

1. All the people who by not doing their job properly could have been the cause of the accident.

2. All the people who are in some way involved in trying to save him (and therefore trying to minimise the disastrousness of somebody's not doing their job properly).

3. All the people other than he who may suffer from his accident and therefore from somebody's not doing their job properly.

1. All the people who by not doing their job properly
could have been the cause of the accident.

Road policy makers;
road planners;
designers;
maintainers.

All the people responsible
for the state of the road.

Car design policy
makers;
car makers;
car maintainers
(previous owner).

All the people responsible
for the state of the car.

Road sign policy
formulators;
designers;
position planners;
maintainers.
erectors;

All the people responsible
for the state of the road
warning signs.

Driver's tutors;
influencers (public
motoring article
writers); other drivers.

All the people responsible
for the driver's skill at
driving.

Driver's doctor;
feeders (wife;
restaurant runners;
food suppliers);
associates.

All the people responsible
for the driver's physical
condition at the time of
driving.

Driver's passengers;
passers by;
other traffic;
radio comperes;
advertisement people;
associates.

All the people responsible
for the degree to which
the driver is concentrating
on driving.

71

2. All the people who are in some way involved in trying to save him (and therefore in trying to minimise the disastrousness of somebody's not doing their job properly).

Transporters:
ambulance drivers;
drivers' trainers;
ambulance makers.

Raisers of money:
government
(taxpayers);
charities (public).

Actual helpers:
doctors;
nurses;
administrative staff;
maintenance staff;
kitchen staff.

Equipment:
suppliers of:
hospitals;
beds;
drugs;
surgical apparatus.

Trainers:
lecturers;
researchers;
writers.

3. All the people other than he who may suffer from his accident and therefore from somebody's not doing their job properly.

All people who have to pay for the efforts to help him: charities; public and industry; government (taxpayers, public and industrial).

All people who cannot benefit from the money he could have spent on their goods and services: consumer goods industries; dependents of above; industries which supply above; their dependents, etc.

All people on whom he would have spent his earnings: his family; friends; clubs; charities (public); government (taxpayers).

All people who could have done with the help themselves: victims of natural disasters (including victims of famine caused by drought); man-made disasters; disease, etc.

All people who could have benefited from the goods and services he could have produced: his industry's dependents; his industry's customers; the dependents of the above, etc.

Diagram simplified.

Chapter 6

STARVATION OR PLENTY

To live in health, man must be fed.

It is a sad commentary on the second half of the twentieth century that half the world's people are starving and half of the remaining half are too often hungry. Barely one human being in seven has enough food to meet Western nutritional standards, even allowing for the fact that most of us in the West eat too much.

These figures are neither exaggerated nor imagined; they are positive facts which are gradually being comprehended in influential quarters.* In January 1966, an open letter in the form of an advertisement stating the facts in the most forthright (and frightening) terms was published in the *New York Times*. The opening paragraphs referred to food shortages, the subject of this chapter; the later paragraphs referred to the closely related problem of population growth, discussed in relation to Self-ism in Chapter 8.

I have seen the victims of food shortages far too often, and to my shame have not always understood the awful significance of what I saw. Today, I can close my eyes and see whole villages full of expressionless faces, jutting ribs and sunken cheeks. Rows and rows of statistics become for me a mental image of millions upon millions of gaunt, listless, starving people stretching far beyond the horizon of my mind. Mental imagery only emphasised the appalling reality and made me wonder what I could do to help. Soon, I found that many others were already trying to tackle what seemed to be a hopeless problem; the signatories to this open letter to President Johnson were among them. The letter read:

PRESIDENT LYNDON B. JOHNSON

"The world is on the threshold of the biggest famine in history, according to Dr. Raymond Ewell, former advisor to the Government of India. 'If present trends continue, it seems

* See the Report of the United Nations Food and Agriculture Organisation, October 1966.

75

likely that famine will reach serious proportions in India, Pakistan and China in the early 1970s. Latin America will fall in this category by 1980. Such a famine will be of massive proportions, affecting hundreds of millions, possibly billions of persons.'

"The Director-General of the United Nations Food and Agriculture Organization, Mr. Binay Sen, said recently: 'Either we take the fullest measures both to raise productivity and to stabilize population growth, or we face a disaster of unpre-

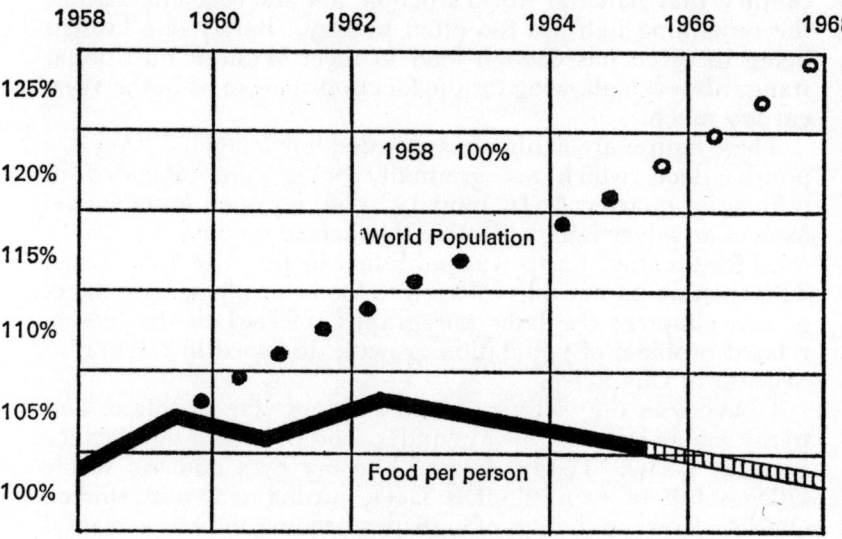

This tells the story

cedented magnitude. In some of the most heavily populated areas the outbreak of serious famine in the next five to ten years cannot be excluded. Problems of hunger and malnutrition which afflict more than a half of the world's population, apart from the human suffering and human degradation that they involve, pose a *serious threat to peace*.'

"U. S. Secretary of Agriculture, Mr. Orville L. Freeman, said: 'Problems of staggering proportions face the densely populated underdeveloped countries of the world in their effort to keep food production in pace with population growth. Both land and time are running out for those countries. In the past, increases in food output were achieved by putting new land under cultivation. But now the supply of readily cultivatable land is nearly exhausted in many of those countries, and new land can be brought under cultivation only at high cost.'

"A generation ago Latin America, Asia and Africa were regions with food surpluses. They exported grain to the industrialized countries, especially to Europe. Now the food flow is reversed and they must import food.

Food into a bottomless pit

"The United States has shipped abroad, since Congress enacted the so-called 'Food for Peace' law in 1954, food products amounting *to the gigantic sum of $12 billion,* mostly on a give-away basis.

"Our food warehouses that were bursting at the seams a few years ago are now largely down to a normal inventory required for reserves. Congress recently authorized Secretary Freeman to go into the open market and buy dried milk to keep up our lunch program for overseas children.

"India receives from the United States more than a half of its wheat at the present rate of *20,000 tons a day.* Observers believe that this assistance is the only barrier against large scale famine and open rebellion.

"With all this out-pouring of American resources we are not making a dent at solving the problem. Even if we were to continue such a program on a vastly stepped up basis, as some suggest, until American farm lands were exhausted, we still could not feed the burgeoning billions of people.

Basic problem: skyrocketing population

"Everything possible, of course, should be done to increase the food supply, but *it is the skyrocketing population that menaces today's world.* Latin America, as an example, increased its total production of food over the last five years, but with 25 million more people, the *average individual* had 7% less to eat. And in another five years at the present rate of increase there will be 35 million *more people* living south of the Rio Grande.

"Mr. President, we applaud your statement to the United Nations last June in which you said 'Let us in all our lands – including this land – face forthrightly the multiplying problems of our multiplying populations and seek the answers to this *most profound challenge to the future of all the world.'*

"But the fact remains that to date the manpower and resources of the various agencies of the Government committed to meet this transcendent challenge rank below a hundred less important projects.

"Every day lost in tackling this matter on a massive scale will compound your problems and those of your successors. For you were right, Mr. President, when you said:

"'I do not believe that our island of abundance will be finally secure in a sea of despair and unrest, or in a world where even the oppressed may one day have access to the engines of modern destruction.'

"There will be 300 million more mouths to feed in the world five years from now – most of them hungry. Hunger brings turmoil – and turmoil, as we have learned, creates the atmosphere in which the communists seek to conquer the earth." *

One of my interests, for many years, has been in the Oxford Committee for Famine Relief, known colloquially as Oxfam, and best understood by Americans if considered as similar to CARE or the Famine Relief of the Red Cross. Helping to raise funds for Oxfam as Chairman and Organiser in Bournemouth and later in Salisbury (England), I was able to study the conditions under which the movement and several other relief organisations work.†

Two things soon became apparent.

As with research into health, the enormity of the problem was far too great for privately run groups to tackle properly; they could at best alleviate the position. And their self-imposed task was made even more difficult by a startling number of people who actively objected to raising relief funds, for a variety of reasons. The main objections were:

(i) Why don't they grow their own food? They'll take hand-outs as long as you'll keep giving.

(ii) They will only turn round and bite the hand that feed them.

(iii) I haven't enough to feed my *own* family properly.

(iv) What's UNO for? Let *them* do the job.

* This letter was signed by a great number of highly reputable individuals; however, Dr. Don M. Yost, of the California Institute of Technology, made it clear that those signing this statement did so only in their personal and individual capacity. Their institutional and business affiliations were "purely descriptive" carrying no implication of authorisation or participation by the organisation noted; an individual could say what he thought true but if a company or corporation did so, it might lose business!

† In Great Britain there are several such organisations, all very active. They include the SAVE THE CHILDREN FUND, FREEDOM FROM HUNGER and WAR ON WANT.

Starvation or Plenty

It is immaterial that most of this criticism is ill-considered and due as much to ignorance as to ill-will. It *is* material that, good though the response to appeals for help may be, it is nothing like as substantial as it could and should be; certainly nothing like enough to solve the problem of world hunger.

Until I first came into direct contact with hungry people, I thought *I* had known hunger. In the First World War, a child in a family often reduced (by food rationing) to a potato or two and a slice of bread a day, I had a nodding acquaintance with it. After that war, in the dreadful Depression days, my family simply did not have the money for enough food. In the Second World War, rationing to a hearty eater caused a constant ache and frequent headaches; I was very sorry for myself.

It was soon after the last war that I saw really hungry people for the first time: in Wilhelmshaven, Northern Germany. I was with three other Rotarians who had also been moved to sympathy by stories of the displaced persons from Eastern Europe; and what we saw appalled us. (Few German people were hungry at that period although their hunger in the early nineteen-twenties had nurtured Nazism.)

There is something both hideous and frightening about one's first glimpse of the awful blankness in the eyes of men and women on the point of starvation. There is something quite sickening about the skeleton-like faces and pot bellies of small children who have passed the stage of crying – *and* lost all desire to play. These were some of the displaced persons: victims of the war, not even remotely responsible for their own plight.

We helped a little. God forgive me, I helped *a little*.

When we returned to our Rotary Club there was a great spurt of interest, but it soon faded. We had our own local aged and hungry, our youth clubs and our annual dinner-dance . . . It is strange, but I feel more bitter about that now than I did nearly twenty years ago.

Soon afterwards, I went with my family on a world trip. We spent three weeks in India – and the experience has lived with me ever since. The bodies, wrapped in rags, of men and women who had collapsed in the streets of Bombay and died of starvation overnight, were carried away later, hideously reminiscent of the carting away of bodies in London's Great Plague.

In India at that time there was no fear, as there was of the plague; for hunger is not contagious, and if one has enough for oneself, one cannot truly fear or feel another's hunger. In the

Indian countryside the people were unbelievably emaciated, their eyes sunken, their bones jutting. Again I saw groups of listless, pot-bellied children. To my shame I remember complaining about a skinny, meatless chicken stew at a *dak*-bungalow rest house, and grumbling because everyone from the boy who opened the car door to the turbaned manager lined up for his tip on our departure.

It was so hot. They smiled so fixedly, tightening the skin over their bones. Our meal to them would have been a feast.

"Why don't they grow their own food?"

All about them was the heat, and the arid land, and the rainless skies.

"They will only turn round and bite the hand that feeds them."

But we neither feed them nor, out of our technical and agricultural knowledge, do we find anywhere near enough ways and means of helping them to grow food for themselves.

So in India, even when life is normal, countless people die of hunger. As I write these words, terrible stories of the famine conditions of 1966 and 1967 are reaching the West.

They die of hunger in Pakistan, in parts of Africa, in Indonesia, in South America, in *Southern Italy*, in the Middle and the Far East, in China – all over the world, except Europe, or except *most* of Europe.

In times of drought and flood and hurricanes – of the destruction of what few crops they have – people who have lived on the border-line of subsistence, whose physical resistance has been worn paper-thin, collapse and die in tens of thousands.

I do not believe they need to die.

I consider their deaths an awful indictment of those of us who are well fed.

And I believe that if we apply the principles of Self-ism, there will be food enough for all the world's people.

(Lurking behind the spectre of food shortage and famine there *is* the other spectre, the population explosion; perhaps the most urgent problem now facing the world. As I shall show, even this can be overcome by applying the principles of Self-ism. But in this chapter, the problem of finding food for today's millions is more than enough.)

It is still said that in the United States, South America, Australia and even Europe, the granaries and the meat suppliers of the world, it would be possible to grow enough food to sustain the world's population properly. This is very hard to believe. Of some 3,500 million people in the world, less than 1,000 millions are well fed, many of them by imports from the traditional grain and meat suppliers. Great Britain, for instance, cannot support her population without importing enormous quantities of staple foods. On the other hand, in Russia and South America, both of which could be self-feeding, many people exist at bare subsistence or below starvation level because the national economy depends on exporting large quantities of staple foods desperately needed by their own people.

When one thinks of the enormous increases which would be needed in farm equipment and machinery, manpower, fertilisers and chemicals, it hardly seems practicable to *treble* the present food production in the lands of "plenty" where modern methods combine with national advantages to produce so plentifully. Even if the starving millions could then get what extra food was available in the world, there would still be much starvation and near-starvation.

Other factors have to be considered:

(i) Even if the world could grow sufficient food, the needy nations could not pay for it.

(ii) Even if the wealthy nations could afford to give the food away (which I doubt) or were willing to (which I doubt of some) they could not send it, because

(iii) existing shipping facilities by sea and air would be wholly inadequate. If every unused Liberty ship rusting in the Delaware and the Hudson were refitted (and that would take years) and every aircraft pressed into service, they would carry only a fraction of the bulk needed to succour the starving.

(iv) Even if sufficient food could be taken to the requisite ports, internal distribution problems of most of the needy countries would be insoluble. The inland roads and railways, trucks and manpower, would simply not be there.

All of these things are true.

Nevertheless, a great concerted effort by all nations with a food surplus and potential increases would alleviate some of the worst conditions. Above all, it would convince the hungry people of the world that a serious attempt was being made to help them. At the moment few of them can believe this, because:

(i) The scale of the help now given, though large in itself, is very small compared with the size of the problem.

Comparatively few people are actually getting the help; virtually none, in isolated areas.

(ii) When this help is in money, it is too often mis-appropriated or mis-spent.

(iii) The actual recipients of the food seldom know where it comes from, for usually it is distributed by local or Government officials who are only too willing to claim the credit.

Some spectacular demonstration is needed to make all the hopeless, hungry millions realise that the have-nations and the well-fed really intend to help them – *if they will also help themselves*. We live in a world of publicity and public relations, yet little effort is made to bring the truth home to the most naïve and impressionable of people, the millions of the Far East, of the Indian sub-continent and of South America. If, next time there is a grave threat of famine, a truly gargantuan effort were made to feed the victims, the repercussions would be felt for many years; new hope would lift the hearts of millions. We often talk of sending aid on a grand scale, but only one such attempt, the Berlin airlift, made a sensational impact. I except the Marshall Plan, conceived and carried out soon after the war, which had great political implications and motivation.

Of course, the political implications of the airlift were tremendous too; it was an act of the cold war rather than a rescue mission. But what would happen if a great rescue mission *were* attempted today? Supposing the Great Powers of the Western World, knowing of a famine, filled their *warships* and their *warplanes* with food? Supposing aircraft carriers and cruisers, dreadnoughts and frigates, corvettes and gunboats, swept through the waters of the oceans carrying food instead of bombs? And supposing the great jet aircraft and the transport planes of the armies and the navies flew mission after mission to do the same?

That would truly be a modern version of turning swords into ploughshares.

It *could* be done. With leaders of courage and vision it *would* be done. And with it, a wave of hope such as man has never known before would surge through the hungry world.

But spectacular, sensational and salutary though such a rescue mission would be, it would be short-term. A much vaster programme is needed to solve the world's food problem. Oxfam and CARE and other organisations are pointing the way, as is the World Food Organisation – but in a pitifully small degree.

Starvation or Plenty

Here are the salient facts:

Enough food cannot be sent to meet the needs of today's hungry – as we have seen, there are not enough ships, not enough transport of any kind.

So, they *must* grow it themselves.

They cannot do so because they lack the technical knowledge, the machinery and the chemicals required, but they *do* have all the manpower needed.

Since they can only be fed if they can feed themselves they must somehow be *taught* to feed themselves. They must be taught that until they help (do good for) themselves, they cannot benefit to the full from the technical knowledge and greater experience of the better-developed nations.

So it is obvious that the needy nations must help themselves, by practising pure Self-ism, before they can (*a*) benefit from the good which others can do for them, and (*b*) get themselves into a position from which they can be of benefit to others (the other half of Self-ism). Moreover, the wealthy nations must help the needy to help themselves before they, the wealthy, can reap the fullest possible benefits of trade from the now needy lands.

Is there a way to show both rich nation and poor the vital need for each to practise Self-ism?

I have been puzzling over this problem for years, spurred on by the information that comes from Oxfam and by the fact that more and more efforts *are* being made to show or to teach the underdeveloped nations how to give up the methods their forefathers used, and to adopt modern methods of agriculture and stock-raising.

First, I thought of writing a book, but I could not envisage enough readers for it.

Next, I thought of a series of novels; but although these might have been widely read, their effect would be slow and – for a long time – negligible.

Finally, I drew up a scheme as a prospectus for a television series, thinking that this prospectus, or outline for a plan of campaign, might well be the most effective way of showing how the need might be met. Alas, no producer has yet realised the tremendous dramatic impact such a series would have.*

No one can tell whether such a television programme would be universally popular, but it would surely be more appealing to

* The gist of these proposals is in Chapter 7.

audiences in the West than many of the conventional series of mysteries (including my own!), westerns, comedies and travelogues. If the proposals were to be taken up by the "have" nations *and* by private industry in co-operation with one of the non-political sections of the United Nations, it could well be enormously successful in a shorter time than most of us dare hope: it could conceivably feed *today's* hungry.* And surely it would make satisfactory profits for all the manufacturers concerned.

Profit?

Why not? There is not the slightest harm in making a fair and reasonable profit out of feeding human beings, and there are more kinds of profit than the short-term one of making money to put into the bank or into stocks and shares. As we have already seen, once the hungry were better fed they could do better work; by doing better work they would earn more; with a higher income they would create a much larger market, buying and eating more food. The more food they ate, the healthier they would be and the greater their rate of productivity. With greater productivity they could make their own nation more prosperous, and the more prosperous a nation is, the more it buys; it has no need to beg or borrow.

With 3,500 million people, less than one in three of them at present able to buy consumer goods in any but trifling quantities, there is a vast potential demand for consumer goods as well as for foods and "luxury" goods. This potential market is, in fact, a manufacturer's dream. The people who would make up this fabulous market already exist: they simply cannot afford to buy. They will never be able to buy until they are properly fed, for until they are in full health they cannot work enough to produce enough to earn enough.

The potential for trade is almost as inexhaustible as the potential for goodness. And when the whole world is one easy-working Common Market – when the raw materials are brought from the hinterlands, discovered by the new prospectors in helicopters (or concievably spacecraft!), to reach otherwise inaccessible places – trade will indeed be drawn from the bottomless well of human needs.

That will be the reward, the "profit", of a skilfully-planned, all-out war on starvation. When man feeds the whole world, he will make all mankind an eager buyer for the world's goods. Can there be a deeper significance in the parable of the talents?

* It is absolutely essential to keep emphasising *today's* hungry. The reason will become very evident in the chapter on *Population*.

Starvation or Plenty

The ultimate conquest of hunger cannot and will not come out of doing good for its own sake. Oxfam and CARE and all the others have shown the way, but the conquest of hunger will come only when all the prosperous nations realise that their own security and their own prosperity depend on the security and prosperity of *all* nations.

It will come when private industry fully realises the enormous potential markets waiting for its products in parts of the world which hardly exist as markets today. Too many manufacturers are content if they thrive within the existing pattern of trade; in only a few, perhaps mostly in Japan and the United States, is there any serious effort to expand all markets to a point nearer their full potential.

The conquest of hunger will come, in fact, from the practice of Self-ism on a vast scale not only in society generally but in industry and commerce, in politics and economics.

. . .

Three incontrovertible facts will emerge as Self-ism is practised more and more:

(i) The health of the world will be immeasurably better when all its people are well fed.
(ii) A surprising number of people will discover that they are directly or indirectly concerned with feeding the hungry in lands they know of only by name.
(iii) Many in the well-fed West will realise that much of their food, and so their wealth and prosperity, comes from those little-known and underdeveloped nations.

It really *is* very simple. If the producer of food is well fed, able to work efficiently and able to use the best modern methods in food cultivation, the food he produces will be of better quality and therefore of greater nutritional value to the consumer.

Surely nothing could be simpler than to digest the fact that if all oranges were as good to eat as Jaffas, more would be eaten and would do more good to the grower and the consumer. Yet it is extraordinarily difficult to apply this principle on a national, still less a global, scale.

There are far too many hungry people in lands of bountiful harvest and great prosperity. There really is no excuse at all for any government to destroy food supplies when its own people are hungry and the means of distribution exist; yet as recently as 1966, one of the great outcries in the United States was against the poverty and hunger-stricken areas in their own great cities. And these cities were within reach of agricultural areas where surplus food was destroyed or its production artificially restricted. A similar outcry was being raised in Canada at the same time, and doubtless should be raised in many other countries.

Hunger in a land of plenty is a matter for shame.

But local shortages apart, where food is concerned there are other matters for shame in the world. The interdependence of people and peoples is nowhere so vividly illustrated as in the production and distribution of food. Consider how many individual human beings are involved at various stages of the production.

In the beginning there are the tillers of the soil . . . but in fact *before* the tillers, in this day and age, there are those who can judge whether the soil to be tilled is suitable for the crop which is to be sown. And except in those areas where the wooden plough is used, there are the makers of the machinery with which to plough the land, fertilise it and reap the harvest. If any one of these machines fails through the failure of one man to do his job properly, it can lead to another man's hunger; perhaps even to a child's death.

For if a plough or a harvester does its work badly; or if the farmer uses it avoidably on the wrong day (in the wrong weather conditions), the final harvest may be poorer than it would have been had the work been done under the best conditions. The failure – even the partial failure – of a harvest anywhere can lead to food shortages in the most unexpected places. For if a farmer anticipates, say, a hundred tons of rice but crops only ninety, either the missing ten tons has to be obtained from somewhere else, or ten per cent less rice will be eaten in that vicinity. The farmer suffers, having less to sell; his workers suffer, having less work to do and so less pay; his family suffers, there being less money to spend; those from whom they buy other goods and foods suffer because not so much can be bought.

These things are easy to see at local, less easy at national, level – and almost impossible to see at global level, where they are just as true. A poor wheat harvest in Australia or Canada can put up the price of bread in England or in Holland. Failure of the Chinese rice crop can seriously affect the food supplies in neighbouring nations which would normally buy rice from China. A drought in the Argentine, killing off millions of cattle, can cause high beef prices and acute beef shortages in countries throughout the world.

Some of these shortages are due to natural disasters or freak climatic conditions and until man has learned to overcome such disasters, such shortages cannot be made up. But many are due to bad farming; bad fertilising; poor machinery; bad distribution; and to strikes and disputes in themselves unrelated to the produce affected. One individual engineer's single mistake can ruin a whole refrigerated van-load of meat, butter, milk or cheese; a dock strike in London over one man's grievance can ruin hundreds of tons of perishable foods – causing rising prices and creating shortages *even for the children of the strikers.*

When the cause and effect are easy to see, the gravity of the consequences can be understood. But the ramifications of such dockside losses stretch far and wide. The cargo of bananas dumped because an engineer kept them at too high a temperature, or a strike delayed their unloading, affects not only the people wanting the food but also suppliers who may be on the other side of the world. The late delivery of foods has serious secondary effects, for if the customers have "managed without" or found other sources or substitutes, then the producer has lost that market at least for a time, and *his* loss inevitably has repercussions on the people who work for him – on their spending power, their prosperity, their health, their living conditions.

And as in health, one man's failure to carry out his job properly – even to the planting of seeds or the driving of a combine-harvester – may not only affect others: it may affect him personally. Certainly the failure of others will affect him, one way or another.

If everyone concerned with the growing, harvesting, distributing, packaging and processing of food were to do his straightforward daily job properly there would be more – much more – food to go round. Where it is now in short supply, it would become plentiful; where it is now plentiful, it would become cheaper.

There are other causes of wastage in food. In too many instances the growers or the distributors do not consider the margin of profit in supplying it cheaply to be worth while; some transactions undoubtedly lead to financial loss. But the fallacy of being influenced by these factors alone cannot be emphasised often enough. Until the world's hungry are fed, they cannot work; until they can work, they cannot earn; until they earn, they cannot buy; until they buy, they cannot make a profit for any supplier.

It is quite normal business practice to make a loss on one transaction if it will lead to others both permanent and profitable. This principle simply has to be applied on a wider scale and on a longer term, in order to benefit the whole world.

There is a good example of adjusting profit margins in the publishing trade. Not infrequently a book is printed in such quantities that the sale of half the total print order at the normal price will recoup the publisher, paying him a fair profit. Thereafter, any copies he sells yield a very high proportion of profit. He could, of course, print only as many copies as he knows he can sell at the normal price, but the more copies printed, the lower the cost per book – so on a lower print order the cost per book would be greater. He might make no profit at all on a lower print order – might indeed make a loss. Publishing is a particularly hazardous business, for the publisher has to gauge the demand for a book very accurately.

With food, this is seldom true.

For example, take cornflakes. There is an unending demand for them, so turnover plus modern packaging methods keep them fresh. If the manufacturer's profit margin were ten per cent net (after meeting all costs, overheads and expenses) on the first £1,000,000-worth sold, he could easily afford to sell another £1,000,000-worth *at no profit at all*, or on a one or two per cent margin. These supplies would be sold to consumers in the "poverty" areas – who by getting eleven packets for the price of ten, would thus start on the process of becoming better fed and so better able to play their part in the national economy and so the international economy. Moreover, work for more men and more machines, more money in wages and profits, would automatically arise out of the second £1,000,000-worth of sales. Financiers who are always seeking *safe* outlets for investment would find this attractive, and so the whole economy would benefit.

That is how industrial Self-ism will *always* work.

If a company sells £1,000,000-worth of its produce at either a nominal profit or a loss it may *appear* to be very generous. In fact, the generosity is a form of enlightened self-interest, because the total cost of producing the £2,000,000-worth is less, per packet,* and so the profit on the first £1,000,000-worth is in

---

* Many basic overheads are static; no matter how much is produced. So that given the proper machines, the cost of paper, packaging goods, printing, machining, maintenance, is lower per unit, and man-hours are not greatly increased. In practically every commodity, the more units produced, the lower the price (cost).

fact higher than ten per cent. This clearly gives an indirect profit on any of the product ostensibly sold free of profit.

This in turn shows that once a society or an industry is launched on a progressive Self-ist economy, existing limiting factors will de-limit themselves.

It is not yet time, however, to discuss Self-ism in industry; that will come later. We have still to consider the full effect of Self-ism on the problem of feeding the world's hungry millions.

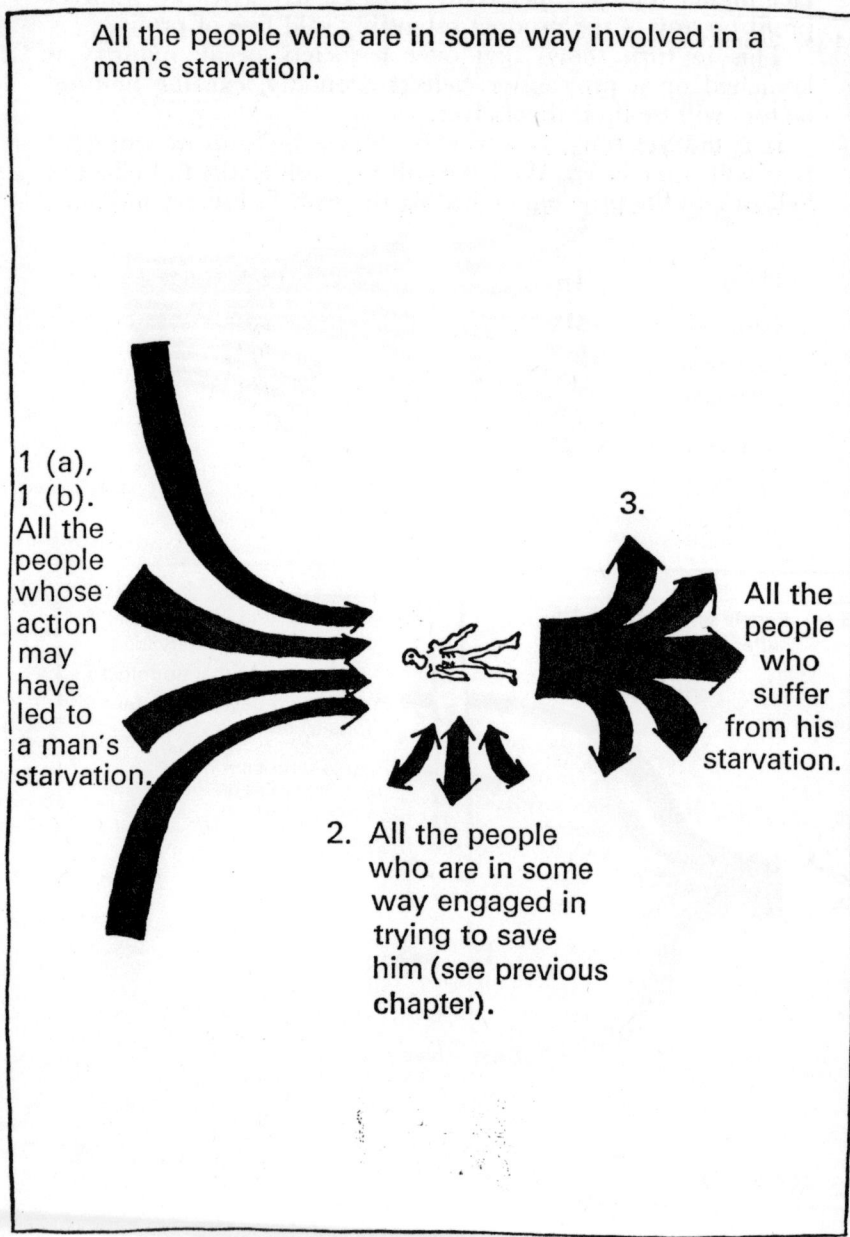

All the people who are in some way involved in a man's starvation.

1 (a), 1 (b). All the people whose action may have led to a man's starvation.

3. All the people who suffer from his starvation.

2. All the people who are in some way engaged in trying to save him (see previous chapter).

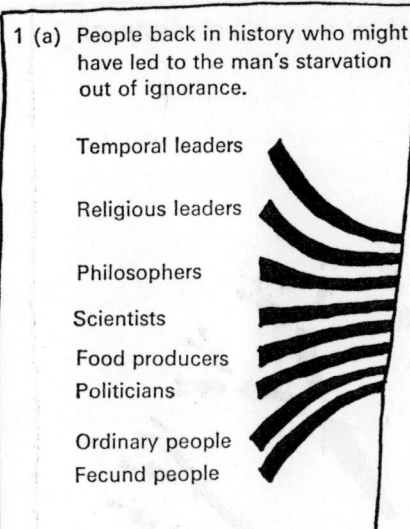

1 (a) People back in history who might have led to the man's starvation out of ignorance.

Temporal leaders

Religious leaders

Philosophers

Scientists

Food producers

Politicians

Ordinary people

Fecund people

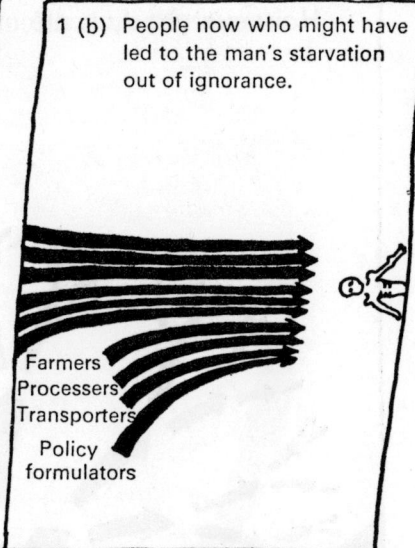

1 (b) People now who might have led to the man's starvation out of ignorance.

Farmers

Processors

Transporters

Policy formulators

3 (a) People who will immediately suffer from his starvation.

People who cannot sell goods and services to him.

His dependents.

People who cannot buy goods and services from him.

3 (b) People who will eventually suffer from his starvation (people in other countries).

People who have to pay for the efforts to help him.

People who cannot sell to or buy from these people goods and services.

The dependents of all these people.

People who cannot sell to or buy from these people goods and services.

People who need the help the starving man is getting themselves.

How everybody is affected by a man's starvation.

Chapter 7

"FEED HIM ALL HIS DAYS"

"GIVE a man a fish, feed him for a day," says the Chinese proverb: "Teach a man to fish, feed him all his days." Here is the crux of the problem of food and hunger; of malnutrition; of starvation and famine. If we can find a way to teach enough men "to fish" – to grow and to cultivate food for themselves – there will be no famine.

In a modern industrial society it is, obviously, impossible for all men to grow food for themselves; some have to grow it for the rest. And some peoples have been born and bred in those parts of the world where climatic and soil conditions, until quite recent years, have made it impossible – even for those who could and would – to grow enough food to keep the community well fed. Means of distribution – from village to village, district to district, region to region, country to country and continent to continent – may have been evolved, but we have seen that these means of distribution are far from sufficient to meet the needs of all mankind.

So some people starve, others have barely enough to live on; and the rest have too much: some have so much that they burn their surplus crops.

It may seem an insoluble problem, for the task of providing the necessary distribution and storage is virtually insuperable. And despite the ingenuity and the skill of modern science, the day is far, far off when climatic conditions can be changed by man. In the foreseeable future, ways of creating rain may well be found, but for many years to come, the incidence of rainfall is not likely to vary sufficiently to influence crop-growing conditions throughout the world. There will still be floods and droughts; humid jungle and arid desert; food surplus and famine.

In recent years, however, there have been two significant developments in the realms of food production. In the more significant, the experiments have been on a comparatively small scale, and in both, political motives and prejudice have restricted the advantages which the development itself offers. New agricultural methods, for instance, are often resisted by backward communities. Many primitive agriculturalists raise the same crops as their forefathers, and cling to the same methods. At the same time, political and business groups in a community often resist change because their own plans might be disrupted, their profits lessened, or their privileges endangered.

In fact all of these people would benefit rather than suffer in the long run. Many are difficult to convince, however, while those who do live and thrive on cheating their neighbours *would* lose this particular source of livelihood. The compensating factors, nevertheless, would give them ample alternative scope for their ingenuity and talents. They would find it more profitable, and far more pleasant, to live honestly, than to live by corruption and chicanery.

The question of improved agricultural methods – dependent so largely on new machinery, fertilisers and chemical sprays to kill disease – has already been discussed. The second, even more significant development has had little attention focused on it, although advanced agriculturalists are watching results with great interest.

I refer to the improvement of strains of crops and of livestock in areas where at present they are stunted and poor.

One of the activities of most famine relief organisations today is to help the people of backward communities improve their methods, and to use different seeds or to develop strains of livestock known to flourish better under certain conditions. Progressive private enterprise, including some world-wide organisations, are constantly busy developing such new strains. UNESCO and the World Food Organisation are also involved and committed in these researches. But at best the efforts are haphazard and limited in scope; so far, they touch only the fringe of the problem.

Yet there is a way of getting to the heart of it – and *soon*.

The British Commonwealth and the United States of America between them, we should remember, contain within their natural boundaries all the climatic and soil conditions in the world.

In an age when man is actually contemplating space research stations, it would be comparatively simple and inexpensive to create a world-wide chain of Agricultural Research Stations to deal with food production in all its forms.*

* This might well be called: THE BUREAU OF RESEARCH AND EXPERIMENT IN AGRICULTURAL DEVELOPMENT. As such it would soon become widely known as BREAD.

"Feed him all his Days"

The task would be simply to concentrate on finding new or improved strains of corn, maize, wheat, rice, fruit, grass or fodder and livestock which would flourish best under a variety of specific conditions.

It could – and surely should – be sponsored and financed by the United Nations; by the United States and the British Commonwealth; by other advanced nations; and by such private corporations and organisations as the Dupont, Shell, and Imperial Chemical Industries.

The immediate task, some of which has already been started, would be to survey all the world's famine and hunger areas, nation by nation and region by region, and then to prospect in the United States and the British Commonwealth for the soil and climatic conditions which approximate most nearly to each of these "famine and hunger" areas.

There is no way of estimating accurately how many survey areas would be required, but let us suppose two hundred areas of the world to be in urgent need of such study, and of help. Two hundred research teams, each with a mobile laboratory, would thus be needed: hardly an extravagant number. Two hundred experimental research areas would be surveyed and all the scientific and technical knowledge possessed by the West would be applied to developing new varieties of produce in those specific conditions.

It would not be entirely new ground, since research very similar to this is already carried out in many parts of the world. Only recently, an American research team developed a strain of rice which is expected to yield *six times* the crop of the best rice harvested today. And the development of varieties of alfalfa in the Western States of America has enabled cattle to grow fat over the very ground where the grazing allowance was once three acres to a steer.

In most Western nations, some such agricultural advisory schemes – usually government-sponsored – are in operation, but it is left to the farmers to take advantage of the research discoveries. In a world-wide plan, teams of specialists would be in constant consultation with those research teams in the needy areas as well as others at the actual research stations. Unskilled labour is always readily and cheaply available in underdeveloped areas, and once promising strains were developed, large-scale experiments in growing and stock-raising could easily be carried out in the very place where the food was most needed. Farmers, workers and government officials, as well as the ever-curious passers-by, would see the improvements being made before their eyes. And once the evidence was there for all to see, local feeling would run too high to allow prejudice or corruption to restrict progress.

When a man is hungry, his first thought is of food. When he sees food available and at hand, he will demand it. In this way food production everywhere could be increased tremendously, and within only a few years – *years, not generations* – there need be no hunger or starvation in the world. The effects of such a social revolution would be incalculable. It would certainly lead, as we have seen, to increasing prosperity among the needy nations, enabling these nations to become substantial customers of those other nations which, in the beginning, helped to create the conditions of plenty.

Man would indeed have cast his bread upon the waters and would find it returning to him not only ten but a thousandfold.

The essence of these proposals is, like the essence of all man's needs, very simple indeed. And their achievement is easily within our reach. The money is there; the facilities for research, the workers, the mobile laboratories, the chemical supplies, the technological knowledge – all are there for the making or training. There is no difficulty in transporting the research teams and their units from place to place; no shortage of manpower where manpower is most needed.

All that is required, I can only repeat, is for man to see and to accept his responsibilities to his fellows. Once he does so, he will himself begin to reap the benefit. There is no good in the world which is not a boon both to those who give and those who receive it.

The greatest material good that man can do for his fellow man is to "teach him to fish" for himself – to practise Self-ism.

Is *this* the true message contained in the parable of the loaves and the fishes?

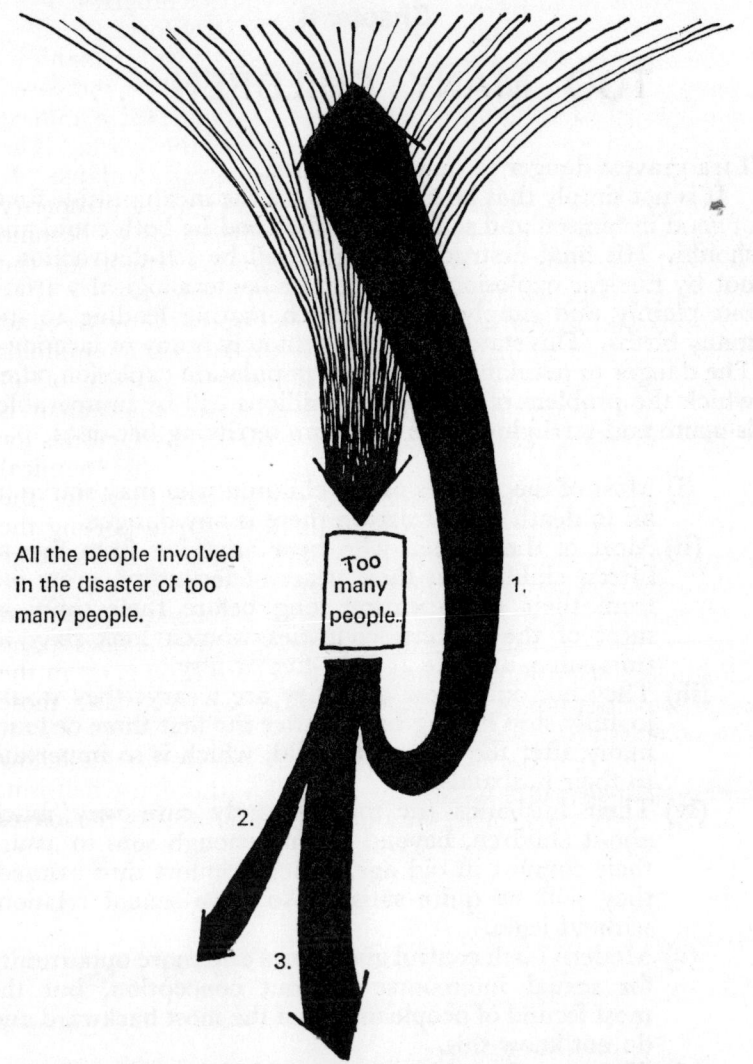

All the people who cause there to be too many people: fecund people who are either ignorant of contraception or fearful of using it or ignorant of the danger of not.

All the people involved
in the disaster of too
many people.

Too many people.

1.

2.

3.

All the people who will suffer from there being too many people:
1. The people who cause it. 2. The people who neither caused it nor who can do anything about it. 3. The people who did not cause it but who are able to do something about it and therefore who must for their own benefit.

Chapter 8

TOO MANY CHILDREN . . .

THE gravest danger to mankind is man.

It is not simply that he may fail to see the inexhaustible fund of good in himself and so fail to do the good he both could and should. His final destruction might well be self-destruction – not by nuclear explosion, radiation or bacteriological warfare but plainly and simply by too much mating leading to too many births. This statement is not remotely funny or facetious. The danger to mankind of an acute population explosion, after which the problem of feeding the millions will be insuperable, is acute and terrifying. It is the more terrifying because:

(i) Most of the parents of the children who may starve us all to death do not dream there is any danger.

(ii) Most of the women who bear anything from five to fifteen children in their years of fecundity, grow old from their child-bearing long before their time; in most of the Eastern countries women look sixty at thirty-five, and die at forty-five or fifty.

(iii) They not only grow old, they are weary; they would joyfully stop having babies after the first three or four; many after the first male child, which is so important to their husbands.

(iv) Their husbands (or mates) rarely care very much about children, beyond having enough sons to assure their comfort in old age. Their comfort thus assured, they will be quite satisfied to have sexual relations without issue.

(v) Modern birth control gives more and more opportunity for sexual intercourse without conception, but the most fecund of people are often the most backward and do not know this.

(vi) The cost of teaching them and helping them to avoid having their unwanted offspring is negligible compared with the cost of armaments; the running cost of one Polaris submarine a year would go a long way towards solving the problem in a decade.

(vii) The Roman Catholic Church excepted, few people believe it wrong for contraceptives to be supplied and used, and vast numbers of Catholic women already risk even threatened damnation by taking advantage of modern methods of avoiding pregnancies.

(viii) Once they do so in their millions – as they will, with the spread of such knowledge – the Church will find a way of condoning the use of contraceptives, since failure to do so would weaken the Church and the faith and loyalty of many of its members.

As I understand it, the fundamental objection of the Roman Catholic Church is that birth control is a form of taking life, of destroying human souls. But the absence of birth control is taking infinitely *more* life, Catholic lives included, than birth control can ever do. When the world problem is solved the Church can be free to apply its own principles, because then it will not be a choice of two evils, as it is today.

Lest this sounds too glib, here is a quotation from a report of the International Planned Parenthood on conditions in Honduras in November 1964:

"We asked a social worker to pull one of the cards at random from her file. It was a case of a 29-year-old woman with ten pregnancies, six births, and four abortions. She had five living children and a family income of $30 a month (£10. 10s.), bare subsistence."

It is years since this kind of report convinced many social workers of the appalling danger of the population explosion, which gave added urgency to the problem of the food situation in the Far East. It is a simple fact that the population of the world, now 3,500 million people, will *at the present rate of increase* be doubled in thirty-five years, that is in half an average human lifetime. We cannot properly feed more than a quarter of the world's people today; the prospect of having twice as many to cope with is utterly terrifying.

And it is terrifying in several ways.

In the first place, if the present rate of increase is *not* halted, untold millions more human beings will be born to almost immediate death through starvation. Many mothers will die while watching their children die, but the birth-rate will be so high that there will be no hope of stopping the overall increase. The men, the fathers, will not accept starvation philoso-

99

phically. With its political *credo* to justify its adherents in overcoming Capitalism by force, and with such an excuse, Communism will not hesitate to start wars – as in fact they have already been started, in Korea, Laos, Vietnam and Tibet. The "climate" which made these wars possible would not have existed but for the amount of suffering due to hunger, or the fear of starvation. Under such conditions, militant Communism thrives and militant Democracy defends. Remove these conditions, and Communism will turn into the benevolent force which some at least of its founders envisaged, seeking peace with all men – since it will be obvious that only out of peace can there come continuing plenty.

No doubt there will be some who will contend that Communism is in itself an aggressive force which prosperity will only strengthen. But is this so? When Communist nations see the advantages to themselves of peace, surely they will honestly seek peace, if only because they will no longer be able to gain anything from war or the threat of war. Is not Russia already (1967) tending this way? And did such a mellowing seem possible a decade ago? Yet such evolutionary change is as inevitable as it is necessary for world peace, and must in time come to all nations, even those who today are dangerously aggressive because they are so acutely underprivileged.

The fantastic increase in population in the underdeveloped nations is, therefore, a present and very real threat to world peace.

Moreover, unless it is checked, the explosion in the rate of population in such areas will be so swift that there will be no time to cope; the hungry small nations *will* seek food beyond their own borders, so wars will become quite inevitable. And the great powers will inevitably take sides. In time, indeed, they will have to fight one another so as to obtain enough food for themselves; more than one authority believes that cannibalism on a mass scale will be inevitable. Here, in its most grotesque form, we would see a nation trying to do good for itself but causing another nation such harm that each would have to fight so as to annihilate – even to feed upon – the other. I wonder how many who survived would remember:

Doing good for oneself is instinctive to man and every act of good swells the sum total of goodness from which all men benefit. Doing harm (evil) to others is not instinctive to man but each harmful act takes away from the total good and so robs all men – including oneself. When this simple fact is understood it will be recognised as a natural law:

100

Too Many Children . . .

when observance of this natural law has become the norm, it will be shown as the true source of human happiness.

* * *

Nothing like the anticipated rate of population increase has been imagined before, still less experienced.

At the present rate of progress, the final explosion of births will come about the end of this century. If, before we are blown up, reason prevails and the leaders of nations agree that nuclear war is ridiculous and must be outlawed, it would still be impossible to prevent our self-destruction.

There simply would not be enough food to go round.

Even if no one actually did battle for more than his fair share of available food, supplies would not be enough. The world would starve. The United Nations Food and Agriculture Organisation in its estimated Third World Food Survey, in 1963, said that to provide a reasonably adequate level of nutrition in the year A.D. 2000, for the predicted population of 7,000 million, the world's total food supply per person would have to be trebled, yet there has been no increase in food production per head of population for five years. This is of course why, when one talks of feeding the hungry, one must think of *today's* hungry: unless we can prevent too many births, we shall not be able to make any provision for tomorrow's. All the grandiose schemes for feeding the world would collapse.

In a luncheon talk to a literary club, Lord McCorquodale, then Chairman of the British Family Planning International Campaign, convinced me of what was happening. I was shattered.

No one else seemed to be. There was a sage nodding of heads and a sympathetic clucking – but no one else asked him if they could help. A few weeks later I found myself on his Committee, and with increasing dismay discovered that there simply weren't enough funds to *begin* to tackle the problem seriously.

Did Governments play any part in this?

Well, they were beginning to, I was told. A little. The Indian Government agreed with birth control and approved – and, yes, helped – but they hadn't enough money for it. This from *India* – with tens of thousands dying every month from malnutrition and her human progeny spawning!

China? Well, yes, China was beginning to realise the gravity of the situation.

Indonesia? Well, what else were the leaders really worried about – except feeding the multiplying millions who might rebel if they were not fed?

Good, God and Man

What about Washington? Well, financial help on a modest scale *was* authorised, but mostly for family planning in the United States, which has a grave population explosion problem of its own in the Deep South and in Southern California, as well as some of the larger metropolitan areas.

The more I looked at the facts, the more I was baffled and perturbed. No one studying the figures could reasonably doubt the gravity and inevitability of what was happening, yet few Governments appeared to be taking this anything like seriously enough. True, there was an earnest and quite impressive conference in London in 1965 – but its high spot was a buffet meal and an evening visit to the House of Lord's Debating Chamber, in all its gilded splendour. *No one*, not even the Indians and Pakistanis whose countries were then in conflict, seemed *worried*.

I began to get scared.

Could I, I was asked, write a book about this, to go into one of my series? By all means. With much help from John Simons of the English Campaign Committee, and some invaluable guidance from Professor J. H. Fremlin of Birmingham (England) University I began the book.

As I saw it, the population of the world would overrun civilisation in less than forty years.* So, I created creatures called *lozi*, which looked like miniature human beings but bred like rats – in fact, worse than rats, the females having litters of up to eleven at a delivery, and a *nine-day* pregnancy. Hardly a pretty story. In the course of it I had to get the *facts*, and Professor Fremlin supplied them in an article of almost mesmeric appeal. Perhaps the simplest way to show what terrified me is to re-quote his estimate of what will happen as the world's population doubles itself every thirty-seven years, although he made it clear that *in fact the rate will be much higher unless there is a limiting factor not yet known to us.*

Today's world population 3,500 millions†
In 2003 7,000 „
In 2040 14,000 „
In 2077 28,000 „

This brings us up to the end of our grandchildren's era!

* I am serious about this; I believe it to be inevitable if we go on as we are now. So do many scientists.
† Different sources give different figures. I use 3,500 millions as this is the official UNO estimate.

Too Many Children . . .

The first part of Professor Fremlin's article says:

"The world population is now about 3000 million and is increasing at a rate corresponding to a doubling in 37 years. In view of the increasing importance attached to the immediate effects of the rapid growth in human numbers, it is of interest to examine ultimate technical limits to this growth. Traditionally, these limits have usually been regarded as fixed by possible food supplies, although, in practice, at least in historical times, the actual limiting factor has more often been disease.

"Diseases are now nearly, and will soon be entirely, eliminated as effective controllers of population growth but it is not at all clear that difficulties in food production will take their place. It is true that there is a limit to the improvement of agricultural output by application of existing scientific knowledge, but by the time this limit is reached other methods of food-production will have been devised. In this article I shall explore the possibility that the real limits are physical rather than biological.

"I shall assume throughout an effective degree of world co-operation in the application of food technology, etc. This is quite evidently essential if the maximum world population is to be reached. There are of course many ways of *not* reaching the maximum, but none of these will be discussed here.

"In order to give a time scale, it is supposed that the rate of increase of population remains constant at the present value – that is to say, doubling every 37 years. In fact the rate is itself accelerating so that, in the absence of limitations, this time scale will be too long.

Stage 1: up to 400,000 million in 260 years' time.

"Using existing crop plants and methods it may not be practicable to produce adequate food for more than four doublings of the world population, though the complete elimination of all land wild-life, the agricultural use of roofs over cities and roads, the elimination of meat-eating and the efficient harvesting of sea food might allow two or three further doublings – say seven in all. That would give us, with the present doubling time of 37 years, 260 years to develop less conventional methods, and would allow the population of the world to increase to about 130 times its present size, or about 400,000 million.

103

Stage 2: up to 3 million million in 370 years' time.

"The area of ice-free sea is some three times that of land. Photosynthesis by single-coiled marine organisms may be more efficient than that of the best land plants. If organisms could be found capable of the theoretical maximum efficiency (8 per cent of total solar radiation, according to A. A. Niciporovic) we should gain a factor of three in yield. We could then double our numbers a further three times more if all the wild-life in the sea, too, was removed and replaced by the most useful organisms growing under controlled conditions, with the optimum concentration of carbonates, nitrates, and minerals. (Of course a reserve of specimens of potentially useful species could be preserved, perhaps in a dormant state.) Again, for maximum efficiency we must harvest and consume directly the primary photosynthesising organisms, rather than allow the loss of efficiency involved in the food-chains leading to such secondary organisms as zooplankton or fish.

"By this stage, we should have had ten doublings, which at the present rate would take some 370 years, with a final world population of 3 million million. Since the world's surface (land and sea) is 900 million million square metres, each person would have a little over 160 square metres for his maintenance – about a thirtieth of an acre – which does not seem unreasonable by more than a factor of two, so long as no important human activity other than food production takes place on the surface.

"No serious shortages of important elements need be envisaged so far, though extensive mining operations for phosphates might be needed, and we have not yet approached any real limit.

Stage 3: up to 15 million million in 450 years' time.

"Many readers will doubtless feel that something unconsidered must turn up to prevent us from reaching the limiting conditions I have supposed. One point of this study is however to suggest that, apart from the ultimate problem of heat, we are now, or soon will be, able to cope with *anything* that might turn up. Anything which limits population growth in the future will, therefore, be something we can avoid if we wish. It would be perfectly possible to choose not to eliminate some major killing disease or to neglect the world food problem and let famine do its work, but this would have to be a positive decision; *it can no longer happen by mistake.*"

· · ·

104

So this awful issue of over-population, like most things which affect man, can now be controlled by man. Could anything make the need for man to accept his responsibilities, to do what is right and good and sensible, more apparent? And can anyone seriously *expect* man to do so unless the natural law of Selfism is applied? In this crisis the only way each man can do enough good for himself is by limiting the number of his children. It will preserve his own and his family's well-being and health, and it will help to save the world.

What greater good could man do to the Self in him?

My *lozi* simply do in a year what human beings could do in thirty-five years if we don't stop them. I made no attempt at all to envisage a situation beyond the first thirty-seven years, because I do not believe mankind can conceivably afford to double his numbers in that time. In fact, no doubt, some nations – perhaps the United States and Russia – would find the means of survival, but it would almost certainly be at the expense of other nations. The only certain way to give all mankind the chance of a good life is to slow down the rate of population growth.

Utterly convinced by my researches, or rather by Professor Fremlin's researches, I went back to the Committee. Money was urgently needed, very little could be done without it. An American general was trying to raise a large sum . . .

Ah! America, land of the rich, the generous and the wise. Could I go and try in America?

I went (partly on my own affairs; it was on this trip that I tried to interest Hollywood in the BREAD-FOR-ALL television series) and was very courteously received. And if American interest in the main was directed at their own internal problem, there was a deep understanding of the immense significance of the problem on the international scale. I asked if I could visit some of the affiliated groups in California; the suggestion was most warmly accepted, and I went first to San Francisco. Here, a very lively, highly intelligent and danger-conscious group had little or no idea of the enormity of the world problem. They were eager to know and anxious to help.

With the New York, San Francisco and Albuquerque groups, I still hope to evolve a scheme which might reduce the birthrate substantially – and *soon*. Meanwhile, in a year in which I had done virtually nothing to help, some *seventy million more human beings had been born and had survived*.

It is utterly fantastic that such a problem should be left to a group of voluntary organisations which raise funds privately –

even though a fourteen and a half million dollars gift from the Ford Foundation was a magnificent contribution in 1965.

This is a problem of the most acute urgency, and the facts of and danger from it need to be told to the world as a matter of absolute priority (see Chapter 10).

Tens of thousands of clinics, hundreds of thousands of nurses, millions of the simplest possible contraceptives, the I.U.D. (no, not the pill – not yet: but that is a long story) are needed. Nationally organised campaigns on a mammoth scale now are essential if the awful danger is to be avoided. It is perhaps the most perfect example of the world need for applied Self-ism.

Each woman, *in her own interest*, must be able to limit the number of children she has. Each husband, *in his own interest* – so that he can feed and clothe himself and his family and do his work properly – must accept this family limitation. For until all women *do* restrict the number of children they bear, not only the children they already have but also their country and all the people in it will suffer – and ultimately this suffering will spread to the rest of the world with disastrous results.

It is therefore in the whole world's interest (and so the interest of every person in it) to help create the conditions for universal birth-control. It is only by so doing – by the practice, in effect, of Self-ism in essence at individual, national and global levels – that man will survive. If we continue to drift on, if the population explosion is allowed to reach its climax of eruption, we shall destroy ourselves.

This is in fact more Orwellian by far than anything Orwell wrote in his *1984*. And, by a bitter twist of irony, if we haven't checked the meteoric rise in population *by* 1984, then Big Brother's only concern will be to find enough to eat. Orwell might have been much more prophetic than even he suspected, but it will not really matter whether we live under Communist, Fascist or Democratic control in 1984, unless about 2,500 million births now statistically scheduled never take place.

There is still time – just time – to prevent the disaster.

The cost? It is hard to estimate. But assuming that for 500 million women, the necessary contraceptives and instructions in how (and why) to use them, could be provided at a cost of one pound each, that would mean £500 million. And spread over ten years, say, the cost would be some £50 million a year.

Let us reduce this to terms of individual Self-ist responsibility. Let us disregard for the time being the French, Italians,

Japanese and Germans, the Spaniards and the Scandinavians,*
the Dutch and the Belgians. Let us consider the British,
Americans, Canadians and Australians as the likeliest pro-
viders – in all, some 300 million people. Halve this number,
for half won't be able to afford it, which means that 150
million individuals would together have to find £50 million (say
$140 million) each year for ten years. That is, *they would each
have to find no more than six shillings and eightpence, or ninety-six
cents.*

Reduced to such terms, the problem would be laughable – if
the danger from over-population were not so hideously real.

There is *some* understanding at top level. In 1964 Prince
Philip, Duke of Edinburgh, said: "We make so many wild
claims for ourselves as human beings, with superior intelligence.
The least we can do is prove our superior intelligence by con-
trolling our numbers and standards of existence willingly."

The Governments of the world should, surely *must*, open their
eyes wide to this emergency; the money needed is a bagatelle
by the standards of today's budgets. In his 1966 State of the
Union message, President Johnson included aid to Family
Planning (birth control) as part of America's duty, but at the
time of writing it is not clear how high a priority it will have.

If the Governments will not act . . .

Who will join those already working in the endeavour to
collect one dollar a year from everyone who can afford it, so as
to save themselves and their children and their children's
children from extinction?

If we assume that by a combination of governmental wisdom
and private enterprise – both inspired by Self-ism – we *shall*
overcome this most urgent of man's problems, we can seriously
begin to tackle those that remain.

In any case, we must at least plan and prepare the ground for
settling them. The first such problem is that of education – or
more accurately today, of ignorance. Ignorance of the dangers
of over-breeding is after all at the root of the population explosion danger, much of it among the masses in the Far East,
in Africa and in South America. Some new approach to
education in the elementary facts of life is becoming increasingly necessary. As things are today we *must* first attack and
overcome the basic problem in feeding and housing – and both
can be done without academic training. Instruction in birth

* The Swedish Government gave a substantial sum to help with this
problem in 1966.

control needs specialised knowledge, however; so does the treatment of all the other major social problems.

How can we teach the world's people what they need to know? Teach them, in fact, their responsibilities?

Do we, today, even understand *what* knowledge they need?

It is worth considering this question first from the point of view of the "educated" West.

Chapter 9

A LITTLE LEARNING . . .

A LITTLE learning is the beginning of much knowledge. One of the first pieces of knowledge needed by any human being is that scholastic training and wisdom are not necessarily the same. One can be very wise, yet have little learning (in the sense of having learned at school or in college). And one can have all the learning in the world and still be a fool if one does not know how to use what one has learned.

True, a man both learned *and* wise is a great man.

As surely, the acquisition of knowledge, particularly about one's fellow men – whether imparted by others, or through personal experience – is most conducive to wisdom. The thing to remember is that the two are not necessarily the same. If they accept this axiom, the wise man will know humility because he is aware of his lack of knowledge, while the learned man will know humility because he is aware that his knowledge does not of itself give him wisdom. Each will be proud in his own right of those qualities he possesses; each will have a proper pride in himself – true self-esteem, the basis on which the theory of Self-ism is founded.

After the age of fourteen I did not attend any school, college or other form of educational institution. There was always too much to do and no time at all to attend evening classes. Anything I have learned since my schooldays has been acquired by living – by travelling, by looking about me: by studying other peoples, other places, other ways of life. Certainly I have not read as widely or as deeply as some will think I should have done. This has not been due to laziness or disinclination. Too often – perhaps misguidedly often – I have not been able to concentrate on books of philosophy or thought because:

(i) Not only did the propositions expounded often seem to me illogical or irrational; too often they started off from premises I could not accept.

(ii) Often, I found they conflicted with my experience of human behaviour and reactions, as if the authors were discussing people of a kind I knew nothing about – and who, to me, did not exist.

109

(iii) Often, I simply could not overcome the dullness or turgidity of style; or the prolixity.
(iv) Often what was presented as a "new" thought or concept proved to be only a restatement of what had been said many times before.
 (v) Often, what was said with great earnestness, intensity and length, seemed to me so obvious that it was not worth stating at all.

No doubt many of its readers will have exactly the same criticisms, or even more, to make of this book. Perhaps the faults I found in those books I did read may at the time have created a kind of arrogance or self-conceit within me. Perhaps I was simply oblivious of the fact that both these characteristics lived within me already, and were the true cause of my reactions. Today, they may well be insuperable obstacles to my obtaining the learning and wisdom I badly need.

I state this unequivocally, so that there can be no doubt as to my own background or outlook on education. I feel certain that in the Western world formal and theoretical learning are held in too much awe, and not enough value is put upon learning by practical experience.

Theory and practice should always go hand in hand. In fact, many kindergarten schoolchildren learn theory by the application of practical knowledge; in one or two trades and one or two countries this continues throughout the early school years. Only in Denmark, as far as I can discover, does it continue throughout college and university life, although some American colleges have practised it for years. In England, where the shortage of places, professors and tutors is acute, the number of students or undergraduates could be doubled if education were intelligently divided between learning the theory and learning the practical application of the theory. I do not mean working in another part of the university or college as one learns – I mean working in an industry, trade, or profession so as to earn at least a portion of one's livelihood.

For the primary and basic responsibility of man *is* to earn his living. Full-time university training, obviously, makes it impossible to do so until a man is 22 or 23. This is too late. Long before then, he should have begun to understand and to feel the sense of responsibility which can only be known with deep and abiding satisfaction when one is earning substantially for oneself. This is a fundamental need of the human male.

In law, an adolescent becomes a man at 21. In time of war, a youth of 18 often becomes "a man". At any time after puberty, a male may prove his virility. Idiots are usually men, sexually. But in fact a man is only truly a man when he *can* earn his own living – "stand on his own feet" – and support himself. It is conceivable if not probable that our higher education makes it impossible for many a male to become a man in *every* sense, until it is too late for him ever to learn properly. As a result, too many healthy, intelligent, married men – fathers – never really become responsible human beings. They think they do; far too often, their parents have good reason to disagree. Some of course can adapt themselves to full-time education and, later, to the responsibilities of manhood. But I believe most of these would have become even better men than they are had the system compelled them to start learning and accepting the responsibilities of earning a living earlier.

Another aspect of this is only too evident in the increasing tendency for young men, and to a lesser degree young women, to make a sudden, often totally unexpected decision to go off on their own in search of independence: to "find themselves". They may go from the best of and well-to-do homes, deserting family, friends, college and comforts in their desperate quest. The older generation is either too tolerant, too understanding and too complaisant with them, or else it blindly and angrily condemns the often-hurtful desertion of the family.

Certainly the parents seldom understand what the young are seeking; no more often, I suspect, than the young themselves understand. Such behaviour is frequently said to result from too loose a parental control, but too tight a control will generally have the same effect. There can be little if any doubt that the young who behave like this are driven to it by a sense of deep frustration, or unfulfilment, which leaves them deeply dissatisfied with their environment and their prospects.

They are in fact searching for the responsibility, the true manhood, which modern society denies them. They are looking for the good, for the best, in themselves.

Yet society not only imposes upon them a morality which minimises the importance of self but creates by its educational system the conditions under which the more intelligent young *cannot possibly be self-sufficient or self-supporting.* Consequently rebellion is almost inevitable for some. So is the resentment of parents whose generosity (and often self-sacrifice) has given their children the very things which the children do not need: utter dependence on a system of education, diplomas, certificates, and passes which restrict rather than develop the growth of one's self – of natural Self-ism. Sir Winston Churchill's intellectual growth was hardly impeded by his failure to pass an examination after the age of 12.

There are, of course, professions in which full-time study is necessary, but these are probably fewer than is commonly supposed. They are the academic professions, in which knowledge of theory is of first importance. English literature and theology have been specified as needing exclusive full-time study, but surely such a claim for theology can be questioned. To teach people religion, one needs a knowledge *of* people and their problems and emotions which cannot be acquired from books alone. Literature, as one of the arts, may be a borderline case, although this is by no means certain. To write about people, one must know and live among them. An author who lives apart or aloof from the man in the street cannot reflect life as it really is.

It is worth going back to the beginning of this chapter and repeating: "A little learning is the beginning of much knowledge." The danger comes not from having limited knowledge of a subject but from thinking that one has much when in fact one has little. This is common enough to make the axiom "a little learning is a dangerous thing" sound plausible. It also makes it deadly, for it gives an utterly false impression of the purpose and the character of knowledge.

Knowledge is fundamental to the acceptance of responsibility; fundamental to behaviour.

Lord Acton, who is not now much remembered for any other reason, gained great renown for his axiom that: "Power tends to corrupt and absolute power corrupts absolutely." This was widely, in fact universally accepted in Liberal politics and in liberal thought, and evidence in support was assumed in the antics of Hitler, Mussolini and Stalin. The axiom is wrong. Power in the wrong hands will corrupt, but not all power is corruptive. The power that parents have over their children, or schoolteachers over their pupils, or managers or employers over their workers, often actively prevents corruption.

It is not absolute power but the abuse of *any* degree of power, which corrupts.

And the abuse of power is due to only one thing: ignorance of how to use it. If Hitler had known how to use his power wisely and well he would be alive today; his abuse of it led to his own destruction, to self-destruction. All ignorance damages the self; too much ignorance can destroy the self.

All *ignorance* corrupts.

Absolute ignorance corrupts absolutely.

In view of my opinion of the relative value of knowledge, clearly I don't mean simply ignorance of the academic, or scholarship variety. Everyone knows that some of the happiest people are those who know very little academically but have learned to use their limited knowledge to the fullest advantage; they know enough for their comprehended needs. But in a modern society lack of some kinds of knowledge can and often does mean that one is ill-equipped for daily life; ill-equipped, that is, to carry out all one's responsibilities. Ignorance of the deadliness of dirt killed thousands, millions, of people, until Lister learned and taught the truth. Ignorance of the tubercular infection in milk killed as many, until Pasteur discovered its existence.

Physically, then, ignorance is a killer.

Politically, it is as bad – in some ways, worse. Ignorance of the truth in any political situation is likely to lead to wrong decisions. Wrong decisions lead to injustices, economic insecurity and often to war. War creates the most intolerable conditions for human life.

Socially, too, ignorance is as bad. The fact that one half of the world *doesn't* know how the other half lives leads to grave misunderstanding, bitterness, despair, enmity – and again often to war. So *much* leads to war. Knowledge of humanity, on the other hand, leads to understanding. One has only to know, to forgive – only to know the truth, to understand. The trouble is that in today's world, what one is *told* about other people is often not believed. Mistrust, born of finding oneself so often misled, automatically turns into suspicion. If one were told only the truth and could be sure that this would always be so, there would be no reason for suspicion, so there would be absolute trust. That is why it is essential to tell the truth – not for its own sake but because of the good which derives from doing so, for oneself and for others.

Truth for one's own sake and *good* for one's own sake are almost equally significant and fundamental to a true understanding of self – and of Self-ism. *Knowledge* for its own sake may be good, but the full value of knowledge comes only when one is able to use or to apply what one knows for material benefit, or for pleasure. There is no value at all in ignorance, only grave danger – because ignorance corrupts the ignorant without their being aware of it. It is ignorance only in the sense of unawareness which is bliss.

There are many stages of knowledge. All people need to

know certain fundamentals; but beyond these, knowledge is important only in relation to the individual's needs or desires. Thus it is necessary for all to be able to read, but not necessary for all to read and be able to comprehend (for instance) philosophy. It is necessary for all to be able to add, subtract, multiply and divide; not necessary to have a knowledge of higher mathematics. It is necessary to be able to write, but not necessary to be able to write a book. One needs academic or theoretical knowledge only in so far as one's work and leisure demand it. In leisure, as we have seen, knowledge of a subject is worth while for the sake of the pleasure and the interest it gives; but to a great many people it need be no more than how to sail a boat, or kick a ball, or play bridge. Many derive great pleasure from reading or listening to music, but are utterly bored by games.

Each individual is wholly justified in being true to himself. Society's task is simply to create the conditions in which he *can* be.

The first – absolutely the first – principle one should be taught is that all learning is good for oneself. A child, when beginning to learn, can be made to understand that learning is good for himself – that certain kinds of knowledge give pleasure, for instance – but cannot grasp the fact that what he is learning may also be good for others. Nor would he care much if he could. As a child one is very, very acutely aware of *oneself*, but aware of others only to the degree in which they affect oneself.

With the positive realisation that what he learns is for his *own* good and benefit, the child will become much more receptive than is general today. Most children are instinctively eager to learn; but, being given the wrong reasons for learning, or being made to learn the wrong (or for them unsuitable) things, they soon lose their enthusiasm. Learning, both in the home and in school, is too often presented as something which should be done for another's sake – ("Teacher says you must learn") – which is a variation of doing good simply for *its* own sake. Consequently, a barrier against or a resistance to learning is erected very early in life, subduing the natural desire for knowledge, and can become so ingrained that it is virtually instinctive. So, from an early age, the human mind is often prejudiced against many kinds of education. This creates a mental block which in some cases is never completely removed, and usually begins to weaken only when the child comes to realise that *certain things he does not like doing are to his own advantage.* Once he recognises this, the child will begin to want to learn those things.

The task of the educationalist should surely be to find a way to foster and develop in *all* children their own innate desire to learn. But this cannot be done on a mass scale (a "mass of people" being only a large number of individuals gathered or considered together, at one time or in one place) unless each child realises that it is for his own good.

So, all waste or superfluous learning must be eliminated. There must be no indiscriminate "teaching for the sake of teaching". One of the most common clichés of the old educational system was that "one goes to school not so much to learn as to learn how to learn". Today, of course, a great deal of work – although nothing like enough – is being done to inculcate the real purpose of learning into young minds. Certainly much is done to make learning more enjoyable; but the danger here is that the young may develop a wrong scale of priorities.

Fortunately, it is fairly commonly understood today that the primary task of elementary education is to open the mind and keep it open. Few things are as wondrous as a child's uncluttered mind; few things more wonderful than the way a child first sees life. Few things are more distressing than the way a child's mind can be gradually cluttered up with prejudices of all kinds, even prejudices about what to learn.

For some people, of course, learning *is* important for its own sake. There is the type of mind which acquires knowledge as readily as a sponge soaks up water. But even such a mind will serve its owner better if he has learned how and why to use that learning so as to do good to oneself without causing loss or harm to others.

There comes a time in the life of every young human being when *a* purpose of learning *is* brought home; when study is specifically for degrees or other diplomas or examination passes which will equip the individual for a specific type of work or position in society.

As we have already seen, a great many young people rebel before they reach this point, and in consequence damage their own prospects. Many rebel in their minds without in fact running away. In some ways this secret revolt does even more harm than open rebellion, because the frustration it causes tears at the nerves and weakens the stamina. This is one reason why drugs are so increasingly used: to dull the sense of frustration which follows a young person's enforced inability to become a full man (or woman) in every sense at a time when, physically at least, he (or she) is prepared to be. The student is virtually blackmailed over the years by constant warnings of the critical time of testing to come at the end of school or college, with his whole future probably dependent on the result. Eventually, he will find himself under severe pressures in the throes of fierce competitive examinations. Thus, there are certain specific things he must learn, in order to get a job and earn his living.

In fact, this is what we permit to happen:

  (i)   The student *must* pass a certain examination in order to qualify for a certain job, carrying with it a certain salary.
 (ii)   He therefore concentrates on the necessary theoretical knowledge, which all too often he is able to learn in parrot-like fashion: he can recite but not apply what he has learned.
(iii)   This gives him a mistaken sense of his own ability and superiority.
 (iv)   Equally, it gives the student who fails because he *cannot* acquire knowledge like a parrot (or machine) a mistaken sense of inferiority.
  (v)   The successful theoretical student will often be placed in a position of authority which his real talents do not justify.
 (vi)   The "failed" student will often be forced to accept a lower position than his real talents warrant.
(vii)   An unending number of dead-end jobs are thus created: millions of "square pegs" are forced into "round holes".

Several methods are applied to try to overcome these defects in our educational system. "Aptitude" studies are made, *mostly based on theory*. The I.Q. (intelligence quotient) test, which is applied more and more, is also based on the theory that one can judge a human being's suitability for a particular job on what he *could* do, instead of on what he *would* do (i.e. how he would apply his knowledge). Thus we build an entirely false situation, creating in the human being an artificial climacteric at the most significant formative age. We make him believe that once he has achieved success in his examination or has acquired his degree, he has surmounted a natural obstacle; whereas, in fact, he has merely surmounted an artificial obstacle which should never have been placed there in the form in which he found it.

This does not necessarily mean that there is a case in the educational system for dispensing with examinations: in some ways these are essential, and the arguments against them have been based on a confusion of intent. The dissatisfaction is not with examinations, so much as with the nature of them. All examinations should be based both on theoretical and on practical, applied knowledge.

Patently, it would be better if the young person studying for any business or profession were to become steeped in its particular customs, requirements and responsibilities from the age of, say, 18. In the next five years, he could spend part of the time at a university or college, part in the profession or branch of commerce or industry for which he has an inclination or an obvious bent. During the first two years the student or apprentice would find out whether he really liked the work. His employer could judge whether he truly had an aptitude, and if so, for what particular aspect.

If the trial period proved satisfactory, then the student – at youth's most impressionable age – would know very much more about what he was likely to do all his life. His understanding in later years would be immeasurably greater than if he had continued to learn only the academic or theoretical aspect of the work until he was 23. If, as happens more and more often these days, he wanted to marry early, he would be earning at least part of his living. The indignity (always present if not always felt) of being dependent on parents or relatives or the State (other people) during the years in which he was coming to full manhood, would be gone. The fact that he was standing partly on his own feet would equip him for full manhood much better and much sooner.

These things combined provide the most effective means of developing the self; of learning responsibility first to oneself and then to society in youth's most critical, formative years.

We who live in the West tend to assume that whatever its faults, our educational system gives every child a reasonable chance to learn. However, it depends what one means by "the West". *The United States Population Bureau* in a report published in October 1966 stated:

"There are about 373 million children of school age throughout the world, but only 115 million of them go to school. The remaining 258 million, about seven out of every ten, get no school education of any kind.

"Almost 750 million adults, half the population of the

117

non-Communist developing lands in Asia, Africa and Latin-America, have had no schooling and cannot read or write."

Such facts point to only one thing: a need for an "education explosion" is inevitable – one which will swamp existing educational methods and systems throughout the world.

In the West, meanwhile, more and more young people want advanced education; and as the "Welfare State" grows stronger, more and more will receive this free. In the East, and in underdeveloped countries everywhere, the demand for education becomes more and more pressing. It will be elementary at first, but there will be increasing demand (through force of circumstances) for advanced forms.

On my first visit to South Africa in 1950, there were a few cheap-looking books in Afrikaans and English in a corner of big book-shops where the Bantu (indigenous African) could browse and buy; only here and there were there a few odd books in the native languages. In 1962, however, large sections were given over to these same people, most of whom were much better-dressed and more prosperous-looking. They were buying textbooks and primers in Afrikaans, English *and* their own languages. This indicates how easily – and in how surprisingly short a time – the hunger for knowledge, for literacy, will sweep through nations whose people are now regarded as illiterate and backward. Thus, throughout the world, the demand for more general education will increase the pressure on places in universities and colleges. They will not be able to cope if the present policy of full-time study persists; there will be neither sufficient space nor sufficient tutors. Great numbers of new universities – possibly akin to the enormous University College of Los Angeles in California – capable of giving part-time tuition to millions, will be needed. As only those specialising in certain specified subjects will spend full time at a university, universities will revert to their original important and profoundly respected place in society: they will become the great sources of learning for all mankind, but they will cease to be schools.

As education becomes more widespread and increasingly attainable without cost to the individual – except in so far as he contributes towards the national prosperity, or "the State" – there will be only one qualification needed for a place in any higher seat of learning, after everyone has received his basic education. That qualification will be proof of aptitude and accomplishment, as well as personal desire to learn. The wealth or the poverty of parents will become less important and influential, but the charge to the state or the community will be greater. There will come a time when the State or community, if it is to advance its standard of living, will be quite unable to afford to allow a large proportion of its healthy, vigorous and intelligent young people to make virtually no contribution to the common funds. So, the young people will *have* to work to earn; the system or policy of part-time learning and part-time earning will become the rule simply because no other rule will work.

Just as the approach to learning will have to change if all people are to benefit from education *to the best of their own ability*, so the approach to the mechanics, or the machinery, of learning will have to change. On a very limited scale, it is already changing. Television and radio – particularly television – are already being widely adapted for teaching. This practice will inevitably become much more widespread, because if television is properly adapted to educational needs it can relieve the almost intolerable pressure on school space, on building facilities and on teachers.

The need for education, indeed the demand for it, will inevitably come much sooner than the necessary schoolroom and teaching facilities can be provided. As the population explosion gets under way, the demand will outstrip the supply of space and teachers at a terrifying rate. Unless the children of the latter part of the twentieth century are to become the most ignorant of all generations, new techniques of teaching must be found and expanded quickly.

And they *can* be.

It seems to me inevitable that closed-circuit television, with educational films in all languages, will have to be adapted for use throughout the world, firstly and most widely in the underdeveloped nations. Each village or town area will need receiving sets which can be housed in churches (even where there is nothing in the way of a hall, cinema or theatre, there is *always* a church or temple) or other meeting places; and in many districts in the open air. A method of supervising the pupils will have to be devised but for such supervision qualified teachers will not be essential – which is as well, since they will not be available.

In backward areas, television and the cinema are centres of fascinated attention. Used as a means of education, they will have none of the disadvantages of "going to school". Graded teaching – elementary, secondary and advanced – can be made available on the same day and in the same place for different age groups. In the early days of this revolution it will probably be impossible to give more than an hour or two a day to such classes, but in most underdeveloped areas children are needed to help in the fields and homework will be necessary to counteract the disadvantages of part-time schooling.

Some valuable experience has already been gained from the radio schools of Australia, New Zealand and other sparsely populated countries. Of much more recent development is an Italian television programme, called *It's Never Too Late* as this quotation from an article by Ronald Singleton in the *Daily Mail* of February 4th, 1967, shows:

ONE MAN TEACHES MILLIONS TO READ

"It's Never Too Late, run by an elementary school teacher is well on the way to eliminating illiteracy in Italy.

"The teacher is Alberto Manzi, 42, whose programme is shown from 6.30 p.m. to 7 p.m. every weekday from November to May.

"Italy had 3,832,000 illiterates in a population of 51 million in 1960 (7·5 p.c.) when Signor Manzi started his programme. Today with a population of 53 million only two million are unable to read and write.

"Signor Manzi's pupils consist of farmers, fishermen from remote islands, prisoners, hospital patients, housewives and young people who are unable to go to school. The present 'class' numbers one million.

"After the war the Government, alarmed by the gravity of illiteracy, launched conventional campaigns with only moderate success and a hard core of 2,700,000 illiterates, mainly adults, remained.

"These adults were too ashamed to attend State schools at night. They believed it was too late to learn.

"The Education Ministry decided that the answer was a television course with an instructor whose kindness and patience would make him acceptable to those willing to learn.

"They found Signor Manzi, a teacher and writer of children's stories who looks a little like the comedian Fernandel.

"He was an immediate success. Often he brought guests to the screen, famous singers, actors, footballers, doctors, whose surnames began with the alphabetical letter he wanted to describe.

"Using charcoal and chalk he taught writing. Sometimes he writes for several minutes to the accompaniment of soft background music.

"The transmission costs little. Guests make no charge. Signor Manzi will accept only the normal elementary school teacher's wages – £17 2s. a week.

"Signor Manzi does not normally speak individually to pupils but recently he could not resist. Among the thousands of letters thanking him was one from a boy named Francesco, a thalidomide baby. His apathy had been the despair of doctors until he saw the programme, learned to write with a pencil in his teeth and scribbled his gratitude."

A television educational system will do two things at the same time: teach elementary reading, writing and arithmetic, while also teaching the improved agricultural methods already discussed; birth-control; health; hygiene and "do-it-yourself" activities in a dozen spheres. Education in the three r's will be incidental, and as individuals show their personal aptitudes, they will be eager to learn everything which will help them to do what they *desire* to do. Even more significantly, such an educational system can teach both the young and the old the personal benefits and the nature of individual and collective responsibility to their society.

Once the manufacturers of television sets and the makers of films realise *their* responsibility, they will begin to plan for this development on an unprecedented scale. Allowing one closed-circuit system for every thousand people, say, will mean an immediate need for two million closed-circuits systems. Allowing one receiving set for every hundred people, will create a market for twenty million sets. These can and should be made and supplied at a marginal profit, because the benefits from an educated (even at first a non-illiterate) world will be enormous (see Chapter 11). Moreover, the side benefits of education in the other spheres will give a tremendous boost to world trade.

The manufacturers of the closed-circuits, the receivers, all the equipment and the film, will benefit enormously; so will the authors, the teachers and the producers.

Almost everyone will profit in one way or another, and one of the major incidental benefits will be the strengthening of communications between man and man, nation and nation.

It has always been commonly accepted that one of the world's most grievous problems is that of lack of communication, but the means of overcoming that lack are certainly available today. Not only television, radio, the telephone, air travel – the *means* of linking man with man, of making nation comprehensible to nation, have long been ours to command. Yet nation still distrusts nation, people can still be roused to hostility against people, there are still wars and rumours of wars.

Obviously, then, deciding and ensuring proper use of communication media is of prime importance to the world. For so long as ignorance causes us to misunderstand one another, we shall continue to mistrust one another. By educating man, by improving men, we shall reform mankind.

Once we begin to do so – as simply and comprehensively as modern visual aids to teaching allow, and on the scale the times allow – then the wonders of science in this potentially great age of communication will finally and truly come into their own (see Chapter 18).

Once men have been made to see that it is they themselves who will benefit most from their own education, they will begin to learn with avidity and enthusiasm. In other words, they will begin to practise the natural law of Self-ism. And those who consciously recognise the fact will then be able to see beyond doubt the great benefit of Self-ism to the poor and underprivileged.

When we who write for our living have learned to communicate with *everyone*, we shall have carried out *our* responsibilities. The benefit of Self-ism to all men should be easily enough comprehended. Surely the most intelligent thing any man can do is to accept and carry out his responsibility, whether it be to teach, or to learn, or to help others to teach or to learn.

From the basic human needs, such as birth (population) control, increased food production, sanitation and rudimentary standards of health, to the higher learning in science, the arts and sociology, there is so much to be discovered, so much to be taught, so much left for man to learn, to do and to see – perhaps even to experience on sensory planes as yet unknown, perhaps even to feel in depths of emotions not yet dreamed of.

Only after man has won his basic needs for himself, can he develop a detached attitude to politics, to the first step towards the true democracy – which can *only* be built upon Self-ism.

But first – how shall all men build a roof over their heads?

How everybody is interdependent

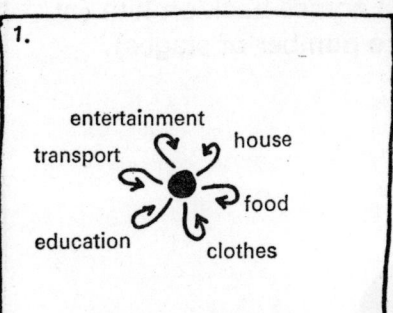

1.

entertainment
transport
house
food
education
clothes

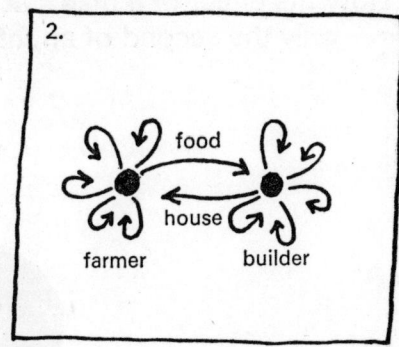

2.

food
house
farmer
builder

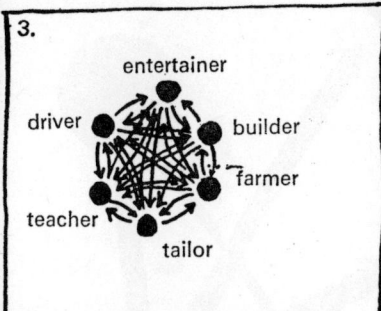

3.

entertainer
driver
builder
farmer
teacher
tailor

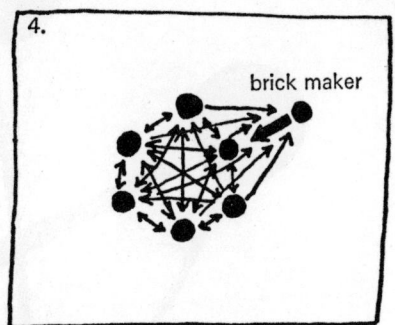

4.

brick maker

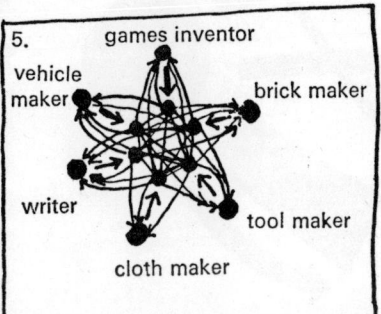

5.

games inventor
vehicle maker
brick maker
writer
tool maker
cloth maker

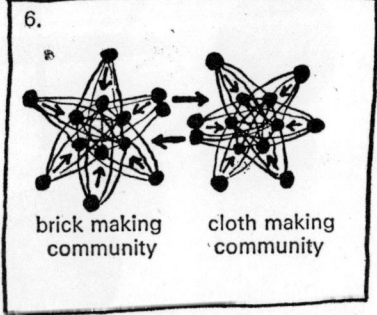

6.

brick making community
cloth making community

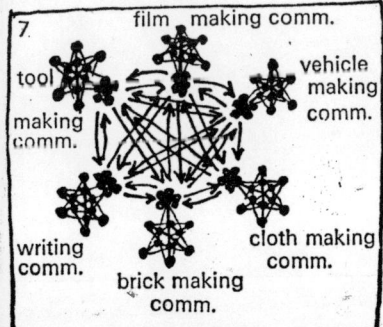

7.

film making comm.
tool making comm.
vehicle making comm.
writing comm.
brick making comm.
cloth making comm.

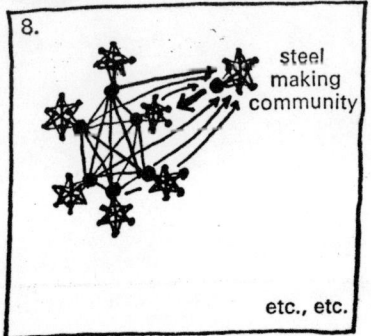

8.

steel making community

etc., etc.

How the effect of a man's action comes back on him (at only the second of an infinite number of stages).

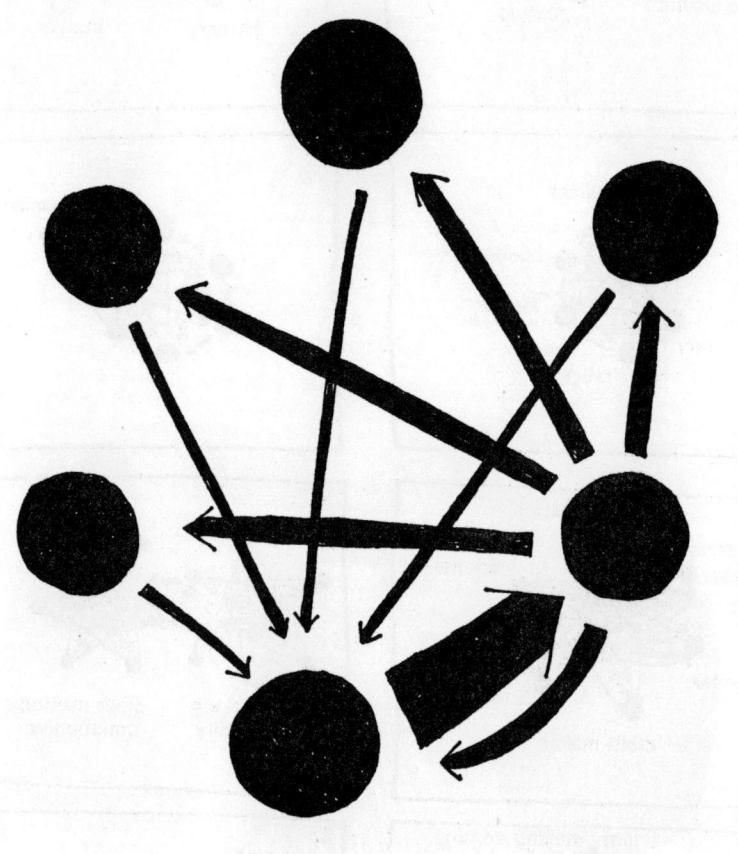

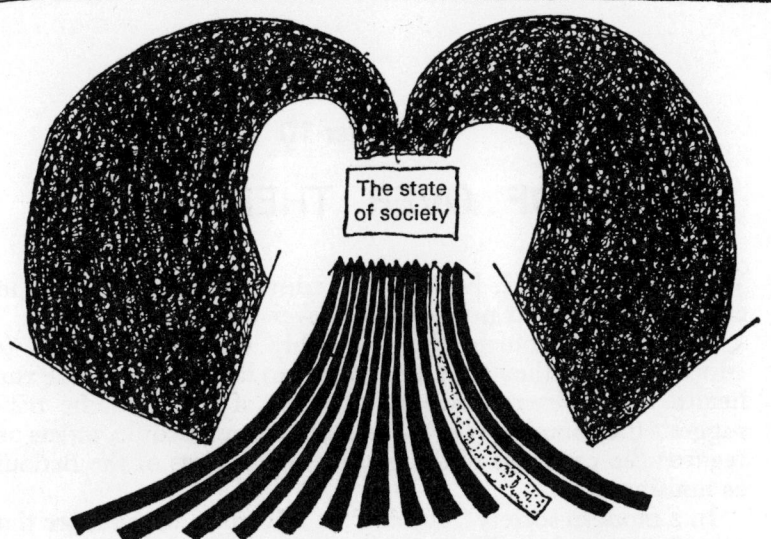

The communities which both cause the state of the society they make up and which are affected by it. (In this case, because one is not playing its full part—possibly because it cannot—none is getting a full return.)

The same communities as above (but here, because all the communities are both able to play and are playing a full part, all are benefiting from a correspondingly full return).

Chapter 10

A ROOF OVER THEIR HEADS

WITH a people fed, healthy and educated according to their capacity, their next need is a roof over their heads.

Actually, of course, they probably won't be healthy (or educated) until they have somewhere to live, although the rude health and boisterous vigour of some of the nomadic tribes suggests that housing is not an essential for all people, unless one regards the caravans of the gypsies or the tents of the Bedouin as housing.

In a modern society "housing" is, of course, much more than a roof over one's head.

It might be worth pausing to consider what a modern society is. All of us know what our own is like but we also know the wide differences between, say, modern community living in a mammoth new block of apartments, and in a rural village; between a sprawling residential estate project on Long Island, New York, and the magnificent homes in Mannaroneck, or the exclusive luxury of California's Beverley Hills and the slums of Watts, only a few miles away. It is convenient to forget these enormous discrepancies between standards of living, easy to forget that the causes of political differences and unrest in the non-Communist world lie buried here, to fester and at times of stress erupt their poison into riots and strikes.

None of these things would happen in a society in which everyone knew he was getting a square deal. And as the impact of Self-ism is felt, more and more people will find themselves being fairly treated (see Chapter 15).

These disturbances, with the resultant dislocation of daily lives, the hardships and the distress, simply would not happen if all men *did* obey the natural law of Self-ism: if all men *did* always carry out those simple, everyday tasks which are their personal responsibilities. It *is* an answer which no political theory or ideology has ever been able to provide, because political theories are always developed (whatever their original inspiration) in the interests of one section of the community.

Take Communism, for instance. This particular ideology has both roused more hope and sparked more hatred in human

126

beings than any other single political concept. It gave birth to a bloody revolution and makes most of its progress through war; sometimes bitter and bloody, sometimes cold and cruel. However well-meant the original purpose of its conception, Communism, in practice, creates antagonism and hostility out of itself.

Self-ism, on the other hand, will win by peaceful means the hearts and minds of men wherever they are, whatever their political beliefs.

Whether one believes in or hates the very idea of Communism, one must agree that it has drawn attention to the appalling conditions in which many millions of people live. And one doesn't need to be a Communist to know that bad housing leads to overcrowding, inefficient or inadequate sanitation, and so disease as well as discontent. Another harmful effect of it is often overlooked. Man, to give of his best, must have self-esteem – respect for the dignity of man is one of the essentials of Self-ism.

If he is living in overcrowded rooms, if he cannot sometimes be sure even of privacy when with his wife because his whole family is crowded into one room, a man's pride and self-esteem suffer terribly. True, there are whole communities which live together in one huge, communal home; but these always have space, usually ample space, for a man to live his own life whenever he wishes. Overcrowding as we know it today is a modern phenomenon except in ghettos.

But despite the wide gaps between have and have-not communities in the West, a kind of composite picture of modern society can in fact be drawn. It enables us to see waterproof, damp-proof and even soundproof rooms and houses. It envisages plumbing, constant hot and cold running water, water-closets and controlled temperatures so that one need never be too hot or too cold. It shows electricity or gas for cooking and labour-saving devices piped into the house. It shows television aerials and piped or picked up radio. It shows sewerage and sanitation, roads and highways, shops and offices, cinemas and theatres, schools and churches; in fact, the whole life of the community. Yet one of the fascinating sidelights, even of a small community, is that one half rarely knows how its other half lives, or what it stands most in need of.

The teetotaller doesn't need a pub or a bar, and the churchman is less likely than most to need a betting shop. But because of the way modern society develops, a great variety of amenities are desired by one person or another: we depend on others as they depend on us. Sports and pastimes, places for relaxing, beauty parlours and bowling alleys, libraries and public galleries, means of transport and places to eat, clubs and societies – all of these and many more are today regarded as essential in every modern community. In some communities they may be luxurious and costly, in others commonplace and inexpensive; whichever they are, they all have to be provided because the people need them.

Within each community, obviously, each person has his own particular responsibility.

Within each community, all the people *are* interdependent, whether they realise it or not. The electrician who pulls a wrong switch and plunges a whole town into darkness causes untold invisible harm, even though the general effect is obvious to all. The builder who puts up bad or jerry-built houses affects hundreds of people, not only those who live in the houses or those who suffer because of the inconvenience or harm caused by the bad building but also the builder himself and his family, through the damage to his reputation and so his future earning capacity.

It is as easy for the community-minded, as it is difficult for those who withdraw from the community, to recognise their mutual interdependence; to realise how much they rely not only on the honest goodwill of others but also on the efficiency with which they carry out their responsibilities.

How *is* a community born?

In past centuries, "planning" as such was purely incidental. Sites would be chosen for availability of water, defensibility of terrain, sources of food and the grazing, mineral or other value of land. Thereafter, cities and towns just "grew" – pleasantly or otherwise according to the vision or the foibles of the men with the money and the artisans with their tools. It is possible to guess how such a city as London came into being; the Londinium of Roman times developing out of a large village community centred around the river which was both its reservoir and its highway. It is much easier to trace how New York began, for the plans of the southern tip of Manhattan, then New Amsterdam, are there to see. But despite this, one doesn't know *how* it grew, cannot follow it through step by step, because there was no town planning, only haphazard building, for many years.

Today, one can follow a community's development from beginning to end, for whole towns are conceived on the drawing-boards. Yet it is interesting that the old mining towns,

A Roof over their Heads

the "boom" towns, developed "naturally" along much the same lines as a new town does today.

I discussed this with a local builder, who explained what happens in this way:

"The initial planning from scratch would be covered by an architect attached to a big development company, who would be in the picture from the moment his clients had a site in view until it is produced on paper and sent to the local Town Planning Officer. The architect would probably also be able to cover the initial surveying procedure and also the part played by the quantity surveyor and the preparation of plans and quantities to enable estimates to be received. On this point presumably one would need some discussion with a solicitor on all the legal aspects up to the completion of the official contract, after which the contractor would take over and the architect's and quantity surveyor's work would then be supervision, instruction and periodical valuations.

"All further information would then be required from a contractor who would proceed on the following lines:

"(1) Survey site and set out roads and buildings.
"(2) Proceed with main drainage, water, electricity and gas supplies.
"(3) Lay out the roads up to the point where they could be used for building purposes.
"(4) Put down foundations to buildings.
"(5) Erect buildings, in which there are dozens of different procedures according to the type of building, whether steel, timber, concrete or prefabricated."

But neither this nor the drawing-board shows how each person who comes into the community is dependent on the work done by those who came before; and how those who have been there from the beginning grow to depend on the newcomers. There is nothing at all new about this process, but it is not always seen and understood – for among the human being's most trying habits is that of taking the good for granted. The bad, of course, seldom goes unnoticed. One sees and buys or rents a house, and only after one has lived in it does one begin to realise how well or how badly all the people involved did their share.

People inevitably notice the bad if it directly affects them; they notice it much less often if the effect is indirect. This is one

I   129

of the gravest problems of society and of human beings – the difficulty of becoming aware of what affects oneself *through others*; of recognising how one's own life is affected by comparatively trivial incidents in the lives of people of whom one has never heard.

How many Western men, living happily in their pleasant, warm houses in a community which offers practically all they need, think more than occasionally of the countless human beings who are homeless? I don't mean the world's nomads but agrarian or urbanised families who would love to have a house of their own but have to crowd into one or two insanitary rooms. These are the people who, seeing the houses of the wealthy, are envious with good reason, for not only do they lack what it is reasonable for them to *desire*; they lack even what they undeniably need. Worse, they are in danger of contracting, even dying from, diseases which are the direct consequence of huddling together with others without sanitation, or food, or protection against the weather.

Countless thousands in Africa's shanty towns are there through no direct fault of their own and no direct fault of the local or national authorities. Hong Kong faces a constant and alarming population increase whenever the borders with China are opened and the masses swarm into the New Territories of Kowloon. The tragic shanty towns in the hills overlooking the city are never empty; as soon as one group is housed in big new apartment houses, others swarm in to take their place. In Aberdeen, only a few miles away, eighty thousand people live in junks and sampans on the water; some families have been there for generations, many are born and die there. Sanitation is non-existent. There is no electricity, only candles and oil-lamps. Water-borne mobile stores visit them and tens of thousands never go ashore. I have stood and watched the barbarically picturesque scene, junks stretching as far as the eye can see against a background of brown hills and flawless pale blue sky marvelling that no plague has yet struck all the people down.*

In parts of South America, the conditions are certainly as bad; people in their tens of thousands squat outside some of the cities under conditions which are evil beyond all imagination.

In parts of the United States living conditions are so appalling that it is hard to believe one is in the country with the highest standard of living in the world. In Glasgow, Scotland, there are still slums too revolting to believe in. On the borders of Israel and Jordan, Arab squatters live in conditions which

* As I write, Hong Kong has been declared a cholera area.

make the heart bleed. In India and Pakistan, indeed everywhere in the East, similar conditions are common. And in these places lurk the seeds of aggressive Communism, Fascism, revolt and war. But it is not only in preventing the danger to the West that the West's self-interest lies, although that cause is great enough. It is in the astonishing waste of opportunity involved. For it needs saying again and again that the people living in those conditions of squalor and poverty could *quite soon* become an important market for goods which the West can supply, as well as for machinery for heavy and light industries with which to build up their own prosperity to undreamed-of heights.

It may be asking too much to expect people comfortably established in the West not only to comprehend the conditions in other parts of the world but also to realise that it is in their own truest interests to help improve those conditions. The evidence has to be made clearer and brought closer. It has to be unmistakable and undeniable.

And there *is* a way to produce the evidence.

If a man living in London, or any city, with all the advantages a modern society has to offer, has difficulty in comprehending the situation abroad or "seeing" its relevance to himself, he can at least be shown the effects of interdependence on his own doorstep. If he does not realise that prosperity anywhere in the world is a fillip to his own prosperity, at least he will know that prosperity in his own country is extremely important to him. He knows that if there is a recession or a depression, wages and salaries fall, unemployment figures rise and taxes are increased. Any one of these endangers his own prosperity and reduces the amount he can buy or save.

When there is a fall in wages, the effect is obvious; he feels it immediately.

When unemployment figures rise, it is less obvious, but he soon begins to sense that there is less money about, a tightening in credit and the danger that he himself may soon be on short time.

Whenever there is an increase in taxes, he feels the effect of it very soon, and resents it immediately.

Because of all these things, he longs for a prosperous country, not out of patriotism but *for his own sake*.

Yet within thirty miles of the metropolitan boundaries of London there are villages and small towns without sewerage; thousands upon thousands of homes without running water, even more without both hot and cold water, far too many without electricity or gas.

The farther one gets from London, the worse this position becomes. In the midlands, the north, the southwest, in Wales and in Scotland, the proportion of homes which have few if any "modern amenities" is much greater. And the same situation exists in all the *large* European and Western nations. Very few are free from these underdeveloped areas, although in Sweden, in Switzerland, Holland and Denmark, they are increasingly rare. In the United States the situation is particularly bad, especially in the Deep South.

During a visit I made to the Harare Township, in Rhodesia, there was a great deal of talk about "native" dissatisfaction and of political unrest because of housing. In that township some housing *is* very bad, but some new residential areas would make many English people extremely envious.

"Why don't you send for some photographs of some of our back-to-back hovels at home, and show them on the screens?" I demanded.

"They wouldn't be believed; the people here would think they were faked," my guide replied.

Would all of them have thought so?

Would the incontrovertible visual evidence that some native Africans were housed better than many white people in England *really* have no effect? Surely there would be some; possibly a very great deal. There would probably be a great stirring of pride, a sense of self-esteem, that might well do much towards easing such tensions as those engendered over Rhodesia.

In Self-ism, self-esteem and pride are worthy emotions; as natural as breathing. If a man does not think well of himself, how can others think well of him? Just as self-esteem is an integral part of Self-ism, so is pride – pride in one's body, pride in one's children, pride in one's home. With a home which compares reasonably with his neighbour's, in fact, man has a good beginning for home as the base on which to build life.

He may have a good appetite and good health, but unless he is a physical fitness devotee, he has no conscious pride of possession in either. He may own a weapon and be proud of that, but in this age he is more likely to take pride in the possession of a television set, a motor-car or a refrigerator. Often in the United States poor peoples' houses have television antennae jutting out of rotting roofs, and modern iceboxes in kitchens where the floorboards are rotten with dry rot or termites.

"They can afford television sets," the Southerners often comment bitterly.

A Roof over their Heads

There can be no *pride* in a rotting house; there perhaps can be some, if only a little, in even the oldest television set.

There can be no *pleasure* from owning a rotten house; there can perhaps be a very great deal from television.

Pride and pleasure are both warming to the hearts of men, as their hearths are warming to their bodies.

When the people of the world are well-housed, well-fed and in good health, more reasonable attitudes will be shown at the conference table, and much less bitterness, simply because there will be much less cause for dissatisfaction.

However, even this is not enough. Even when a man has food, health, rudimentary education in living and a roof over his head, he needs more; after these essentials, he needs educating at a higher level. He can get by without it, but an ignorant man is only half a man; his body may be healthy but his mind is under-nourished and could perhaps become sick, for the mind directs and controls the body.

In order to be fit to take his proper place in society – a society in which he has a voice, or a vote; in which he realises how dependent he is on others and how dependent others are on him – he needs the clearest possible guidance. Because from that moment on he will soon *want* a say in his local or his national affairs: in his own, his nation's and the world's prosperity.

Surely he has been groping for this, throughout history.

. . .

The interdependence of people is nowhere more evident than in the building of a house; a village; a new town.

It is simple fact that each different job is wholly dependent on the previous one being done well. The surveyors, architects, builders and services suppliers are dependent on those who have come before. If the site of a building is badly surveyed, then it will be more expensive to build, will probably take much longer than it should, and might be dangerous. A surveyor overlooking some sandy patches in hard rock will specify the wrong materials, so the quantity surveyor will start off on the wrong foot – and the error, or a degree of error, will be perpetuated. Subsidence can follow, causing all kinds of damage, from cracks in the wall to complete destruction.

The number of individuals involved in creating a new town is very great indeed. It is easy to forget that the counterparts of all of these, and more, were involved in the creation of every city and town, every great metropolis. Moreover, such places

133

must be maintained and serviced day in, day out, by countless individuals, each with specific responsibilities and unarguable rights, each dependent on an incalculable number of others. No one needs telling what happens when one of the services fails. I was in New York in January 1966 when the whole city walked to work for over two weeks because of a strike of bus workers. Incalculable losses were suffered by the corporate city as well as losses and great inconvenience by most individuals. Many, overtaxing their strength, fell ill. Some died in the months which followed – Michael Quill, the leader of the strikers, among them.

Few would blame the strike for his, or for any, death; but can there be any doubted that it was partly to blame?

True, some people benefited. Garment manufacturers and other firms making consumer goods outside New York received orders for goods which the transport-starved city could not supply. But New York lost, heavily. And the places and people which benefited did so on the strength of others' loss; no aggregate good was possible.

A society which cannot find a way to avoid such strikes is not carrying out its group responsibilities. Either the strike is justified, which means that the employers are failing in their duty; or it is not justified, which means that the workers are failing in theirs.

The building of a great city takes centuries; so a city with its throbbing, ceaseless vitality feeds not only off today but also off yesterday; and the lives of the people of tomorrow will depend on the way we live and the things we do today. This is well enough known, of course, but how often does it influence our actions? Do we *live* as if we have a great deal to do, not only for ourselves but for our children and their children? The very life of a city and all the people in it can be seriously affected if a few individuals fail to carry out simple obligations which cost them virtually nothing.

In London, tens of thousands of fires a year begin because in each case one – *one* – person tossed away a lighted cigarette or match. In New York, many more fires a year are started, *each* by the carelessness or the indifference of one individual. The total cost is enormous and is inevitably borne by the rates and taxes; a share of the cost falls on every citizen.

The maintenance and daily life of communities are fascinating in themselves, but there is perhaps a greater fascination in the build-up, already touched upon, of each new city and town. Thousands, tens of thousands, of people are involved, and negligence or an error by any one can be disastrous; or costly; or deadly. To watch the gradual build-up of the actual material and physical structures, is almost awe-inspiring. To know that one man's failure to do his job can cause infinite harm, is both sobering and frightening.

Once the building of a new town is finished, there is need for different services and different people: the doctors and nurses, teachers and librarians, shopkeepers and wholesalers, accountants and lawyers. Take any single group away, or weaken it seriously, and the whole city will stop functioning properly; that is how much we depend on one another to do our own jobs well.

The reason why the *world* does not function properly is that too many groups – national or party-political or social or industrial – seriously weaken it *all the time* by failing to do what they could and should. The basic cause can only be that man does not realise the consequences of his failures as an individual or as the member of a group. No man, no group of men, can *wish* to do harm to his own life, or even to that of others except in time of war.

It is simply that no "morality" or "philosophy" has yet shown Man what he should do and why he should do it. But surely it is becoming easier and easier to see? As we have noted, faster means of communication must help us to understand such simple truisms, as: *We* depend on others and *they* depend on us. *To help ourselves we must help others. To build for ourselves we must build for others.*

Whoever heard of a city built to house one man? How right John Donne was when he said: "*No man is an Island, entire of itself.*"

How people's actions both come back on them and influence the actions of succeeding generations.

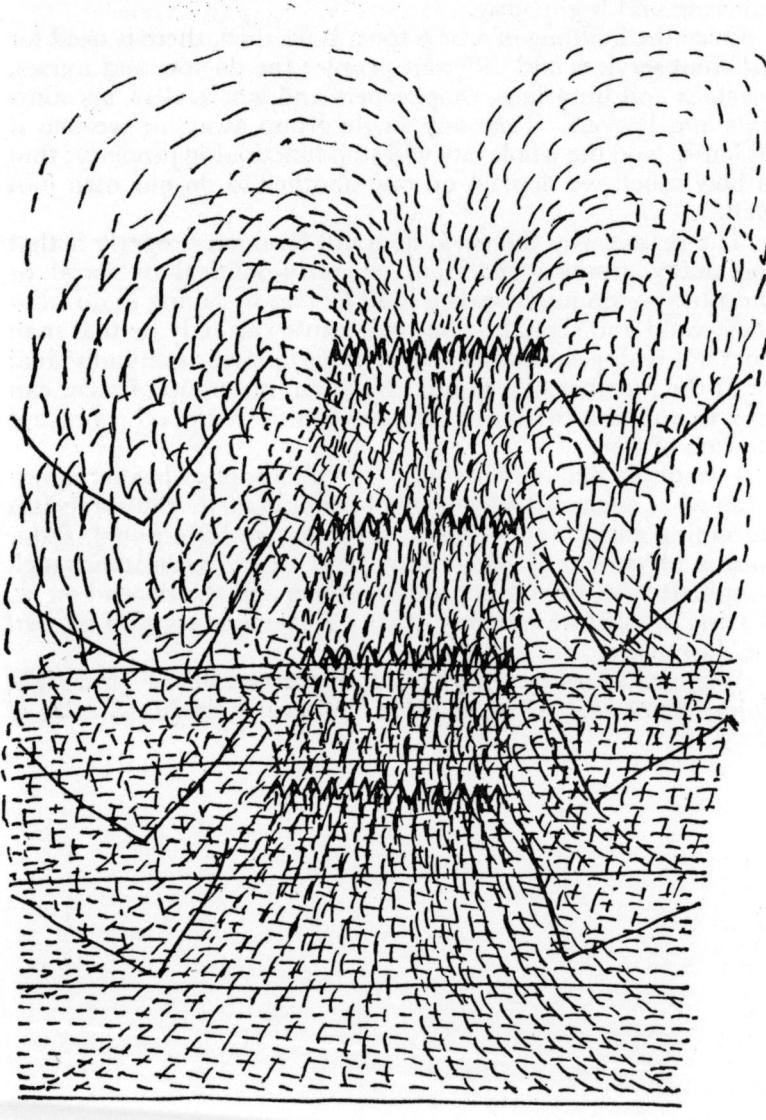

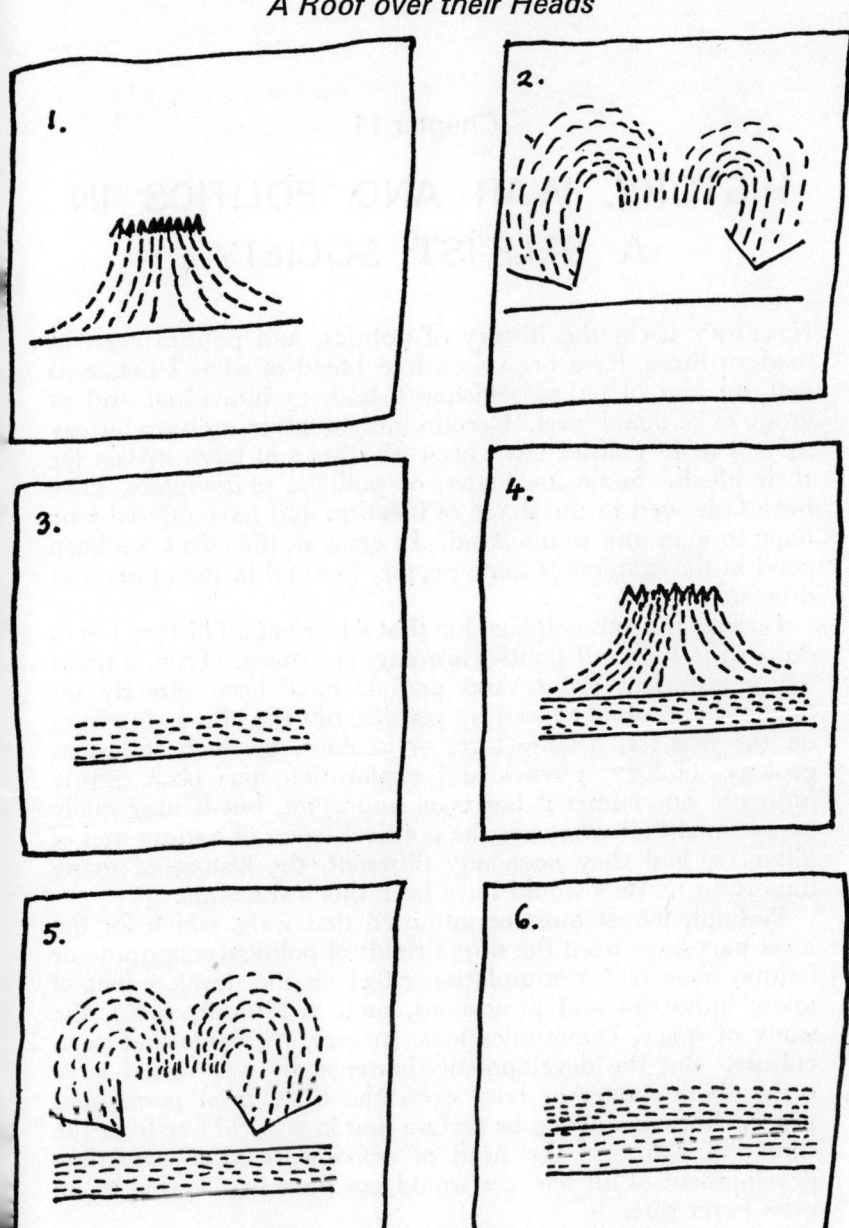

Chapter 11

HISTORY, WAR AND POLITICS IN A SELF-IST SOCIETY

HISTORY itself, the history of politics, and politics even in modern times, have been a curious blend of what I define as Self-ism and of naked selfishness, both at individual and at group or national level. Certain individuals in military history as well as in politics have been idealists and have striven for their ideals. Some ideologies, or political philosophies, have been fashioned in the shape of idealism and have offered true hope to man and to mankind. In general, the effect has been good in the opinion of some people, harmful in the opinion of others.

Perhaps it needs emphasising that while not all history has to do with politics, all politics are part of history. True, a great many historical events and periods have been directly influenced and often caused by politics, but the effect of politics on the arts, on architecture, on science, on such things as geology, biology, physics and exploration, has been mostly indirect. Sometimes it has been important, but it may safely be assumed that whatever the political tenets of nations and of alliances, had they been any different, the history of many important matters would have been much the same.

Perhaps, too, it must be admitted that wars, which for the most part have been the direct result of political ineptitude or failure, have had a stimulating effect on the development of many industries and professions, such as aircraft, radio, the study of space, communications, surgery, medicine and agriculture. But the developments hastened by war would have come about sooner or later even had there been permanent peace. Nor can anyone be certain that in a world free from the threat of war and the need of armaments, the peace-time development of all sciences would not have accelerated at an even faster rate.

It is difficult, almost impossible, to imagine a world without the fear of and the preparation for war. In the comparatively peaceful Victorian era, the possession of military and naval

138

power was a decisive factor, and there *were* wars; communications being slower, the facts of these wars became clouded, so their importance and their cost in money as well as in human suffering was never properly appreciated. The American Civil War was fought in the middle of the great Victorian Age; it is doubtful whether many English or French, Germans or Italians, Dutch or Belgians, knew very much about it – unless, by chance, they had relatives involved or their own businesses were likely to be affected.

Physical courage, heroism, endurance, ingenuity and patriotism, have all been seen at their finest in war. And since the days of the crusades – indeed, since the beginning of time – there have been people ready to fight for their convictions; fighting such as this is a form of idealism. In some ways, man has been nearer to idealism in time of war than in time of peace; for it is when he sees that he might lose what he already possesses, particularly his freedom, that what he possesses becomes more precious.

Whatever may be the truth about wars in the past, whether any have been justifiable, or even useful, there can be no shadow of doubt about their effect on the human race. Throughout history, countless young men in their physical prime, many with brilliantly promising minds, have been slaughtered. War, together with poverty and pestilence, has been responsible for the dreadful philosophy that "Man is born unto trouble, as the sparks fly upward"; that misery is the lot of man, that human happiness is brief and fleeting, quite unattainable as a constant factor in life. Job may have been sorely tried when he said it, but what a belief to live by!

Is it really necessary to believe any such thing?

Isn't it more likely that except for natural disasters, man's unhappiness, his misery, his poverty, his sickness, have all been due *to* man? To his lack of true knowledge of himself, his ignorance about disease and its causes (now decreasing), to his failure to comprehend the simple truth that until he carries out *all* his responsibilities to his fellow men, he cannot receive his own privileges, or "rights"? That until he has helped to make others happy, he cannot be happy himself. *He may not always realise this, but it is, in the light of Self-ism, an inescapable fact.*

War has shown man's inhumanity to man at its ugliest.

War has also shown man's humanity to man at its noblest.

If goodness can reveal itself in the hideous aspects of war, then properly understood and with its strongest motivation – good for *one's own sake* (i.e. the acceptance of responsibility for one's *own* benefit) – man's humanity to man can surely turn happiness into a constant factor in life; then, it will be misery and unhappiness which are brief and fleeting.

This is idealism certainly; it is also the true realism – the reality – everyone longs for. Here again, we see idealism and realism as identical twins.

Politics has given the world a great number of idealists. No one can doubt the idealism of Abraham Lincoln, Wilberforce, Winston Churchill, Mahatma Gandhi, Sir Thomas More, Franklin D. Roosevelt and many others. Moreover, no one can seriously doubt that in original concept Democracy, Socialism and Communism were all idealistic – as well as ideological – even though in practice they have become corrupted in certain aspects and impracticable in others.

Can one doubt that *some* good has come and more can come, from them all? Indeed, from all political systems?

Little useful purpose can be served by any further attempt to analyse the character, causes and effects of war. It is to me unthinkable that another major one will ever be fought, and as unthinkable that war as such – the destruction of the self in others; perhaps hundreds of millions of others – will not cease.

All moral aspects apart, war will surely become a thing of the past if only because another major conflict would mean that most of us would die. Once we fully realise the acute danger of war to ourselves, we will compel our governments to outlaw it. For we do not want to die, and we know now that there is no *need* to die through war – any more than there is need to die through avoidable accident, avoidable disease, starvation or poverty; we need accept death only as the inevitability of age.

This is why interdependence is as true of nations as it is of individuals, nations being simply great numbers of individuals welded together with a common birthright, specific characteristics and common loyalties. It is self-apparent that in time of war, nations need help and so need one another; thus, two groups of warring nations fight each other on a clear-cut issue: to win or not to win. (In a nuclear war no one can win and no nation is likely to fight a war it cannot win; this is the clearest justification for optimism about the unlikelihood of future world wars.)

One nation's need of help from another nation is much less apparent in peace than in war. Even today, this is still true, for peace-time needs are usually less urgent, less obviously vital and much less dramatic. However, nations are coming to realise that national independence, the refusal to acknowledge the

140

need one of another in peace, is a contributory factor to war. The "have" nations can get by on their own, the "have-not" nations cannot; so in desperation the "have-nots" will often join together to try to win economic security through war, in the hope of taking prosperity away from those who have it.

The aid which America in particular and the West in general is giving to certain underdeveloped countries is a clear indication of how much better these things are understood and accepted today. Nevertheless, the relationship between the nations is woefully far from satisfactory. Even friends (or allies) fall out: the United States and Great Britain, for instance, and France and Germany. Most nations quarrel at some time or another: a fairly recent example is in the American resentment at the British trade with Cuba. This is because:

(i) Interdependence is not yet fully accepted, and the need for it is resented by one side or the other.

(ii) There is too little understanding that Governments are not nations; nations are simply millions of human beings, who would never willingly seek war. It is true of human beings that good for one's own sake is essential for the good of all; it is equally true of nations. *War can no longer serve any good purpose for any nation:* it simply leads to more war, or to sanctions against the nation concerned, or to grave economic problems.

If wars should cease, what then of politics?

Obviously the conflict of all ideologies and of all political groups will continue until one simple fact is realised: there is only one essential ideology. That ideology is the idealism inherent in a world without war, poverty, hunger or disease, a world in which people of all religions know they must tolerate the people of all other religions if they themselves wish to be tolerated. Once this has all been accepted, there will be no need for bitter conflict in politics; instead, it will be understood that *all* politicians (like all persons) must work together for the common good.

Is it conceivable that Communist and Fascist will live in peace together?

They have done so, surprisingly often.

Is it conceivable that Democrat and Republican will work together for peace?

In some degree, they do now; and they have shown that whenever they agree on what the American nation needs, they will work closely together.

Good, God and Man

Is it conceivable that Conservative and Socialist, Liberal and Independent, will work together in amity?

They have done, so they certainly can again.

Why don't they do so all the time? Why don't politicians realise that their obligation – their public duty – is to work *together* to seek out the best policy for any given situation? Why don't they, these representatives of differing parties and groups and factions, realise one simple basic fact which cannot be stated too often: that the good of all *is* the good of one?

The biting irony is that until all people, and therefore all politicians, *do* work together, there cannot be enough material benefits to go round. But before industry or commerce can be fully effective there must be a reappraisal of the purpose of politics, a reappraisal which influences the minds and so the behaviour of men. As soon as we can reach the ideal of "Government of the People by the People and for the People",* which was foreshadowed by the Greeks and the Romans and much later by the British, when King John signed the Magna Carta as long ago as 1215, we can forge ahead and give all men their full rights in true democracy.†

In the past few decades lip-service has been paid by *all* ideologies to democracy.‡ Today, the Communists claim theirs is the true socialism, and so the true democracy; the Fascists call themselves National Socialists; the East German Republic calls itself the People's Democratic Republic; Socialists everywhere call themselves democrats; the Republicans in America accept democracy as the proper form of government and the Liberals claim to be the only true democrats.

The Christian democrats and Christian socialists, even the "Gaullists", all pay tribute to the ideal of democracy. And, of course, they all appear to believe that their way is the only way *to* true democracy. The British certainly consider themselves a democracy, having deep (and surely justifiable) pride in their "Mother of Parliaments", but they are still in fact a long way removed from democracy.

There has never been a finer or truer definition of democracy than Lincoln's, and it is doubtful whether there ever will be. *All* Western politicians pay lip-service to it, and most are

* Lincoln's Gettysberg Address.

† Some aspects of this are briefly touched upon in the chapters on health, food, education, and housing; they are mentioned more fully in the chapters on industry and commerce.

‡ The South African Government would by some be regarded as an exception.

142

absolutely committed to the belief that democracy *is* the best means of government. However, let us take a closer look at "democracy" as it exists in Great Britain today.

It is a simple fact that in forty years only one British government has been elected by an actual majority of the voting public; *more than half* of the electorate have been unrepresented in national policies or legislation throughout all those years and a great number, almost one in every five, *have never had any voice at all* in government decisions.

Since Great Britain is still considered by many a model democracy, and since many democracies have been based upon it and have become nearly as undemocratic as ourselves, it is worth analysing the political and economic conditions of Great Britain (see Chapter 13). The purpose is to show that a democracy must represent all the people in all phases of a nation's life, in industry as well as politics, in the social services and in the arts. Whether it be a democracy based on Socialism, Liberalism or Conservatism, if it is truly for all the people and not merely for one section of them, then it must be fully comprehensive. It must allow for differences in personality, ability, health, wealth and breeding. It must enable all people to work together for a common cause while developing their own talents to the full.

Neither Fascism nor any other form of totalitarianism can work this way, and such extreme political groups will drop out of existence once true democracy is established; they are all born out of the failures of democracy.

In a true democracy, all people, all parties and all groups will work together for the common good because it is the *only* way in which all or any of them can get the best out of life for themselves.

In politics as in all else, the natural law is Self-ism.

And in politics, as in all else, the ideal *is* attainable.

Without the ideal of peace and plenty, what do we have? Angry, conflicting groups; strikes; cold wars; economic crises; crime; poverty; hunger; starvation; bad housing; avoidable sickness and accidents; enormous waste of money; misery. These abound in too many, perhaps in all, nations. They are the same factors which have been responsible for all the worst of man's inhumanities to man, from the smallest of personal injustices to the most devastating of wars. They were responsible for the awful plight of the North American Indian (still a reproach and a continuing social problem in a "great democracy") and they were the cause of the virtual elimination of the aborigines in Australia. Further, they were the cause of the unspeakable treatment of the Irish by the British in the days of the famine.

If we, the nations of the world, go on as we are doing, injustices as appalling as these will recur and will as inevitably reap their long and bitter harvests in the hearts and minds of men.

Yet simply by accepting and applying Self-ism, we can between us make such outrages impossible. And when fear and want are replaced by peace and plenty for all, the bitterness and resentment which so injure the self in man, will die.

So will the cause of and the will for war.

So will the cause of and the will for strikes and lock-outs, the industrial wars which are waged so bitterly in many parts of the world.

So will the cause of and the will for crime, for law-breaking, the war against society which at present, particularly in the United States and gravely enough in Britain and other Western countries, seems only to grow fiercer and become more injurious to the State as well as to the individual.

Until the natural law of Self-ism is recognised and acted upon, I believe such wars as these will continue in all their destructiveness: evil feeding upon good.

It may be easier to see these facts in the light of specific historical events. We are all aware that if Hitler had won the Second World War, freedom as we know it would be denied mankind: tyranny and brutality would have flourished in a new Dark Age. If there had been no war, millions now dead would have been alive; men sacrificed to war would have been able to apply themselves to the progress of a free society. We all know that if no one had invented gunpowder or split the atom the world would be a different place. We all talk, sometimes glibly and with half-knowledge, of the influence of the Romans, for instance, on modern civilisation. Historians know it chapter and verse, but the man-in-the-street has little more than a tourist's acquaintance with it. The effect of the great days of Greece, of Troy and Sparta, of the great philosophers, are obvious even in our language. No one needs telling that the history of Christianity has influenced all lands and all religions; or of the effect on the world of the American War of Independence against the British; the world repercussions and consequences of the French, and, much later, the Russian revolutions. All of these things are part of schoolday history lessons.

What is less widely understood is that the success of many a great historical figure, often the actual course of history, has turned on one ordinary man doing his simple duty. There have been many heroes, but we are not discussing heroes, we are discussing the ordinary man in his ordinary job doing it with simple honesty. The effect of the work of millions of such men is incalculable. During the Second World War it was the duty of one man to waken Winston Churchill at times of emergency and crisis; what might have happened had the man on duty failed to do it?

Throughout history, major decisions affecting the future of mankind have been made by great men (or by men possessing great authority). Almost invariably these decisions have been carried out by ordinary men doing quite ordinary jobs. We follow the lives of Hannibal, Julius Caesar and Cleopatra, Henry VIII, Napoleon, Lincoln, Mahatma Gandhi and countless other great historical figures with intense interest, but seldom stop to think that these leaders were served, waited upon, informed and advised by many who have no claim to distinction but who none the less played a significant part in history, simply by carrying out their daily tasks.

All of us today are playing a significant part in tomorrow's history.

And we are living in a world created by millions like us who lived and died in bygone days. In so far as they did their work well, we live well; in so far as they did it badly, we live badly. Countless men in lands we have never seen have influenced the course of history and so have influenced our individual lives. But once we are here we live our own lives, and only we ourselves can make our personal contribution to a better world.

No one can act for us; we have to act for ourselves.

How people that are **ignorant** in a certain way **both** suffer from their own ignorance and the ignorance of all other people.

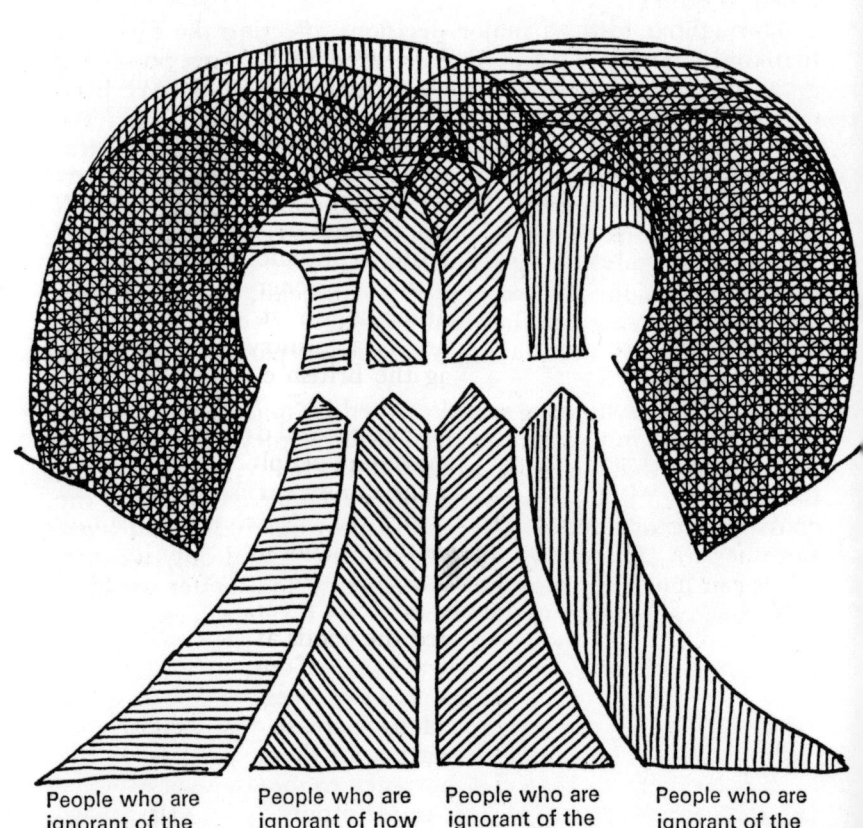

| People who are ignorant of the danger of not doing their job properly. | People who are ignorant of how to do their job properly. | People who are ignorant of the necessity of teaching them how to do their job properly. | People who are ignorant of the necessity of providin them with the necessities of living until they have learn to do their job properly. |

Chapter 12

ONE MAN, ONE VOTE, ONE DANGER

I ONCE asked a Professor of Economics if he could define "economics" in a simple way, and he quoted Lord Robbins as saying that "economics is the allocation of scarce resources among alternative uses". I still consider that an unnecessarily complex definition, but economists profess to find it simple and appear not to realise why laymen do not. Since most politicians are laymen in economics (with exceptions: for instance Mr. Harold Wilson was an outstanding economics scholar and the youngest ever don at Oxford) there is generally nothing surprising in the fact that politicians do strange and often dangerous things to the economy of a country.

They have been endangering the British economy for many years.

Economics, to me, is the law of supply and demand governing all commodities needed by any group of people. The economics of a family are simply whether the family earns enough to buy enough for all its needs, provided the goods are there. In most Western countries the goods *are* there; and acute shortages are either seasonal, or caused by strikes or wars. The economics of a country are exactly the same: whether it earns enough to buy enough for all its needs, provided the goods are there. So far as I can discover, the goods *are* always there if one can afford them, and manufacturing processes having been speeded up by automation, all that is needed to increase the supply of all commodities is an economic market for them.

The days of raw material shortages are nearly over now that synthetic materials are in such ample supply. And with nuclear reactors already in use the problem of supplying energy for manufacture is obviously one of diminishing significance. Of course, other factors than these are involved. For instance, countries with substantial resources can if necessary live partly off their capital; but this never lasts for long. No countries (and very few people) inherit enough to pay for all their needs throughout an unlimited period of idleness. If a man does

147

inherit enough, not only can the fact that money came easily to him spoil his pleasure in what he can do with it but it removes the necessity of his having to persevere in an occupation which he may well find arduous. In other words, it removes the necessity of any form of self-discipline, which we know from experience is essential for every one of us.

We in Great Britain lost much of our inheritance in two world wars; in relaxing after these wars, many believe that as a nation we have become complacent and flabby. However, we have low reserves of capital and few hidden exports left, and we do not earn anything like enough in world trade to pay our way.

Let us look at the effects of this, as well as the causes.

I have taken the British political and economic situation as an example, but am convinced that all of the arguments are acutely relevant to the situation in other countries whose circumstances vary only in type and degree. If the principles are adapted to meet the particular circumstances of any nation, they will have a significant impact on that nation's economy.

For the main thesis I have accepted Lincoln's definition of democracy, elaborating or developing it to mean that the views of *all* the people, including minorities, should be taken into account throughout the life of every government; that no single party, still less any single person, should have the right to run a country without constant consultation with members of all other representative parties and social groups.

As I have shown, we have come to think of "realism" as something less than the best: as merely the "best attainable". Time and time again in modern history, a so-called "realistic" policy has meant a compromise between good policy and bad. Industrial as well as social policies have also been approached on the basis of this false concept of realism. "We must," say such realists, "cut our coat according to our cloth." Or else they say: "Politics is the art of the possible."

Acceptance of these clichés has led the world to two global wars, to Nazism, Communism, the slaughter of the Jews, the bitter "cold war" between East and West, the universal fear of nuclear weapons, a world of haves and have-nots, famine and squalor for hundreds of millions of people, corruption in high places and interminable political and international enmities.

Socially, it has led to almost unbelievable inequalities in nations with a high standard of living; to slaughter on the roads, crime on a vast scale, and a widespread deterioration of integrity and honesty.

In Great Britain, there is a growing sense of cynicism; more

148

and more people give less and less value in work and in service
to one another and to the community. Discourtesy and in-
civility seem continually to increase. Youth is given divided
leadership or none at all. The economy of the nation becomes
weaker and weaker. The disunity among the people is more and
more apparent: not only is the country divided into three main
political camps but each camp is divided within itself, often
bitterly.

An alliance of *all* the parties in which each supplies its best
men for office, seems to me the *only* form of government which
can possibly enable the nation to get the best out of the people,
for it is the only way to end disunity and create the necessary
conditions of political – and hence social – justice. Once these
are achieved, attitudes will change, productivity will rise and
the economy cannot fail to improve. The nation will be strong
in itself and will be able to influence world affairs by example,
as well as by its economic and moral strength. This is what we
urgently need. And this is precisely what our present form of
one-party government fails to give us.

The only practical realism/idealism is one which will
enable us to get the best out of life in time of peace. On the
political realism of an All Party Alliance such as I have out-
lined, I am sure an ideal society can be built. There will be
enough cloth to cut a coat of any size; and it will be clearly
demonstrated that all problems are soluble through practical
politics.

Whether we like it or not, we in Britain have too few of certain essential goods to go round, so they have to be spread thinly
and priorities have to be decided. Here the "allocation of
scarce resources to alternative uses" comes into its own. As
Donald Tyerman, former editor of *The Economist*, put it to me
after studying these arguments:

"This is not just a moral and personal matter; it is a technical,
economic and political matter as well. It is not at any moment
of time *right* to build a school and not a road, and *wrong* to build
a road and not a school, *right* to invest in an agricultural enterprise and *wrong* to invest in an industrial one, or the other way
round.

"These *are* matters of choice to be worked out and argued
about according to the balance between costs to be incurred and
benefits to be got, and the aims to be sought; the choices are in
themselves not moral, though they ought to be morally pur-
sued, but technical, economic and, in a democracy, political as

well. This is the justification (indeed the necessity) for both economic calculation and political disputation.

"That is the core of my comment. These are matters not of an automatic moral verity but of economic choice (not between right and wrong but between this or that) and, as you say at one point, of 'political opinion' – according to the political or social aims you or the other chap (*both* good men) may be seeking."

Clearly there can be no serious refutation of such reasoning, but the economic and political factors *can be very greatly influenced* by the application of Self-ism – under the influence of which every individual involved in economics or politics will do the best he possibly can.

No one can ignore economic truths; Self-ism simply claims that if everyone accepts his full responsibilities, and recognises the full implications of interdependence, the problems of economic priority will automatically resolve themselves.

To illustrate the political approach to this, I shall quote in full my memorandum on the principles of government by ALL PARTY ALLIANCE, first promulgated in September 1965.

Many of the conditions discussed in it are true in part or whole in every democracy. Certainly the basic fact that after a general election one party usually takes absolute power is true. Democracy, I believe, has outgrown the need for this. What would the United States and Great Britain have thought, for instance, had the Communist party been elected by a minority vote in France or Italy and then proceeded to take absolute power – as the winning party invariably does in Great Britain, and very nearly does in the United States?

Such a situation could never arise anywhere if the principles of an All Party Alliance were generally accepted.

The full memorandum reads:

"It is perhaps self-evident that no society can truly prosper without the co-operation of its individual members. Only if a nation prospers can all its people prosper, but only if all *do* prosper can all be asked or expected to give of their best.

"Since a political system satisfying to at least the vast majority is an obvious prerequisite of such co-operation, it follows that a properly-functioning democracy must provide the most fertile soil for a sound and flourishing economy. And since our present economic situation leaves so much to be desired, our political system must plainly be at fault.

One Man, One Vote, One Danger

"Great Britain is allegedly a political democracy today. But consider these facts:

"(i) For over thirty years, no party has gained office on a majority vote of the electors. Government has been by whichever party won more seats at a General Election than any other single party, but which nevertheless had more votes cast against it than for it.

"(ii) Thus under our present system, we are regularly subjected to one-party rule by a Government which cannot and does not represent all the people, yet can and does force through legislation based on the interests of the minority it represents. The Opposition's voice may be heard, but the Government is at no time compelled to heed it – and very seldom does.

"(iii) This system makes it virtually impossible to have the nation's best political brains in the Government: instead, we have only the best brains of the party in power. As a result, more often than not some very able men are idle when their party is out of office, while less able men carry the responsibility of ministerial duties.

"(iv) At the whim of any Government the country may be faced at any time with a General Election. The retiring Prime Minister may claim that the time has been chosen in the best interests of the nation: in fact it is invariably chosen in the best interests of his party.

"(v) When a minority-elected Government has a very slight majority of elected Members, much time, energy and ingenuity are spent in maintaining the Government (party) position, leaving too little for single-minded concentration on the affairs of the nation.

"Not surprisingly – since these facts in themselves surely amount to a negation of what I believe to be democracy – there is considerable dissatisfaction among all classes and income groups, and resentment, distrust and cynicism are increasingly widespread.

"With interests represented by different parties and factions continually pulling against one another, industry and commerce consistently suffer major disruptions, often arising from the pettiest of disputes. Compared with other nations, the growth of British productivity is slow and the quality of many of our products poor. Service from supplier to consumer is too often

151

negligent, inefficient, off-hand and unreliable – both from the retailer to the customer at home and from the exporter to the customer abroad. Thus in far too many fields, we are simply not competitive. As a result, the gap between import and export is always too great, and we are in a state of constant crisis or near-crises in our balance-of-payments with other nations.

"At home, too, we shift from crisis to crisis, and are in continual danger from inflation. Almost without relief, the political and economic mood has for years been one of pessimism and gloom, punctuated by an occasional burst of unjustifiable optimism. Taxation is held at crippling level, and in itself restricts industrial development. And due to our industrial weaknesses this country, which fathered international banking and, via the industrial revolution, changed the whole course of world affairs to lead directly to this age of scientific achievement, is today a debtor nation.

"The effects of our unstable economic and political position are obvious and grave. Commonwealth member nations have to seek financial and economic aid and even political guidance from non-member nations, including Russia. The countries of the Common Market so lacked confidence in us that for years none dared go against the virtual dictates of France. What influence we do exert in the world today is out of the seriously-depleting reserves of our past greatness, because international respect has to be underwritten by economic strength.

"In the financial capitals of the world, a strong Britain is deemed an essential cornerstone in Western security and economic growth. For that reason the World Bank, International Monetary Fund and 'lending' nations have consistently bolstered our economy by loans – originally made to help us recover from the war and put our industrial and so our economic house in order. But a number of factors are clearly beginning to alarm world monetary sources:

"(i) The increasing indications that successive British Governments are coming to regard massive loans as automatic; to expect continuing help, whatever the circumstances.
"(ii) The fact that much of our borrowing is simply to pay back earlier loans (or interest due on them).
"(iii) The lack of any indication of successful attempts to deal with the problem at source: i.e. to increase our productivity and the quality of our goods, so 'working' instead of 'borrowing' our passage.

"(iv) The growing conviction among some international bankers and political interests that we shall never be able to put our house in order, and that it is useless to continue to lend us money or extend our credit.

"(v) The fact that if this view should harden, and loans be refused or withdrawn, the £ sterling would collapse, resulting not only in disaster for Great Britain and near-disaster for any Commonwealth country whose economy is integrated with our own, but also having serious repercussions on every Western currency and economy.

"It is plain that this last eventuality, with its obvious advantages and opportunities for the Communist half of the world, is the basic reason for the continued support we at present receive. It is equally plain that this help must one day be drastically curtailed if not actually withdrawn, simply because it can no longer be afforded – either materially or politically. There are limits to the economic resources of those nations on whom international funds depend, and certain commercial interests in some powerful nations do not share the general desire for an early revival of British economic strength.

"At all events, it is clearly in the vital interest not only of ourselves but of the whole free world, that Britain should begin forthwith to remove the causes and so the danger of economic collapse (which would be disastrous for so many other nations). To do this we must:

"(i) Bring our balance of payments into credit.

"(ii) Keep our balance of payments in credit by economic growth, so that we become a 'lending' and not a 'borrowing' nation.

"In simple language, *Great Britain's first responsibility is to herself.** Only by restoring her own fortunes can she pay her debts and meet her responsibilities to others. And only by carrying out her responsibilities to the world can she achieve the greatness which her history, her tradition, her wealth of experience *and the qualities of her people* deserve.

"In the final analysis, after all, a nation's wealth lies in the qualities of its people – and World War II alone proved just how great those qualities can be. The people of Britain saw

---

* Political and national Self-ism. Britain's recovery is not possible until she puts her own house in order.

their responsibilities to the nation and the world, and shouldered them unhesitatingly: for those who needed guidance, Winston Churchill was the beacon lighting the way.

"But duty in war is easier to define, and the goal is obvious. The responsibilities of peacetime living are less apparent. Lack of urgency or of recognisable common aim, ignorance of the essential interdependence of all individuals in any society, uninformed acceptance of prosperity at home at the expense of the export trade and balance of payments: all these contribute to the couldn't-care-less, 'I'm all right, Jack' attitude so rife today.

"The fault does not lie with those who cannot see, but with those who have failed to provide the beacon. To draw again on those dormant seeds of greatness, we must first provide the unifying sense of mutual purpose and demonstrably mutual benefit those 'Valiant Years' evoked. And I believe that this will be achieved only when all the British people have become effective members of a true democracy.

"Only in a true democracy can each individual really feel that he is part of the whole and *responsible for that part*. Only then will he give the best that is in him. And only when the British people give the best that is in them can British productivity increase enough to strengthen and enrich the economy and thus restore Great Britain to her rightful position as a great power, able once more to exert that much-needed influence and leadership in the Commonwealth and the world.

"Clearly, such a restoration of her power and prestige never will *or can* be achieved under our present political system. I am convinced that what we need, *and most urgently*, is a Government which consists of all the best elements in all the political parties: namely, a government by ALL PARTY ALLIANCE.

"Such an ALL PARTY ALLIANCE can and should be created at *the next General Election*. The political parties should fight that election (and all future General Elections) on the usual party lines, advocating their policies and winning as many votes from the electorate as they can. Thereafter:

"(i) Once the Members are elected, the Leader of the party which gains the most votes in the country (*not* the most Members in the House) should be called upon to form a Government.

"(ii) The Prime Minister should be required to appoint his Cabinet from all the parties, in direct proportion to the votes cast for each party at the General Election.

"(iii) Bills should be presented to the House during each session in the same proportion.

"(iv) All Bills should be submitted to a free vote of the House, so that all Members could vote according to conscience on each issue. The Whips would ensure that Members went into the Lobbies; *not* that they voted in any predetermined way.

"N.B. In order to allow the fullest opportunities for stable government, we should adopt a fixed-term policy of four or five years for each parliament; *not* a term to be decided by a party or party leader.

"Given these revisions, *every vote would matter*, since none would be wasted. Thus the people would feel the Government to be truly 'theirs', as all shades of opinion would be represented in the Cabinet – and thus, in the legislation. The party system would operate at its best, since each party could concentrate on policy – in the knowledge that its best policies would be submitted to the test of debate and decision in the House.

"Since the elected leaders of each party, including the Shadow Cabinet, would be always in office, their invaluable experience and expertise would be always available. And with the most able men from all parties in the Cabinet, Ministerial appointments could be based on ability, *not* mere expedience. Any sudden changes in Ministerial office would be dictated solely by the interests of the nation, *not* the party. Other nations would be able to rely upon continuity of basic policy for all Commonwealth and Foreign Affairs – and we and they could be assured that the best available men were in charge of Great Britain's relations with them at all times.

"I do not claim that of themselves such political changes would adjust the economy of the nation. I do claim that given these revisions, the mood, temper and spirit of the people would improve tremendously, and that Britain would indeed become the first fully operative true democracy, encompassing all sections of society and all shades of political belief. And I do claim that such reform would provide *for the first time ever* the climate of national opinion essential to the creation of the conditions in which fully effective and amicable labour/management relations could exist."

I have discussed these principles with people from all walks of life. Only *one* asserted that although this might be true democracy, he was satisfied with things as they are. All the others

155

agreed with All Party Alliance in principle, but most suspected that its realisation would be baulked by one thing or another. Some held that "human nature being what it is, you'll never get the parties to agree". Yet as we shall see, such a form of government would improve each party out of all knowledge, *and moreover, would ensure that each was always represented in the government of the day.*

Some said: "Politics is a dirty business; you'll never clean it up." But under All Party Alliance, all the conditions which make for political huckstering and nepotism would be gone. Some said: "The professional politicians would never stand for it." But it is the only way by which the really able professional politician could *always* play his part in Government, no matter which party was in power.

Some said: "It's only a coalition, and coalitions never work." But while All Party Alliance has all the advantages of coalition government it has none of the disadvantages. Any of the member parties to a coalition can withdraw at any time, and so bring down the Government. No party can withdraw from All Party Alliance, which is a system of government, not simply a form of government within a system. Moreover, in a coalition there are parties or groups which oppose the Government for the sake of opposition, whereas in All Party Alliance, opposition would be to bills presented; bills could be defeated without bringing down the Government. It should be remembered, too, that of the three coalitions Britain has had, the two in war-time were outstandingly successful, and even the 1931 "National" Government pulled us through the immediate crisis. Coalitions only fail when the participants begin manoeuvring for political advantage, begin to put their parties' interests above the nation's.

Some said: "But if all the parties were in the Government, there would be no opposition." In fact, as I have shown, the Opposition under our present system is virtually impotent, but the Opposition in an All Party Alliance will come from *all* the parties and will be able to defeat any bill: the first *effective* opposition in British politics for over a hundred years.

The majority said – and it seems to me shocking that this should be the most common plaint: "If only it could be made to work – but it never will." The need for it is, unquestionably, widely recognised. All that is lacking is the *will* to demand it.

And that is likely to come as soon as the political parties themselves are examined more closely by their own supporters.

Such an examination will show, quite clearly, what does not yet appear to be realised: that the need for each party to gear itself chiefly to win elections is its greatest weakness, as well as its strength. Each party has to attempt to become all things to all men, to trim its sails simply with a view to winning over the wavering or uncommitted voter. Its leaders "hedge" on major and on minor issues. Its Members of Parliament have to walk the party line carefully; only the boldest will defy party opinion and campaign for what they fully believe.

Moreover, during debates at conferences and in committee each party caucus has constantly to try to soothe rebellious elements, to try to find a formula which will both please its members and attract more of the electorate. This continual polishing of the party image in the public eye has a debilitating effect on the party itself. Members to the right or left of the official (vote-catching) line who are brought to heel by disciplinary action, often seethe with discontent. All too many are afraid of saying what they really believe, for fear of harming their party's election prospects.

Yet it is the aggressive, progressive-minded rebels who give a party not only new ideas but also fresh vigour and vitality.

With All Party Alliance such rebels would only strengthen and enrich a party. Given a substantial representation in the Government – whether the majority or not – no party need ever fear, or indeed suffer from, the clearest possible expression of *all* points of view.

This will greatly influence those voters who stay away from the polling booths out of disgust with or disinterest in party politics; they will have much less reason to abstain.

Moreover, the competition for office among the best men of each party will of necessity become much sterner. At present, the Government party has about one hundred ministerial posts to fill, and many are filled by uninspired, if competent, party men. With All Party Alliance, the majority party is unlikely to have more than fifty-odd posts. Competition among the members of each party to qualify for a post will be a far greater stimulus to efficiency than any that exists today – and the nature of the system will demand that it be honest competition, allowing the truly best men to obtain posts. "Jobs for the boys" will become a thing of the past, because ministerial performance will be under close scrutiny from fellow ministers of their own *and* other parties.

Furthermore, at each General Election *each* party will have to give an account of its stewardship in ministerial posts, some of cabinet, some of minor rank. It will no longer be enough simply to blame the other party. A Minister who is able to gain continued support from *all* the parties, if he is to hold his post, will clearly be much stronger and more capable than one who can rely on the support of his own party whether he is right or wrong.

So with All Party Alliance, each party will have constant incentive to increase its own strength – again a form of Self-ism. With its own proportion of bills to sponsor in every session of parliament, each party will have to review its policy regularly, forever working to strengthen its effectiveness so as to win the support of its opponents. It will thus be in the interests of every party to make itself as sincere and as honest as it can be. There will be no question of "watering down" policy so as to make it acceptable to the other parties: any weak policy will automatically unite the opposition against it.

To justify itself, therefore, each party will *have* to keep itself at peak strength all the time. And if each party is at its best, it follows that the Government must be, also.

I don't doubt that for some time there may well be a great deal of unthinking and prejudiced opposition to these proposals. Every new political movement risks misunderstanding and misrepresentation, deliberate or otherwise, and All Party Alliance has proved no exception. Many people hearing about it for the first time are apt to think it a new political party, for instance.

It is not.

A new political party would represent the views only of a proportion of the electors, whereas All Party Alliance is a new concept of government by which the views and the policies of *all* parties are considered *all* the time. With All Party Alliance, no session of parliament would ever be devoted only to bills sponsored by one single party; all would have a share.

The essential purpose of this new political concept is to create *all*-party government, based on the *policies* of all parties. There would always be room for a new party in All Party Alliance but there would never be any risk that a single party, new or old, could take over the Government and by clever legislation perpetuate itself in power.

It is provenly true that:

No single party can assure us of democracy for all time; All Party Alliance can.

No single party can represent and speak for all the people of every age, in every walk of life, for all the time; All Party Alliance can.

One Man, One Vote, One Danger

No single party can attract into politics and so into government the best minds of *every*, or of no, political conviction; All Party Alliance can.

No single party can ensure continuity of policy both at home and overseas; All Party Alliance can.

No single party can get the best out of all the people and so create the conditions for a new national team spirit which will enable Britain to compete successfully with the rest of the world; All Party Alliance can and will.

Just as I believe that the principles of Self-ism will pave the way to social and economic evolution in Great Britain, so I believe that once Great Britain has demonstrably become a true democracy, it will become a model for new democracies both in the old, historic nations and in the newly-emergent: each one independent and yet interdependent, each one playing its full part – accepting its responsibilities – in the prosperity of peoples and the conditions of happiness for mankind.

Chapter 13

INDUSTRY IN A SELF-IST
SOCIETY – I

INDUSTRY is a positive and yet at the same time a too-vague term. As a word it is commonly understood and yet often has shades of meaning which differ from person to person.

There are basic, heavy and light industries, and the common factor among them is that they all produce goods. Industry might be called organised production; yet it varies so much in its nature, from country to country and even region to region, that often there appears little or no organisation about it.

It is haphazardly run in a capitalist society and too often inefficiently run in a socialist society; yet it can be shamefully inefficient under private enterprise and magnificently efficient under socialism, or at least under nationalisation.

Few industries are better run than that of the Swiss Railways, which are nationalised; few, surely have been more inefficient of late than the British shipbuilding industry, which is privately owned. Of course, the shipyard owners will blame the industry's bad record on the workers and the workers will blame it on the shipyard owners, but any industry which can lose so much trade in so short a time to Japan, Germany, the United States and Holland has been deplorably inefficient, whoever was to blame.

The Fairfield experiment of co-ordination between the labour force and management is a heartening indication of a change for the better if one believes, as I do, that one thing alone will bring about essential reform throughout industry all over the world: good labour/management relations.

Bad labour relations are to blame for most of the economic ills of our time, perhaps of all time. It is often said that in the "good old days" – when *were* those days? – the relationship was perfectly amicable, and the craftsman or workman took a great pride in his job. One has a vivid picture of a nine-year-old girl squatting in a coalmine tunnel, opening and closing a canvas flap for exhausted, black-grimed men to crawl through; or a six-year-old boy having his buttocks burned to make him

160

climb into the terrifying darkness of a hot and stinking chimney to brush away – and blind himself with – the soot. Or a galley slave, being flogged at the oar which is pulling out his life; or a farmer's boy, up at five o'clock and working until dark for his pitiful "keep"; or a shop-assistant, working from six-thirty in the morning until ten o'clock at night. The list is endless.

The truth is that in the days when labour/management or employer relations were allegedly "good", the employers representing the terrifying face of CAPITAL, did not give the workers anything like a fair deal. Had they done so, the revolt against capitalism would never have come about. Whether in the extreme as with the Russian Revolution of 1917, or whether in the mild form of British Trade Unionism, the effect of the revolt is still with us. The tragedy, of course, is that the revolt, even though justified, is inevitably *against another part of oneself*. That is why, as things stand, there can be no end to the revolt; why we live in a world of constant industrial turmoil and economic instability *and* why there is so much usually justified complaint about the quality of so many goods, even those ordinarily of high repute.

It is unlikely that any motor-car, from a Rolls-Royce to a Volkswagen, will be driven for its first thousand miles without developing a fault which gives cause for legitimate complaint, each such fault being due to the provable fact that one among the long chain of workers at the manufacturers failed to do his job properly. A peculiar system of alibis or "passing-the-buck" has become common among all motor-car manufacturers. The manufacturer does not accept full responsibility for the car *he* delivers or makes available to the customer. It is generally the accessory manufacturers who are blamed: the suppliers of lamps, upholstery, windscreen wipers, battery or tyres – the variety is quite remarkable. And shameful.

It is also shameful that any qualified and trained person, workman or manager, should fail to do his job properly. In the industrial world of the second half of the twentieth century a great deal of culpability is evenly spread among all sections of every industry. This culpability ranges from the man at the workbench who takes too long over his tea-break, to the manager who goes off too early for his golf. It also ranges from the supplier of the raw materials to the salesman of the finished product who exaggerates, lies or misleads when selling his wares. I have selected the motor-car for these strictures because they seem to me symptomatic of an age when manufacture of all commodities could be near-perfect, but so seldom is. I can remember the disgust on an African carpenter's face when he showed me a dozen screws from a gross box, each without a head, or without a point, or without a thread.

"And they come from England, Baas," he said.

In the same year I remember the disappointment on the face of my then seven-year-old son when he saw in a toy carpentry set bent over like brown paper. It had "Made in England" stamped on its "blade".

England, of course, is one of many offending countries from America to Switzerland, countries where flaws in work should be absolutely minimal. Possibly the Swiss and the Germans produce fewer faulty goods than anyone else. Again, this is an example of applied Self-ism: they have realised how much their own success, and so well-being, depend on goodwill from their customer-nations. Without this goodwill their trade would fall away seriously.

The Japanese, also, are better than most in the standard quality of their goods today, whatever they were in the past. Yet like the Germans, they have had to break down a great deal of ill-will caused by their aggressive wars. The Swiss, with no native raw materials, dare not let their quality fall. For some undiscoverable reason, the Americans, French and Italians don't seem to think this matters much; nor do the British. Too many people in Britain seem to live on faith in a remembered seller's market, which in fact they can maintain only if they restore the quality of their goods.

For more and more consumers are becoming more and more selective, particularly those from the poor nations, to whom money is scarce and value for it essential. It should be essential to all – but so slack, for instance, is the average English customer in his own self-interest that he accepts poor quality goods with a shrug and a "What's the use of complaining?" A form of destructive *laissez-faire* is spreading a dangerous corruption throughout industry, grave enough to threaten the economy of whole nations.

It is *all* due to a mistaken concept of self-interest. In fact, inefficiency always works against the individuals responsible: it could lead them to disaster in the form of mass-unemployment and economic collapse, as it has already led them to economic difficulties and a crushing burden of taxation. They blame the Government, or the low wages received by workers in competitor nations, or dumping by those nations which have a surplus; they blame tariffs which are too low, while complaining that tariffs put against *their* goods by other nations are too high.

The harsh fact is that the industry concerned is to blame, and each industry is made up of individuals. The industries fail to give of their best because too many individuals in each give less than theirs, or tolerate less from others (sometimes from fear of what will happen to them if they don't). All failure is due to individuals failing to carry out responsibilities which can be quite easily fulfilled.

These strictures may be rejected outright, or criticised in detail, but I believe they are fully justified in the Western world. There is hardly a service or a commodity which does not at some time arouse and usually deserve the harshest criticism. In an age when we can and should make the best, we far too often make the worst. In an era which can put men and machines into orbit round the world, we are constantly forced at both private and national level to put up with indifference and inefficiency in everything from transport and telephone services to the maintenance of machinery and the manufacture of consumer goods.

I have travelled in forty-nine of the U.S.A.'s fifty states; in all but five of the countries of the British Commonwealth – including Canada, Australia, South Africa and New Zealand – and in all of Europe except Rumania, Greece, Finland and Albania; and I have never been able, *anywhere*, to rely upon finding the standard of service, civility, quality and efficiency which should be common to all people of all nations.

This state of affairs had so developed in the U.S.A. that, writing in the *Daily Mail* on June 28th, 1966, Jeffery Blyth said:

SHODDY WORK IN EVERYTHING
FROM SUITS TO SPACE SATELLITES

"The U.S. is experiencing a rash of shoddy workmanship.

"A LORRY fleet owner, trying out his new truck, puts it into first gear – and the vehicle goes backwards.

"A STEEL company orders new machinery – and finds that all the screw holes have no threads.

"A REFRIGERATOR is delivered without brackets to hold the compressor unit.

"Manufacturers blame the business boom, which is overloading factories with more orders than they can handle, the shortage of skilled labour and the demands of the U.S. Government for supplies for Vietnam.

"Although most American goods, from cars and radio sets to men's and women's clothes, have 'built-in obsolescence'

and are not designed to last forever, at least most used to leave
the factories in perfect condition. But no longer.

· · ·

"In the past few months five different U.S. car companies
have had to recall more than 1,500,000 cars to replace various
defective items – from latches to faulty brake-linings.

"One Los Angeles store owner reports: 'Our service engineers
have to spend 50 p.c. more time in customers' homes these days
making sure that new appliances are working properly.'

"The Defence Department estimates that shoddy workmanship costs the department more than £1,000 million a year.

"The National Aeronautics and Space Administration, which
expects '100 p.c. reliability' in its rocket 'hardware' and satellite
components, has just launched a campaign, which is costing
nearly £200,000 to persuade engineers, electricians and other
space mechanics to be more 'quality conscious'.

"The campaign was launched after several recent instances
when faulty equipment not only cost millions of dollars but also
endangered spacemen's lives.

· · ·

"The GEMINI 8 mission came within a hairsbreadth of disaster
because of a short-circuit. And because of battery trouble the
plan to put a huge telescope satellite into orbit was a failure.

"The satellite, which cost £20 million, is today orbiting the
earth *like so much dead metal*.

"On the Gemini 9 mission the failure of workmen on the
launching pad to follow the instruction manual properly
resulted in the 'target vehicle's' protective shroud failing to
open. NASA officials are still deciding how much to fine the
contractor responsible.

"Heavy industry is experiencing the same problems. One
big firm in Michigan, which assembles railway coaches, reports
defects in the steel castings it buys from foundries. A works
official said: 'Measurements are off, tolerances are not good'.

"Out of 22,000 forgings delivered recently 9,000 had to be
sent back."

Protests along the same lines from sources nearer home
appear from time to time in the national press. On September
27th, also in the *Daily Mail*, Elizabeth Gundrey wrote:

SHODDY GOODS, SHODDY WORKMANSHIP

"Mrs. W. of Wooburn Green, Bucks., had a washing machine that broke down after two months. It was put right but within days it went wrong again. For a fortnight no service man came. When he did arrive, he said it was Mrs. W's fault – water spilt on top of the machine was getting into the works. There was no warning in the instruction book that the machine wasn't waterproof.

"Mr. C. of Liverpool paid £400 for a central-heating system, put in by an installer 'approved' by the Coal Board. The house was damaged during installation and the immersion heater dangerously connected. Room temperatures never went higher than 58 degrees and because pipes had been wrongly connected there was no hot water at all. To put things right cost nearly £400.

"Mrs. B. of Southall took an eight-months-old tape recorder in for repair (it wasn't recording). After collecting it, and paying 30s. for labour, she found it still didn't work and took it back – five times in all. It took five months to get it right: the company meanwhile alleged new tapes were needed and that the machine had been damaged in transit – neither of these excuses was true.

"Just why does bad workmanship get by? Regularly products leave the factories with faults; service men fail to locate and rectify them.

"Wallace Heaton have found so many faults in cameras that they have set up their own inspection department: one camera in five has to be adjusted before it is sold.

"The Society of Shoe Fitters say that, of every hundred pairs of shoes that are delivered to the shops, five have to be sent back.

"Because central heating installations are a costly source of trouble (and a frequent one, a *Which?* survey revealed) I asked Bernard Hodges, secretary of the Institution of Heating and Ventilating Engineers, why there are so many complaints of bad workmanship.

"Heavy advertising of central heating has created a sudden demand before enough men have been trained to meet it. Any amateur can *call* himself a heating engineer and cash in on the shortage."

One could go on and on; the truth of this appalling failure to do simple jobs properly cannot be doubted. What may be in doubt in most men's minds are the harmful effects of such failure, and I can best illustrate this with an example of my own.

In my early twenties, I worked in a factory where rubber motor-car tyres were made. One of my jobs, my responsibilities, was to make sure that stocks of all the commodities used in the manufacture of the tyres were in ample supply. In all, over three hundred – *yes, three hundred* – different commodities were used, some in the direct preparation of the mix of rubber and pigments (chemicals) out of which the tyres were made, some in the general maintenance and supply. To check my memory, I recently asked my then employers if they would remind me of the actual constituents. The reply came quickly:

RUBBER

"Current tyre production absorbs approximately 40% of Crude Rubber and 60% Synthetic Rubber.

"Six grades of Crude Rubber are used for varying purposes and are imported from South East Asia, Ceylon and Liberia.

"Eleven different grades of Synthetic Rubbers are used and consist of varying grades of Styrene Butadiene, Polybutadiene, Poly-Isoprene and Butyl. All of these grades are available from U.K. production.

FABRIC

"Fabric is purchased on a large scale and can be analysed as follows:

Rayon Tyre Cord	9 different constructions
Nylon Tyre Cord	9 different constructions
Cotton Bead Chafer & Reinforce	3 different constructions
Rayon/Cotton Bead Chafer & Reinforce	3 different constructions
Nylon Bead Chafer & Reinforce	3 different constructions

"In addition a large variety of square woven fabrics ranging from cotton, rayon and polypropylene construction are purchased for liners, i.e. interweaving with unvulcanized stock for conveyance during production. In all there are about 32 different types and widths for varying purposes.

"Large quantities of Polyethylene Film are also used for backing unvulcanized rubber gums mainly for repair materials and of this there are 2 grades, 4 different colours and 5 widths. In all 40 items.

166

CARBON BLACK

"11 different grades of U.K. produced furnace blacks are used and 1 special grade imported from the U.S.A.

WIRE TYRE CORD

"2 types of Wire Cord are imported from Belgium.

BEAD WIRE

"2 types (diameters) are produced in the U.K.

SPECIAL CHEMICALS FOR RUBBER PROCESSING

"16 different types of Accelerator Chemicals, 12 types of Antioxidants and 3 types of Retarding Chemicals are used in tyre production. Of these all Accelerators are made in the U.K., the bulk of Antioxidants consisting of 2 types are imported from the U.S.A. and the balance together with the Retarders are made in the U.K. The total is 31 different materials.

"These, without doubt, are the most important materials used in the rubber compound since the Accelerators and Retarders assist vulcanization to give the utmost toughness without deterioration and the Antioxidants protect the final product from deterioration due to climatic conditions and from Ozone. It is essential that the correct material is used for the final purpose required.

OTHER COMPOUNDING INGREDIENTS
Major Ingredients

Zinc Oxide	2 types	Made in the U.K.
Sulphur	2 „	Imported from France and the U.S.A.
Clay	2 „	„ „ the U.S.A.
Stearic Acid	2 „	Made in the U.K.
Waxes	2 „	Imported from the U.S.A. and China
Whiting	2 „	Made in the U.K.
Oils	5 „	Refined in the U.K.
Resins	5 „	Imported from France and the U.S.A.

Minor Ingredients

"There are approximately a further 100 ingredients, ranging from small quantities of Petroleum Solvents to Glycerine and Mineral rubber all of which are in regular use and available from British sources.

OTHER MATERIALS

"A further 40 items are purchased which are not incorporated in the rubber stock but are essential for processing. These consist of lubricating materials such as mica, mould release agents, water treatment chemicals and various acids and solvents for degreasing. All are available in the U.K. but a special grade of mica is imported from South Africa."

These different materials, then, come from various parts of the world. No one needs telling that the natural rubber might come from Malaya, Indonesia, India, Ceylon, Africa, Mexico or Brazil, or that the carbon black might come originally from any country with great oil deposits – the United States, say, or Arabia, Bahrein or Venezuela. The other constituents also come from widely separated parts of the world.

In the preparation of any *one* of the constituents, at least ten people were probably involved – helping to mine, crush, mill, refine, pack, ship, deliver, submit to laboratory test, and suchlike all before its actual use in the rubber tyre mix. At a conservative estimate, clearly, at least three thousand people were involved in preparing the raw materials before they reached the tyre factory.

Any *one* of these three thousand could, by failing to do his job properly, seriously affect the quality of a raw material before use. And the quality of each constituent is of vital significance in the quality of the tyre, which is one of the most important accessories to a motor-vehicle.

Some of the individuals involved may seem remote – like the Malay plantation worker, for instance, whose job is to collect the latex from the rubber tree. Yet if they do their work badly or carelessly – that is, irresponsibly – their presence can hover about the scene of an accident like the shadow of death. On the other hand, everyone concerned in the preparation of the constituent materials may do his job properly up to the time that the product leaves the plantation, the factory or whatever source is involved. Even after that, each of the raw materials is subject to damage and deterioration in a variety of ways, and such deterioration can at any stage be due to a single person's failure to carry out some ordinary, everyday responsibility.

Many thousands of people – individuals – play some part in a diversity of jobs from that of finding the raw materials of cotton and iron ore to that of producing the finished, processed fabric (these days, often nylon) and the steel.

The fabric prevents a blow-out.
The steel wire, or "bead", holds the tyre on to the rim.
Both are essential to quality and to safety.

I had no idea that I was also essential to safety when I went into the storage yards and checked the barrels of pigments and oils, into the store sheds and checked the sacks and other containers, into the fabric sheds and made sure no weight or size was in short supply.

Obviously, a heavy-duty, or heavy car or lorry tyre needs stronger fabric, stronger wire and a tougher rubber than the materials needed for a mini-car tyre. In a dozen processes it would be possible to use the wrong strength, or weight or quality. Unless every job by every worker, no matter how simple or routine, is done properly, danger is inevitable.

The job I failed to do properly was to check stocks of a certain hardening or toughening pigment, one of the anti-oxidants, of which very small quantities were used. Delivery of new supplies was delayed, and stocks were down to the last barrel. I had not examined this closely and did not know that an acid from a cracked container had leaked on to the lid, seeped through and damaged the contents.

When delivered from the supplier, the pigment had been sampled by a laboratory chemist and tested to make sure it came up to specification. After removing the lid to take the sample, someone (labourer or chemist: no one ever knew or ever admitted) did not secure it properly; had the lid been secured there would have been no seepage and so no deterioration. As it was, the damaged pigment was sent through to the mixing room and mixed into a batch which was tested and approved; even under chemical analysis it appeared to be up to specification. So the tyre cases were moulded and "cooked" or cured at great heat. They were then inspected, subjected to physical tests and passed; the deterioration did not set in until they had been in use for several hundred miles. By freak chance, one was put on a van of a local firm, who soon reported poor wear. When the tyre was checked, both rubber and fabric were shown to be deteriorating at an alarming rate.

"Anyone driving on those tyres might have a blow-out any minute," the service manager said. "We've got to call them in."

Recalling those tyres took weeks. It cost a great deal of money. Step by step the cause of the deterioration was traced. The fact that I had allowed stocks of the pigment to run low came out, so did the fact that both I and the man who collected

169

the barrel had noticed that the lid was loose and "damp". I
shall never forget the expression in the eyes of the manager,
when he said:

"You're a lucky lad, Creasey. If we hadn't got those tyres in,
you would have a man's life on your conscience."

In fact, if the alarm hadn't been raised in the way it was, the
cause of any blow-out would never have been discovered, so I
should have known nothing about any resultant death or injury.
But there would have been no *risk* of death or injury due to
bad quality *had I done my job properly*. That job was simply to
make sure that the factory held sufficient stocks of a material
which might not go into a tyre mix for many months – and
even when in the completed tyre, might not be in use on the
highway for months, possibly years, after it was made in the
factory.

It is surely self-evident that if everyone did his or her job
properly, such things could not happen. It is unarguable that
we, the individuals, are to blame when they do. *We*, the
workers, the service and maintenance men, the technicians – all
of us who contribute to poor quality in any kind of human
activity. *We*, the consumers, the users, the customers, who pay
for goods of poor quality and accept without protest inefficient
and often insolent service – we are to blame, for we tacitly
connive at the situation. *We* contribute to it, by omission or
commission. *We*, who suffer so much because of the shortcomings of others, who are burdened by economic problems, by
high taxes – *we* are as culpable as anyone, for the shortcomings
are ours every bit as much as "theirs".

If we practised Self-ism, as individuals as well as in groups,
these shortcomings would vanish. They are due *only* to the fact
that vast numbers of us simply do not do our daily job, which is
easily within our grasp, as well as we can and should.

Thus we lose much and gain nothing. Industry and its twin,
commerce, play a grotesque game of "heads everyone loses;
tails no one wins".

There is another aspect of all this – the manufacture of indifferent or low quality goods by the underdeveloped, non-
industrialised nations. Such countries manufacture, export and
sell poor quality goods on their home and export markets *not*
because they don't care, but because they lack the economic
resources to pay for the proper machinery, raw materials, skill
and technical know-how. It is all the greater tragedy because
in some of these countries the consumer goods manufactured
before the war were of such excellent quality.

So the world is divided into three groups:

(i) Manufacturing nations which possess everything needed to make first-quality goods but fail in their responsibilities.

(ii) Non-manufacturing nations which cannot afford to buy such consumer goods, and for want of raw materials and lack of technical knowledge, make shoddy ones instead.

(iii) A few nations (and industrialists in the nations listed as (i)) who make top quality goods *and so prove that it can be done*.

This, then, is the state of industry today. Too many of the prosperous "have" nations *do* not – and the needy "have-not" nations *cannot* – produce the quality goods which would set each nation's economy on its feet and spread prosperity throughout the world.

Yet it is an axiom that trade, like good, thrives on itself; for trade creates trade. And as we have seen, the problems of raw material and of power need no longer limit industrial output. Nothing *need* be in short supply again, once we have applied Self-ism to banish famine, strikes and war.

Any trade which stagnates adversely affects the prosperity of other trades. All trades which prosper increase the prosperity of other trades, provided these are run efficiently. All industries *need* other industries to support them. There is an enormous, world-wide complex of manufacture, distribution and supply, involving a system of shipping, road transport, aircraft and raw material production, which beggars the imagination. This complex works on exactly the same lines as a village community. If there is enough work and prosperity in the village, the village shop flourishes; if there is enough work and prosperity in the world, the world will flourish.

If it is true that food (and consequently health and strength) is at the root of production, and if it is true that trade begets trade, then if the law of Self-ism is followed there can be an abundance of both. The examples cited were of books and cornflakes, and what is true of those is true of all foods and all consumer goods. Since the basic industries flourish according to the prosperity of the secondary industries, it is also true of these.

No one needs to be reminded that the more money people have, the more they spend; as obviously, the more they spend, the more other people have. Some economists may take me to task for over-simplifying this fact, but it is doubtful whether any will attempt to disprove it. Critics may attempt to say that before the expanding circle of income can come about, certain conditions have to be met, that the increasing supply of raw materials is not as easy as I have suggested, for instance; and that there is still the problem of producing or finding enough machines and trained men.

Two of the key factors undoubtedly are manpower and machines. With enough of both, who can doubt that the raw materials can be obtained and turned to industrial and so to social advantage? As there is *no* limit to raw materials, there can be no *known* limit to the amount which man and the right machines can produce. It is, after all, precisely because we can today produce what mankind needs in so much less time, that sociologists are so deeply concerned with helping man use his increasing leisure in the best possible way.

In the past, national economies, and so industries, have been largely self-supporting. Today, industrialists are acutely aware of the fact that industry is part of one world. The nations of Europe, particularly Great Britain, which once had the world almost to themselves are now in fierce competition not only with the other industrial but also with the newly emergent nations, many of whose needs Great Britain both created and supplied.

Here is the irony and the tragedy.

The world is crying out for consumer goods, from bicycles to radios, motor-cars to toy trains, books to blankets: goods of a vast, almost inconceivable range and variety. At the same time, industry is crying out for markets. But the customer cannot afford to buy at the prices the manufacturers can afford to sell, although the raw materials, technology, means of distribution, machinery and manpower all exist. While one part of the world has a super-abundance of indifferent-quality goods, the other part has desperate need of goods which will increase its standard of living and so its prosperity. All – *all* – of this is because of the failure of management and labour to recognise and eradicate the causes of their conflict.

They can only eradicate this conflict by working together; when both sides work together each will be serving its own *and all mankind's* best interests.

The beginning of a new industrial era of prosperity will come not through automation or technicological advance but through a meeting of men's minds in understanding of this problem. But their minds cannot meet until all men realise their *own* vested interest in the prosperity of others: until they *give* of their best so as to *receive* the best.

I believe this can be achieved simply and quickly by the

application to industry of the basic principles of Self-ism. And the first essential is a clear understanding of the industrial interdependence of people and of nations. Awareness of this truth is second to none in importance. It is not even second to health, because until we have prosperity and so plenty, we cannot have a wholly healthy society. Those among us who are well-fed must, in the beginning, produce the goods which will create prosperity for others who are not, and those others will in turn keep the well-fed prosperous *and* well-fed.

There are the two major forms of industry:

(i) The basic industries.
(ii) The consumer-goods industries.

Food is essential; thus, agriculture is a basic industry.

Health is essential; thus, medical services and after-care are basic.

Education is essential; thus, schools are basic.

It is true that except for agriculture these are not commonly regarded as basic, but a little reflection will show how fundamental they are to human needs.

Housing is a basic industry, too.

So is the production of power – coal, electricity, gas, oil and atomic energy.

After these come the more commonly accepted basic or "heavy" industries: the manufacture of steel, fabric, rubber, paper, wood products, plastics and synthetic fibres, heavy and light machinery.

Moreover, the distributive trades, shipping, rail transport and road transport, are in fact basic industries, as air transport is fast becoming.

The production of *all* raw materials is basic; such as mining, or the drilling for and refining of oil.

Twenty-nine basic industries are named above and each of these has many subsidiaries: certainly no less than ten. In each basic and each subsidiary industry, many different tasks have to be performed. Not dozens but hundreds, *many* hundreds of individuals are involved in each instance – and exactly as in the example shown in the chapter on health (Chapter 5), each individual is dependent in some degree on all the others, and all are dependent in some degree on each.

An illustration of this is the big electricity black-out, or power-failure, in New York early in November 1965. Just how effective that was, and how paralysing, I know very well. I was there. For me, it was almost an adventure and it caused me little inconvenience. For millions, it was fear, hunger, anxiety, fatigue and distress. For those trapped for hours in elevators high in great buildings, mostly without explanation, and those trapped in subways, and in cellars, it must have been a terrifying ordeal, as it was for those in hospital, or bedridden at home, the aged, the lonely . . . How easy it is to forget the lonely, and how much worse is loneliness when it is accompanied by fear.

Even today, "they" say, no one knows the actual cause of the failure.

Even at the time one knew that in fact at least one or two, perhaps three or four, experts at their job did not do that job as well as they know how.

There is absolutely no way of telling how much harm can come from a single, momentary failure to carry out one's responsibilities. It is so *very* easy to bring about the death of that man on the operating table.

The responsibilities – and so the opportunities for irresponsibility – are endless. The producers of the steel for the table itself, for the equipment, for the instruments . . . the manufacturers of the rubber for the surgeon's gloves . . . the makers of the fabric from which the garments and the masks are made.

The masks?

One tear in a mask, one germ from a single cough, one sneeze, one instant of infection – any or all of these can mean the difference between life and death. So can one moment's carelessness by any one of all those involved in the manufacture of the mask and its packing, sterilising, unpacking, examining, donning and adjusting. The prime requisite, the most fundamental one of all, is the absolute need for awareness of the possible harm that can come from the most trivial-seeming failure to carry out one's responsibilities, *and* of the good, or benefit, which can come if one *does* carry them all out.

There is no difficulty in it; and no problem, provided always that every task, every responsibility placed on a man's shoulders, is within his capacity: whether a natural capacity or one he has acquired by training or education.

There is little excuse and no need at all for failure.

Putting the blame for failure on "human nature" simply will not be a good enough excuse any longer.

We have seen that failure comes from the abuse or neglect of certain qualities *in* human nature, not from human nature itself. It is to blame for the traditionally-held belief in the frailty of human nature. Human nature is not frail at all; few men are frail in tending their own interests.

Self-ism is the answer to those who claim that what has become accepted as basic human nature, cannot be changed; for Self-ism will show men clearly what their true interests are.

Human nature is prone to error only if we allow and encourage it to be.

It is prone to ignorance only if we fail to teach it.

It is prone to sickness only if we fail to do our utmost to prevent and to cure sickness.

It is prone to hunger only if we fail to produce enough food.

It is prone to cold and exposure only if we fail to produce enough warmth and housing.

It is prone to poverty only if we fail to produce enough riches from the earth and from our labours.

It will be prone to dreadful overcrowding on this earth *only* if we allow too many children to be born.

And it is prone to shortages in consumer goods, our daily needs, only because we have not found the *incentive* to produce enough.

As our attitudes to all of these things improve, human nature will also improve, out of all knowledge, in its capacity for kindness and for goodness. But this improvement will only come when the self is recognised for what it is, when the natural law of Self-ism is accepted and practised by all.

What is easier to practise than the care of one's own interests – so long as one knows what they are?

Management and labour are simply two groups of men with the same basic natural needs, likes and dislikes, and desire for happiness and comfort. They will each be able to take care of their own – and thus, automatically, of their mutual – interests, once they fully understand what those interests are.

The interests of one, remember, are the interests of the other.

However, simply to say that Self-ism would solve the labour/management conflict, would be to beg the issue. One must demonstrate just what this would entail. Again taking as example the situation in Great Britain, with which I am most familiar, I shall show in the next chapter exactly how Self-ism can be applied to industry. And as the situation in other nations is simply a variation on the British, what I call Alliance in Industry may well be adapted to help solve the problem in every nation.

Chapter 14

INDUSTRY IN A SELF-IST
SOCIETY – II

FEW will disagree that good labour/management relations are
fundamental to a sound and expanding economy.

For years in Great Britain, this relationship has fallen
woefully short of what is needed. Consequently production
is far lower than it should be, and the quality of many
goods is not high enough. Crisis after crisis has had a grave
effect on international confidence in Britain's stability,
and it is worth repeating that the stability of the *whole*
sterling area is vital to the economy not only of Great Britain
but of nearly half the world. Once Britain has re-established
her prosperity, she will be able again to share her wealth with
others.

Moreover, with a sufficiently high rate of quality production
Britain could reduce taxes and improve social conditions
generally, so increasing both her prestige and her influence
on countries outside the sterling area. I believe all these things
can be achieved simply by improving labour/management
relations.

It seems unlikely that the existing machinery for improving
these relations will ever be effective, however. The three
currently accepted methods are:

   (i) The normal labour/management negotiating machinery
     in industries run by private enterprise, involving the
     trades unions.
  (ii) The relationships, very similar to (*a*), which have
     developed in the nationalised industries.
 (iii) Co-partnership, as advocated by the Liberal Party and
     practised in industry on a very restricted scale.

Although often denied, the general practice is to look after
the interests of one side only, either labour's or management's:
each fights to gain what it can for itself, without regard to the

other; so inevitably the pull is too often against each other, too seldom together.* Yet it is a simple fact that only if the *whole* firm (or industry) is flourishing, can either side obtain the fullest benefit.

Co-partnership (*c*) has failed to capture the interest of either management or labour in Great Britain for one obvious reason: it is not enough for the working man to share in profits – or even in management also. *He must share in capital, too.*

The underlying cause of present labour/management attitudes can be traced through a long history of mutual mistrust. To put our economy on a strong basis, these two sides of industry must get rid of this mistrust and recognise their inescapable dependence on each other.

Great Britain's economic and financial difficulties both at home and overseas, her erratic balance of payments position and her crippling rate of taxation, are due to this one basic factor: *we simply do not make enough to sell enough to buy enough for all our needs.*

The cause of the mistrust is simple: the old basic antagonism between capital and labour, and to the working man management always represents capital. In production failures, labour blames management and management blames labour, while capital (like the consumer) blames both. It would obviously be extremely difficult to eradicate that damaging mistrust if both parties continued to regard the problem as an issue between two groups with opposing interests.

However, the natural law of Self-ism will present them with a completely new perspective.

It is simple fact that no side involved will put its best into all endeavours *unless* convinced that it will receive a fair share and a square deal. But once each group concerned becomes fully convinced that it can *only* get for itself the best possible rewards (in wages, salary, production and dividends) if the other *also* gets the best possible rewards, the problem will be solved.

The first step is to make clear to labour that management and capital are *not* in fact the same, that indeed, as the situation is today, both capital and the consumer blame management and labour equally.

Once this step is taken it becomes apparent that, as management and capital are not the same, then there are not just two but *three* interested groups involved. As no reform in industry can be satisfactorily attempted until this fact is recognised and

* The Fairfield Experiment is a noteworthy exception.

accepted by all concerned, it might help to set out the three interests involved thus:

(i) Men (labour).
(ii) Management (administration, sales and research).
(iii) Money (capital).*

I have called this Self-ist approach Alliance in Industry.

To labour, capital is a vague and often menacing or hostile phrase, whereas money means only one thing: the wherewithal for one's own (and one's family's) needs. Once it is seen that capital is simply the money by which industry and commerce can get what they need (including labour), attitudes will change. "Money" is acutely personal – everyone knows that money is a necessity – whereas to most people capital is something quite remote.

In simplest terms, the three interested groups might be explained as follows:

(i) Capital – money – serves no purpose and earns no interest (privilege) if there is nothing to do or buy with it. And it would have no value (could not even buy the barest necessities of life) unless management and men used it to produce, sell and distribute the goods and services essential to the community.
(ii) Without both men and money, management has nothing to do and can serve no purpose and obtain no privileges.
(iii) Without management and money to supply the basic needs of machinery, materials, sales organisation and administration, men in industry can do nothing, so they can earn nothing, buy nothing, and obtain no privileges for themselves or their families.

The three M's are three vital parts of the same body and are quite indivisible: take one away and the others cannot function.

Once this is recognised by all concerned, then the first step of Alliance in Industry has been achieved.

No man, evidently, can be expected to feel deeply interested in money which is not even partially his own. (To this degree, at least, everyone will admit to being a Self-ist!) So to make men realise that money is not only valuable but essential to

* Money, of course, is impersonal, but it is used in this sense as a third force in industry: a force in its own right, as management is, but – also like management – made up of the contributions of many individuals and groups.

their industry or firm, they must have direct personal interest in some of that money.

They must be made to understand, eventually, that they themselves are in effect a part of their industry's capital. But the one absolutely certain way to bring home to them the true value of that capital, is to ensure that they themselves *own* a part of it.

There are at least two ways in which this could be arranged:

(i) For all the trades unions concerned in the running of a firm or industry to invest in that firm or industry.
(ii) By making available (free) to all workers and employees, shares and stocks in the Company for which they work, on a basis of years of service.

The trades unions, which too often appear to be concerned only with the interests of trade unionists, would then obviously be vitally affected by the success of the firm, just as vitally affected, in fact, as management and capital. So, naturally, would labour, since every employee would then have a direct interest in his firm's share values, not simply a share of any profits made. If the firm had a bad year, the employee would be affected in the same way as any other shareholder, because what would in effect be a bonus, often a substantial one, would not be there to have and to spend.

Now if labour owned part of the capital it would obviously be necessary (and fair) for management to own part also. Again, there are at least two ways in which this could be arranged:

(i) By giving all employees in Managerial, Selling, Buying, Research and Development departments, etc., the option of taking part of their salary in shares, which would of course be bought on the Stock Exchange in the normal way.
(ii) By allotting all such employees a number of free shares, also to be allocated on a years-of-service basis.

(N.B. The shares might be allotted on a basis of ten for every year of service, or a specified number for every £100 of annual salary waived.)

Moreover, all employees, at whatever level, should also be given the opportunity to buy shares in addition to those acquired by means of (i) and (ii).

The benefits of Alliance in Industry to labour, both at trades union and personal level, and to management at all levels, become self-evident. The benefits to the capital investor, whose sole part is to put up the money, may at first be less evident. However, the purpose of capital investment is to earn dividends – and the purpose of Alliance in Industry is to increase profits, and so increase dividends: this is what every investor, large or small, primarily requires. If Alliance in Industry is successful, the benefit to the capital investor will be self-evident, *in better returns for his money.*

This new and much closer association between the worker and his job is perhaps the only way of making it possible for him, in this mechanised age, to take the pride in his work which the olden-day craftsman took in his. He would certainly have a more vital interest in the over-all success of his firm than the purely wage-earning old-time workman. And once he realised that the skill and efficiency of *his* work would have a direct bearing on both his own and his firm's well-being, he would have good reason for such pride.

Obviously the key question is: *Can* Alliance in Industry succeed? I believe it cannot fail, once it overcomes the existing prejudice within industry and commerce. It is the only way in which:

(i) Men, management and money, can benefit to the utmost.

(ii) All three can *see* that what benefits the others also benefits themselves.

(iii) All three can *see* that none can truly flourish unless *all* flourish.

In the course of these proposals "firm" and "industry" have often been bracketed together. It has always seemed to me that one of the great weaknesses in modern industrial structure has been the organisation of the unions into trades.

The most effective operating unit, surely, is an industry. It is transparently unfair and unrealistic that the car industry, for instance, can be disrupted by a strike of its electricians, or engineers, or drivers, caused by the dissatisfaction of a group of their fellow tradesmen in some other main industry in no way connected with car manufacturing.

It is an obvious corollary of Alliance in Industry that if no firm can be wholly efficient unless each section is content, no single industry can be wholly efficient unless all the firms in that industry are. Yet no plan can guarantee that a firm or an industry will not suffer from a change in local conditions or, say, the loss of export orders. There will also be the normal shifts in population, and a variety of other reasons for individuals to change employers. To cope with this and so lessen the hardship of changes and recessions, Alliance in Industry would create a national "pool" of resources and privileges in each industry, so that:

(i) It would be practicable for an industrial worker in Glasgow, say, to move to London and exchange his shares in his Scottish firm for shares in his English one. (This is only a variation of Stock Exchange dealings.)

(ii) Pensions and superannuation benefits could be transferable in the same way.

(iii) All other benefits could be transferable, including those arising out of years of service: these years to be calculated on those spent in the industry, not spent in any one firm.

(N.B. All of these things would be a two-way traffic, except in the case of local depression; in which case, Government aid would be needed.)

Government, or State, participation in industry might eventually solve the major taxation problems *and* the problems of State-owned or nationalised industries. It may well be valuable to examine this possibility in the light of conditions in Britain as I write.

We now know beyond doubt that nationalisation does not have all the answers to the problems which bedevil industry. We also know beyond doubt that private enterprise and big business do not have all the answers, either.

Single-control industry, like single-party government, fosters the "Them *v.* Us" mentality by splitting the people into two conflicting groups, each fighting against the other. Yet, as we have seen, the best interests of each group can *only* be served by working *with* the other.

What we must do is rid ourselves of both 100 per cent nationalisation and 100 per cent private enterprise, and what we might well have is an alliance of labour, management, trade unions, big business *and the State.*

With our present system, big business operates under threat of State take-over or take-over by a bigger company (as happened when the Chrysler Corporation took-over Rootes); of strikes, and of sudden changes in government policy. In fact, nothing is certain for big business except that it will pay more and more taxes and face more and more difficulties and threats.

If Alliance in Industry included the State all this might change completely. Certainly, big business would no longer have absolute control, but no one would resent or want to take away the share it retained. By allying itself with the other groups, it would take the brakes off industry, and both production and profits would rise sharply. The amount the big businessman received as his share in the total profit would be nearly as great as the amount he received when it was exclusively his, with none of the headaches of sole risk or responsibility, and without resentment from any, since *all* would have their share.

Such an Alliance in Industry could start in three fields: steel (there is still time), shipbuilding, and the docks. And after that, the mines, all the fuel industries and the railways – which between them certainly could not be less successful than they are today.

The changeover should be staggered say, by ten per cent each year, so that the whole transition took ten years.

As success in these key industries was proved, others would want to adopt the system. A new, and predictably popular, industrial revolution would sweep through Britain, bringing with it another tremendous revolution – *in the very economics of the country.*

Since the State would own a big slice of industry, it would make substantial profits. The more successful the industry, the greater the State's profits – which could be set against general taxation and so reduce it from its present incentive-crippling level.

It is taxation which puts up the cost of living; so as trading profits rose, prices, like taxation, would come down.

With such a system, everyone – whatever his job or political views, whether earning £10 a week or £10,000 a year – would have overwhelming encouragement to give of his very best. So by giving of their best in industry men would not only increase their own earnings and the national prosperity but would rid themselves of much of the great taxation burden they carry in a modern state.

What could be clearer indication of the potential value of the law of Self-ism as applied to industry?

No cause or justification would remain for political conflict over the issue of nationalisation, since each section of the community would have its fair share of industry. Existing nationalised industries and services might well become profit-bearing. All restrictive practices such as the closed shop, even the avoidance or evasion of taxation, would become pointless.

I have little doubt these proposals can and will work once the initial objections, and perhaps initial hostility, are overcome. The trades union leaders in particular might fear a weakening of their power and influence, but in fact, if the economy of the country is improved, they and the workers they represent would benefit also. In their early days, the unions had one supreme task: to improve the lot of the workers. That is *still* their task. The law of Self-ism through Alliance in Industry can enable them to carry it out simply by bringing greater prosperity to *all the people*, enabling them to share in the prosperity while never getting less than their fundamental or basic wage.

Moreover, the trades unions will be partners *in* the management and they will obviously have a representative on the Board of Directors as the simple right of substantial shareholders. And surely it is obvious that if the intelligence and acumen shown in running trades unions at a profit are applied to the industries concerned, the industries will benefit enormously.

Once Alliance in Industry begins to show results, *everything* and everyone to do with industry will begin to flourish, the unions, the people, the management and the "money". Greater production will lead to the expansion of both exports and imports, while the quality of production will improve because man will have the natural Self-ism incentive to take full pride in his work.

The white-collar worker, the schoolteacher, the postman, the nurse, and all who are not directly involved in production, will be affected in two ways. First, with the national economy greatly improved, they will share in the benefits which will come from quality goods being in plentiful supply at reasonable prices; from a cost of living which always keeps pace with wages and salaries. The police, the armed services and the civil service generally would receive these indirect but substantial benefits. White-collar workers and those in maintenance, administration and distribution, *services absolutely essential to industry*, would have to be given the same rights as the producing workers: *shares* in whatever they are doing. True, most postal services run at a loss; but they need not. True, the National Health and Medicare Services run at a loss; but under Alliance in Industry, they need not. The same will be true of the railways, of the coalmines, of the power industries. In an expanding economy and with incentives which simply do not exist under nationalisation, these can and will make money.

In a Self-ist society, the slacker and the dodger – both largely the product of our present-day society, which gives little incentive to absolute honesty in any of its aspects – will inevitably disappear. And with even the slacker and the dodger acutely aware of how everyone will suffer if anyone does his job badly, there will be no patience with or place for the "passenger" in society.

There is, moreover, a basic fairness in the human being, one which is particularly apparent when, as an individual, his own well-being is not in danger; there is also an understanding of the differences between individuals. No one will deny, for instance, that the slower-witted man needs to earn just as much as the quicker-witted, to support his wife and family. In a Self-ist society, if he carried out his responsibilities *to the best of his ability*, he would deserve and earn the respect of all his fellows. No man could or should be expected to do more than his demonstrable best.

Here, then, is the shape of democracy in industry as I see it. I believe it is what the people of the Western nations want and the rest of the world needs. The industrial proposals offer to *every man and woman* the share they themselves earn in the nation. They show clearly what each individual's responsibility is. They also show that only if he accepts his own can he expect others to accept theirs too, and only if they do can he expect to receive the utmost reward from the society he is helping to create.

Once such a true democracy exists in Britain, the people of the world will be able to see and understand the advantages of it, and the fears of all will be allayed. For we shall have proved that a just and stable world, which men of all nations can create together, is simply a matter of time.

Chapter 15

COMMERCE IN A SELF-IST
SOCIETY

JUST as the intellect is what one thinks with and intelligence is what one does with what one thinks, so is industry what one makes and commerce what one does with what one makes.

This isn't an over-simplification. Industry *is* what is made or produced, and trade and commerce *are* the means of distributing and selling the goods. If one could make a million television sets, they would be worthless unless they could be distributed to the shops, the shops could sell and deliver, and the buyer could plug them into a power socket to make them work (see Chapter 10).

A television set is a good example of a central item in a chain or sequence of events. From the makers and suppliers of all the raw materials – the wood, plastic, glass and metal – to the makers of the infinite variety of parts – the wire, screws, screen, aerial, loudspeaker, switches, controls, cathode tube, valves or the substitutes for any of these, that is, *everything* in the set – there is a very wide range of trades, and so of people, involved.

Not only has the set to be made, polished, tested and passed for service; it has to be packed, distributed to wholesaler or dealer, unpacked, delivered to the retailer, installed and serviced for the customer. Also part of this chain of events, which so many of us take for granted, are the electricity, the electrician, the truck- or van-driver, the paper, the carton maker, the printer of labels and instructions and guarantees, perhaps the railway-yard men, train driver, platelayer and all the others who help to make and maintain the railways and the roads – *and* all who supply the raw materials for or build those railways and roads.

Are there more? Yes; a great many more. The clerk or accountant who sends the bill, the bank which honours the cheque when it is paid, or the bank or hire-purchase company which has financed it, as well as all the makers and operators of the machines used by the banks and the credit company. A veritable host of people are involved. If only *one* of these does the wrong thing at a crucial moment, the television owner does not get his picture when he should have it.

And what about the picture itself?

The actor, the announcer, the technician, the cameraman, the floor manager, the director, the producer, the script writer, and other individuals almost *ad infinitum*, are involved. So many people are concerned with the pleasure one gets from watching television, from the myriad involved in the manufacture of every item in the comfortable room, to the flickering picture on a screen. So many possibilities exist, therefore, of spoiling that pleasure, of preventing perfect reception by some distortion of vision or of sound. Most such distortions are simply due to the fact that someone along that production or supply line has not done or is not doing his job properly.

Where does the commerce come in? And the trade?

By strict definition, perhaps, in the manufacturer–wholesaler–retailer–customer chain, as well as all the incidental subsidiary or contributory vocations involved. But the retailer must have a service-man or men, so must the electricity company; a shop-keeper or tradesman needs insurance which is commerce but not trade; evidently there is no clear-cut distinction between trade and commerce.

However, trade and commerce can be seen most clearly in a narrower perspective.

No one needs telling what a trader is: he buys and sells. Trade, then, is buying and selling, although it must be remembered that some communities still barter a great deal, exchanging goods for goods. The West may regard such societies as primitive, but the fact remains that in England there is a *very* popular weekly journal called *Exchange & Mart*, and that some of the large circulation women's magazines have run such exchanges, while one can drive through the once wild and still fairly woolly West of the United States and hear similar exchanges offered by radio. (I once heard a grand piano offered in exchange for a watch-dog.)

We know what trade is. We have a fair idea of how trade is carried out, of the actual mechanics of trading. We also know that in general a trader or dealer who cheats or over-prices his goods soon goes out of business. To stay in business, for his own sake, he has to do well by other people. This is a truism in almost any form of trade, in any wholesale or retail business. We also know, whether we like it or not, that there is a great deal of concealed over-pricing, of concealed cheating in the sense of putting a false value on commodities by lying or exaggerating about what one sells, or by taking too large a margin of profit.

All three of these practices are virtually accepted as normal, at some stage or other in trade.

No one really believes all the salesman says; it is generally accepted that much of the average "sales talk" must be taken with a pinch of salt. If one's friend has been "sold a pup", a common phrase in our society, one is inclined to laugh, secretly or openly, because he should have been too alert, too wide awake, to "fall for it". Of course, a great many salesmen sell simply on the quality of their goods, but the vast number sell on the glibness of their tongues. My brother once told a would-be buyer of containers for electric lamps that one could toss the container he had invented – with a lamp inside it – from a tenth-storey window, and the lamp would remain intact.

"Let's try it," said the buyer.

My family was doubled up and almost choking with laughter as my brother mimicked his own agony of suspense while he waited to find out what would happen.

The lamp stayed whole.

"I've never been so relieved in my life," he confessed. And everyone roared with laughter.

Now that he is dead, I hope I may be forgiven for wondering whether he would have taken the order for a million or so containers had the buyer accepted his word and not put it to the test. I daresay he would. He was a *very* good salesman.

The fact is, too many goods are sold by misrepresentation. If this were not so, there would be no reason for the existence of the Consumer Protection Associations which flourish in the United States (and no doubt elsewhere) and the British magazine *Which?* – renowned for exploding claim after claim made for everything from cars to contraceptives and even, to someone's unbelievable shame, to life-jackets for use at sea. Some life-jackets, I understand, actually *create* a hazard when a wearer hits the water, for the head may be jerked back with enough violence to break the neck.

The practice of misrepresentation is a wicked one. Many legal steps are taken to reduce its incidence, to satisfy the protective associations. But the ugliest feature in the whole sorry story of misrepresentation seems to me the fact that to a degree at least it is today regarded as normal trade practice.

Is that statement nonsense? Is it unjust?

If it were, why need such stringent demands be made today on manufacturers of all drugs and patent medicines, to state (*a*) exactly what the medicine contains, and (*b*) to make no false claims for it as a curative? Why is it that so many makers, not only of patent medicines but also of household cleaners, detergents, soaps, polishes and a host of everyday commodities, appear to compete with each other to make claims which *are* inside the law but nevertheless can mislead the unwary?

The answer is that a limited form of misrepresentation *has* become an accepted part of trade.

(And not only trade. Misleading or downright lying to customs and income tax authorities is commonly accepted, too. We no longer feel shocked, may even feel amusement or even admiration at recitals of others' cleverness at customs evasion. There is less open boasting about income tax evasion, since that more obviously harms the next man, and so everyone – we *are* all Self-ists! – is more sensitive on the subject.)

Nor is it only the actual traders and their representatives who are guilty in this respect. We, the buyers of the goods, are also guilty. We make allowances for their exaggeration, and if we ourselves have anything to sell, are likely to emphasise the good points and draw a veil over the bad ones. "Likely to", needs repeating; many individuals *not used to trade*, will be scrupulously honest – and as often as not, suffer or be censured or derided for it.

The custom, habit or practice of misrepresentation in selling is so deep-rooted in modern society, so much the norm, that it might seem almost impossible to remove. It will, undoubtedly, be one of the more stubborn obstacles that Self-ism will overcome, because Self-ism as applied to this aspect of trade says uncompromisingly:

"You think that by making a little extra, being 'smart' on this deal, or in this way, you have gained an advantage. In fact, you have rendered yourself liable to every kind of misrepresentation, cheating, lying and half-lying. You are inevitably a victim of your own malpractice. If you want to be assured of getting full, honest value in every deal you make, you and everyone else must always give full, honest value, and must not exaggerate or lie."

A Utopian concept?

Some will say so. But remember, I believe that realism and idealism are identical twins; and I also believe it is inherent in Self-ism that the ideal can be attained if everyone does his job properly, *and so to his own best advantage*. Even more, I believe that when these beliefs are universal, then human happiness will be just around the corner. In such a concept, anything less than the best *cannot* be good enough. This is self-evident. We *all* want, wish for, even long for, the best for ourselves and those whom we love. To settle for less, when we *can* get the best if we try, is lunacy.

A Utopian concept of trade is perhaps more difficult to envisage than Utopia in other spheres of life, yet it should not be. Trade is the life-blood of any nation and cuts across all the other fundamentals. If we take away trade, how can we be fed? If we take away trade, how can we maintain health? If we take away trade, how can we keep a roof over our heads and our home as we like it?

We cannot live without trade; either we must accept some degree of corruption in it, or we must fit it smoothly into a Self-ist society. Those with a desire for "making a quick buck", the urge for actual acquisition of more money, as such, will find it hardest to apply Self-ism. Most of us, indeed, will find it difficult to accept the paradox that by making less money we may do ourselves *more* good!

This proposition cannot be considered objectively until we have considered all the aspects of trade and commerce, not necessarily the obvious ones. Banking, both a basic industry and an essential to over-the-counter trade, plays its obvious part. So does insurance. So does accountancy. So does the law. Both bankers and accountants may prefer to consider themselves professional rather than commercial men, but they are more closely related than most other professions to trade and commerce.

The bankers supply or obtain the money for industry, trade and commerce and the accountant helps to use the same money to the best advantage for the group or individual. The solicitor or lawyer protects the group or individual from the legal pit-falls, and the insurance man protects the money against accidental loss. All four work together for their own and the common good. One does occasionally come across a defrauding banker, lawyer or accountant, or an insurance man who will cover goods at false values, but in general these professions are made up of men who are honest. If they do cheat they harm not only the professions they serve but also themselves, since discovery means automatic expulsion and thus the loss of their livelihood.

So in trade there are many who are not very close to the practice of Self-ism and others who by the nature of their work are closer to it than most people. The Lloyds broker whose "word is his bond" cannot continue to deal if his promise proves false; that is, he cannot harm others without harm to himself.

So it begins to look as if the task of fitting trade and commerce smoothly into Self-ism might be quite simple. In fact, *all* trades-people do accept in principle the desideratum of absolutely honest trading, but we have allowed the snow-white of honesty to become tinged with too much grey.

In this respect, one group in particular presents a problem and a contradiction, at once a cause for hope and for despair. This group is closely allied to the sales-force of industry at large, and certainly its members all have something to sell, whether consumer goods, a personality or an idea.

These are the publicity men, the advertising men, the newspapermen.

The simple fact is, that publicity and advertising men far too often stretch the truth. Many of them don't relish being told so, and rush to defend their profession, often only too obviously protesting its innocence too much. Many, I am told, worry about the things they must do to retain their jobs. But they do them. They will emphasise or over-emphasise the merits of an article, and under-emphasise or conceal the demerits of the same article – like the salesman, forced by economic pressure to conform to his job's requirements in a society in which some exaggeration is anyway accepted as normal.

Perhaps the obvious truth is that they cannot do their jobs with absolute integrity unless their principals do the same. Here is the clearest possible case of the dependence of one group of people on the behaviour and attitudes of another. And because certain producers and suppliers and their employees provide such dubious and exaggerated claims in the selling of their goods, the consumer protection associations and the Government authorities are forced to provide an effective opposition.

What a ludicrous waste of time, energy, ingenuity, intelligence and money!

If only the whole truth were told always, less money need be spent on advertising and none at all on consumer protection. If less money were spent on advertising, more could go into the pockets of shareholders or employees or management, or into the quality of the goods, or the quantity in a packet. *Everyone* would benefit. The skill, imagination and experience of these advertising specialists could be diverted to more positive uses, in the design of goods, or their presentation. Advertising is only one, and by no means the most important, aspect of commercial art. Such changes in emphasis or occupations and professions are the inevitable consequences of progress. As a result of these particular changes, people would buy the goods advertised, in the knowledge that they could rely on real value for money.

Another inevitable move would be away from "pop" to "quality" advertising. And as all advertising, publicity and newspapermen are in some degree artists or writers, this would enable them to put more of their true selves into, and so take real pride in, the work they do. They could concentrate on expertly and interestingly telling or publicising the simple truth, rather than on attempting to make a one-sided case attractive.

Newspapermen in particular are often called upon to present a case in accordance with the likes and dislikes, and political opinion or prejudices, of their editors or owners. Newspapers carry considerable influence with the public and make a great show of integrity and fairness in presenting the news. Indeed, news of a certain kind, particularly about natural or sporting events, disasters, accidents and such obvious occasions as a State Visit or the opening of Parliament or the State of the Union Message, is almost invariably presented clearly, objectively and honestly. In such matters, the Press is beyond praise. So are its front-line correspondents in time of war. So are its reports on current historic events, such as the various space-craft ventures.

As vehicles of opinion newspapers could be equally invaluable, but far too often they emphasise their own opinions in such a way as to suggest there can be no other. Far too often they will misrepresent a situation by omitting a simple, relevant fact. I remember reading in a highly reputable newspaper an article on certain conditions in Southern Africa which seemed to me most misleading. I wrote to the editor, who wrote back politely, saying that his paper was not interested in presenting all aspects of the situation. I recall attending two meetings in a by-election at Bournemouth in England, each sponsored by a different party. Reading the reports in a newspaper renowned for its trustworthiness, I found the audience at one meeting described as "crowded and enthusiastic" and at the other as "apathetic"; these "labels" should in truth have been reversed. I remember an article about New York by Ian Fleming in which he quoted two American lawyers stating as fact things I knew to be untrue; to my great relief, most of my rebuttal was published.

On political and social affairs, newspapers are in general unreliable whenever they present *one* point of view. It is not uncommon for the staff of a Right-wing paper to be made up substantially of Left-wingers who apparently cheerfully present situations with a Right-wing political slant; equally, there are Left-wing papers served by Right-wing staff writers. These writers, for their jobs' sake, write what they do not believe. Moreover, they write with the positive purpose of persuading their readers of their arguments, if necessary by misleading – in exactly the same way as those salesmen, advertising and publicity men. I recall the picture in a Conservative newspaper of four candidates at a British election, photographed side by side by a Left-wing photographer and used unblushingly by Left-wing editorial staff. Only one, the Socialist, was photographed so as to bring out his good points. The others were taken at deliberately unflattering angles, or with unsuitable lenses. I myself made the fourth (the A.P.A.) candidate in a by-election at Brierly Hill in 1967. Near polling day the trusted *Times* published photographs of the other three candidates with a caption which made it appear as if I were not standing. The *Daily Telegraph* also virtually ignored my existence as a candidate.*

On the one hand, then, newspapers *are* the champions of truth, and on the other the defilers of truth – and this is seldom any particular individual's fault. One editor of a great London newspaper to whom I appealed for editorial help in fighting road accidents, felt deeply about the useless slaughter. But as an editor, he said:

"John, road accidents are dead meat to us."

"Road accidents," he meant, "do not sell newspapers and so do not help sell advertising." Nor do they. But they might kill the editor, or his wife, or his child. They certainly kill thousands of newspaper readers every year.

Are newspapers really as much a part of the commercial scene as this suggests?

Undoubtedly they are the vehicles of trade, just as they are the vehicles of opinion and of news. Any one of them, ready to risk losing advertisers or readers by advocating the principles of Self-ism, would find an enormous response from the general public and in turn have an electrifying effect on trade in general.

And as we have seen, trade and commerce affects all people, vitally.

If the industries produce the goods and the trades distribute and sell them, and if everyone has done his job properly so that all the goods are fairly priced, then no one will ever feel cheated. And once the economy is strengthened – as it as-

* This chapter was written before the by-election except for these personal political references.

suredly will be, by the application of Self-ism – inevitably *all will buy more freely than ever before.*

To encourage freer buying is the purpose of trade and commerce.

The best way to achieve it, the best way to achieve all human objectives, is by following the natural law of Self-ism.

Doing good for oneself is instinctive to man and every act of good swells the sum total of goodness from which all men benefit. Doing harm (evil) to others is not instinctive to man but each harmful act takes away from the total good and so robs all men – including oneself. When this simple fact is understood it will be recognised as a natural law: when observance of this natural law has become the norm, it will be shown as the true source of human happiness.

Some may, by now, be prepared to accept this law for individuals. But is it really true of groups, and of nations? At the moment, many groups and many nations appear to be misfits in today's world.

How can they be brought into the main stream of community, civic, national and international life?

Chapter 16

NATIONALISM AND SELF-ISM

ONE of the great problems the world faces is the effect of the intensely patriotic feeling that many people have for their own country. As simple patriotism it is good, not bad. Whenever it grows into aggressive nationalism, it is wholly bad, and yet in most cases quite understandable.

A great deal of nationalistic fervour arises out of a sense of injustice, which creates an acute sense of injured pride. The great wars of 1914–1918 and 1939–1945 were aggressive in character, yet due at least in part to one nation's *need* for expansion being baulked by neighbours or near-neighbours. One might doubt Germany's need of territorial expansion in view of the thriving economy of West Germany today, but there can be little doubt that Germany's prosperity is largely due to the fact that she concentrates on the German good and is unconcerned about the harm this may do to other nations.

Once she understands and follows the law of Self-ism, Germany will become a great force for good in the world, for the German people have some outstanding qualities. This is as true of Japan, in fact of all nations with a history of military aggression. Few of these nations yet appear to have absorbed the true lessons of the great wars, that nations are interdependent in peace *as well as war*; and that only while all nations are living peacefully and prosperously, can any one nation be sure of peace and prosperity.

The full, true prosperity of all nations which can be enjoyed without fear of recession, rebellion or invasion will come only when their own people are justly treated from within and from without. Justice is the basic abstract or spiritual need of every human being. Nothing can take its place. Nothing can more despoil manhood than for a man to feel he is denied justice but dare not for any reason attempt to obtain it. Nothing is so likely to erupt into fury, and so into riots, into rebellion, into revolutions. It is more basic than freedom, for man cannot be free without it. He may have absolute freedom in his own land, but if that land is subject to another, from economic or political pressure, he is not free and one day will seek freedom, whatever the risk to himself or those whom he loves, because he knows instinctively that it is man's right – the ultimate justice.

It is equally true if there is injustice in one's nation. The clearest example of this is in the problem of Civil Rights in the United States. The Negro rightly believes himself to be the victim of injustice – political, social and economic. When a start is made in giving him justice, he becomes more acutely aware of how much has been denied him, and demands more and more, *quickly*. But amends for centuries of injustice cannot be made in a decade or two, and the white man resents any effort to attain it so quickly, particularly that white man who is himself the victim of injustice. This leads to violent disturbances, and many in the United States fear a bloodbath. It is all considered to be and is blamed on racial conflict. It is nothing of the kind. It is social conflict caused by the one thing man hates above all others: injustice.

I do not believe there is such a thing as a racial problem; given social, political and economic justice, all races will live in amity. Closely examined, all tribal, all national and all religious enmities such as that between Arab and Jew, or Hindu and Moslem, arise out of injustice in one form or another, some with roots reaching thousands of years into the past.

Injustice within one's own country is perhaps the worst to bear.

We have seen that the people even of most prosperous nations with high standards of living – such as the United States and Great Britain – are far from justly treated. We know only too well how grievous is the plight of many underdeveloped nations which, out of their smarting sense of injustice, their poverty and too often their hunger, become aggressively nationalistic.

No one, seeing their plight against the background of the world situation, can honestly blame them; yet most of us do, at some time or another. Instead of casting blame and becoming angry and vengeful, the time has come for each nation to see the vital importance of helping other nations to achieve justice, prosperity and the conditions of contentment, if it is itself to live in freedom, prosperity and peace.

There is in the world only one organisation which has the machinery with which to do this: the United Nations Organisation. It may be that tragedy will overcome UNO as it overcame the League of Nations, but it has weathered some deadly storms and may well be the ultimate advisory authority among nations. It would certainly become so, if its voice were independent enough and if it could create the conditions by which:

(i) All who worked with it were to be truly benefited thereby.
(ii) All who refused to work with it were to suffer material loss – not by punishment or forfeit, but simply because membership conferred some specific advantage and expulsion was thus to be feared.

In this way, the nations of the world would follow the law of Self-ism.

At the moment, the United Nations is a political battle-ground; the economic and cultural affairs of its member nations being largely each nation's private concern. Yet where UNO does work on economic, health, food and cultural problems, it does so with comparatively little dissension among the delegates. It could become much stronger in all of these spheres but for one major obstacle: the nationalist outlook of practically every member nation.

It is true that the United States and Great Britain give more aid to underdeveloped nations than the rest of the world put together. But much of this aid is given on a *quid pro quo* basis. America may give economic aid in return for promised political support; or in return for certain price advantages, or trading concessions; or even free of all strings except a pledge of "neutrality" towards communism. This "free" aid, given unstintingly and in great quantities, is in fact a form of Self-ism. The United States *is* doing good for herself, by protecting what she believes to be the West's need for political freedom and freedom from major war, by doing good for others.

In different ways, British aid also has strings tied to it, some visible, some invisible. Inevitably, our aid goes to those nations most likely or most ready to accept the strings; to be friendly, or, later, to do trade. This creates *blocs* of interest and influence, and in consequence generates a great deal of ill-feeling among nations otherwise well-disposed towards one another, simply because it is not just; not fair.

It is this inequality of aid which is the cause of so much resentment and aggressive nationalism, and the cause of such inequality is this unilateral system for aiding the under-developed nations. One obvious consequence is that there is a great deal of corruption in its distribution. There is a limit to the available resources, so while some nations which do not urgently need such aid receive it simply because of advantages they can offer the donor nations, others cannot receive what they desperately need.

Consequently, the development of newly-emergent nations is very uneven. If a way could be devised of enabling each to progress more or less at the same speed and in the same spheres as others, there would clearly be much less cause for jealousy, envy, bitterness, or for those outbursts of national fervour which so often disturb the peace.

If the machinery of the United Nations Organisation were used to its fullest capacity, it would be possible to distribute aid to underdeveloped countries in a much fairer and so more effective way. This would provide more aid for all nations to share. Normal trade would remain on a nation-by-nation basis, but *all* foreign aid would be distributed by the United Nations Organisation through the International Monetary Fund and the World Bank.

The method I am about to outline is, of course, calculated to serve as a stop-gap or emergency plan until the long-term problems in each category are overcome.

In these emergency programmes, priorities would have to be established. These might well be:

   (i) Food
  (ii) Health
 (iii) Family Planning
 (iv) Housing
  (v) Education

All aid given during any one period of time would be in direct relation to these priorities. If, say, one hundred units of Foreign Aid were available, then any nation suffering from famine would receive more food units than a nation which had sufficient food but needed a better health, housing or education programme. Once the famine was over, then units of a different category would be made available.

Obviously, two conditions would be necessary. First, that all the "have" or donor nations would need to give their aid in whatever form they could best afford, to a central authority which would be in charge of all distribution. Second, that the central authority would have to be absolutely trustworthy. The principle of such a plan is of course based on the law of Self-ism: *each donor nation would be moved to give not only out of compassion but even more because of the benefit it would eventually derive from giving to others.*

The recipient nations, even more significantly, would not

feel they were receiving charity but that this was part of a *quid pro quo* arrangement and was just; this would be of enormous psychological importance.

Until all nations recognised and accepted the law of Self-ism, a means would have to be found of ensuring that the donor nations did in fact receive their fair share of benefits as they became available. Such benefits would obviously be:

(i) Political – since happier nations would create less danger of war.

(ii) Indirect – in that if the donor nation did not have to spend so much on defence (war) it would have more to spare for its own peaceful purposes. And it could reduce the incidence of taxation.

(iii) Direct – in that it would trade with the recipient nation, sharing with other donor nations that nation's improved ability to buy.

All that has been said in this book about industry and commerce is directly applicable here, but principles are of little value without the policy and the incentive to carry them into effect.

I know of no better way to show what I mean in detail than to quote *verbatim* a memorandum which I prepared in March 1966. This was sent to President Johnson on April 4th, 1966. It said:

PROVIDING A BASIS FOR
PEACE IN VIETNAM

A possible solution to the basic problem of Vietnam, via the establishment of mutual good faith between the Republic of China and the United States of America

by

John Creasey

"1. It can be reasonably assumed that the conflict between the Republic of China and the United States of America, now at its most acute in Vietnam, will not cease until:

"(*a*) China is absolutely assured of the good faith of the rest of the world and so free from all fear of the military strength of the West.

"(*b*) China can establish a prosperous economy and so greatly improve the standard of living of her people.

198

"(c) The U.S.A. is absolutely assured that she is in no military danger from China or from any nation within China's sphere of influence.

"(d) The U.S.A. is absolutely assured that no democratic or neutral nation is in military or political danger from China or any nation within China's sphere of influence.

"2. Until the conflict between the U.S.A. and China *is* resolved, the civil, political and social unrest throughout the world – most acute in Africa and the Far East – clearly cannot be resolved, because:

"(a) While too much money, manpower and material resources are spent on war, too little can be made available for peaceful purposes – e.g. improving the economy and so the standard of living of underdeveloped countries sufficiently to prevent such unrest.

"(b) So long as active hostility between these two major powers exists, underdeveloped nations are likely to exploit the situation to their own economic and political advantage, thereby creating internal schisms which cause unrest, and so negating much of the economic and political aid they do receive.

"(c) The cost of the war makes it impossible for the U.S.A. to pay for those social advances which would obviate civil disturbances at home, while the nature of the war creates internal schisms – both of which factors can damage the nation internally and in the eyes of the world.

"(d) To a lesser but quite significant degree, (c) is equally applicable to China.

"Moreover, through the slowing-down of the economic expansion and so the buying-power of the underdeveloped nations, the war restricts the economy and so the prosperity of other nations in both the Communist and the Democratic *blocs*.

"3. Since all the causes of world danger, world poverty and so world hunger and unrest are so closely interwoven, it follows that:

"(a) Even if settlement is reached in one secondary arena, such as Vietnam, the conflict between the two major powers is likely simply to shift to another: experience offers small hope of major settlement following upon minor.

"(*b*) The vital need, clearly, is for a solution of the *primary* conflict between China and the U.S.A. Finding a basis for peaceful settlement in Vietnam (or any other secondary arena) would be greatly simplified when it was no longer part of a global or semi-global conflict.

"4. Plainly, no single nation or group of nations can mediate between these major powers entirely free from self-interest. The UNITED NATIONS ORGANISATION alone has the *potential* influence – and the machinery – to marshal the material resources necessary to provide both China and the U.S.A. with the assurances they need to end their conflict.

"Moreover, success in this all-important issue *would at last establish the United Nations* as the supreme authority on world problems.

"The United Nations should, therefore, without debate and by the authority vested in the Secretary-General, issue forthwith

A PROCLAMATION FOR PEACE

"This proclamation should state unequivocally:

"(i) That lasting world peace can only be built on the prosperity of all nations and that such prosperity can only be built on freedom from fear.

"(ii) That freedom from fear can only come if the Republic of China and the United States of America establish mutual good faith.

"(iii) That the U.S.A. could ensure such good faith by extending to China substantial aid for her own internal use. (Whatever the sum involved, it could hardly equal the cost to the U.S.A. of the war in Vietnam.)

"(iv) That such offer and its acceptance should be conditional upon:

the cessation of hostilities in Vietnam,

the withdrawal from North Vietnam of all Chinese military, economic and political aid – all such withdrawals to be made under the supervision of the UN.

"(v) That such an offer should also be conditional upon:

the fully-effective disarming of the Viet Cong, and

the withdrawal from it of all military and other aid,

the full assurance of a general amnesty for members of the Viet Cong, and

200

the assurance that Viet Cong supporters and sympathisers would have equal rights with other South Vietnamese in the social benefits arising from the settlement –
all such conditions to be carried out under the supervision of the UN.

"5. To compensate both North and South Vietnam for the loss of economic aid from the two major powers, and to ensure substantial benefits to them from the peace, sufficient credits should be made available to both nations by the International Monetary Fund and the World Bank – such credits to be effective from the cessation of hostilities.

"6. A WORLD ECONOMIC AID AND LOAN FUND (WEALF) should be established at the same time as (5), its purpose being to administer *all* foreign aid to the underdeveloped nations of the world, including North and South Vietnam.

"7. To avoid the political and/or economic exploitation of international differences, and to ensure that no nation gives more than it can afford and no nation receives more than its fair share, all nations now giving foreign aid (including the U.S.A., Russia and Great Britain) should continue to give such aid – but to the WEALF, not directly to any nation.

"8. The WEALF should administer such aid through a committee of delegates from the United Nations, the World Bank, the I.M.F., the U.S.A., Great Britain, Russia, China and Japan: this committee to be advised by delegates from their own countries and from *blocs* such as the European Common Market, the Cominform, the British Commonwealth, the Pan-African and the Pan-American organisations.

"9. The only conditions placed upon such aid (which would be assessed solely upon *need*) should be that the recipient nations must use the credits extended to them by the Fund in an agreed proportion with the donor nations only.

"(N.B. The implementation of Paragraphs (7), (8) and (9) would overcome the disadvantages of present *quid pro quo* arrangements and no nation would feel that it was compromising its independence by accepting aid. The opportunities for and thus the incidence of corruption would thereby be greatly diminished.)

"10. Any nation not now contributing substantially to Foreign Aid should be offered the opportunity to do so, in order to become a supplier as well as a donor nation to the recipients.

"11. The credit extended by each donor nation should be in an agreed proportion to the nation's volume of export trade.

"12. The long-term purpose of the WEALF should be to help establish the self-sufficiency and prosperity of each under-developed nation so that there shall be no unjust political, economic and social inequalities among nations – it being recognised, however, that the needs of some nations will now differ, and are likely always to differ, from one another.

"13. The amount of aid extended to any recipient nation should be based on its ability and *its proven endeavours* to help itself: such aid would be given not as a right, but as the means to achievement by self-effort of a higher national standard of living and satisfactory balance of payments.

"14. As each recipient nation becomes self-supporting economically, it should cease to qualify for aid, and when its balance of payments are sufficiently favourable, should become a supplier and donor nation.

NOTES:

"*A*. It would be difficult if not impossible for the United Nations Organisation to refuse to accept such responsibility.

"*B*. If China should reject such an offer, her motives would be gravely suspect even by those nations now well-disposed toward her: she would isolate herself from the rest of the world.

"*C*. The heavy and light industries now concentrating on the weapons of war could at last make long-term conversion to the products of peace, being wholly assured of expanding world markets – many almost untapped – which would more than compensate for trading losses in weapons."

These proposals were submitted to President Johnson with the following letter:

March 31, 1966
New Hall, Bodenham,
Salisbury, England.

"Dear Mr. President,

"In the past twenty years I have visited your country often and, as a professional writer, have travelled extensively through forty-nine states of the Union. Few Englishmen can know your country better. Certainly none has a greater affection for it, nor a warmer admiration.

"And none would more dearly love to be able to help in the grave problem over Vietnam. Perhaps none has more reason

202

to hope that he might, for my interest in politics has been life-long and my travels – and so my studies of social and political situations – have been world-wide.

"I am also encouraged to try because of the interest shown by your State Department* in my proposals – as 'A.P.A.' – over the vexed Rhodesian problem; even more, by the constant call for peace by negotiation in your personal speeches.

"I hope profoundly that these proposals *do* help in the grave task, and until I hear from you I shall keep them strictly confidential. If, however, anything prevents you from making an approach along these lines, I shall either submit them direct to my own Government and to the United Nations Organisation – or simply publish them.

"In either case, it would be without any indication that you had already been consulted.

Yours very sincerely,
(signed) JOHN CREASEY"

On May 9th the following acknowledgment came from the United States Embassy in London.

"Dear Mr. Creasey,

"Your letter of April 4 to the President has been sent to me for reply.

"I have read your memorandum and appreciate the bold scope of your vision as shown by your Proclamation for Peace.

"What you envisage is an ultimate goal for diplomacy. It is useful to look up from the crises which we face daily and to think about distant objectives.

"It took centuries to achieve the goal of creating the United Nations, it might take decades to reach a plateau in international relations where members of the United Nations would approve and implement a Proclamation of the type you outline.

"There are some drawbacks in your suggestion. As you know, President Kennedy very quietly offered wheat to Communist China at a time when it was badly needed and was turned down. It would cost the present Communist Chinese Government a great deal in pride and prestige to accept anything from the United States (see enclosed Point 7 in Secretary Rusk's recent statement of our policy on Communist China). Yet we believe their attitude will slowly change. I doubt that most nations would now agree to placing all their economic aid

* In a letter to Olga Stringfellow, dated January 28th, and signed by Michael P. E. Hoyt.

203

programs under international supervision. Yet the international aid organizations, such as the UN, which is supporting the Mekong Valley Project and the International Bank are slowly becoming more important. They need good publicity as much as they need more funds.

"I'm afraid it's a bit early for your Proclamation, but it is a worthy ideal.

Sincerely yours,
(signed) Chalmers B. Wood
First Secretary of Embassy"

On June 6th I sent copies of the proposals to Mr. U. Thant at the United Nations, and to leaders of British and Commonwealth countries. In the same month the proposals were released generally to the Press through the Newsletter *Insight*. Slowly, slowly, slowly, acknowledgements came in.

In Montreal two weeks after this letter was received, Mr. Robert McNamara, America's Defence Secretary, made a remarkable speech to the American Society of Newspaper Editors revealing an almost revolutionary change in America's attitude towards the problem of China and of co-existence with Communism. The speech clearly showed that Mr. McNamara shared the "bold scope of vision" and "worthy ideal".

But it was not, could not be, good enough. The basic attitude revealed in Mr. Wood's letter, the timid, frightened approach towards the enormous power of the weapons of peace and the totally unjustified faith shown in the weapons of war – which never bring peace or justice but only a respite in man's struggle for them – the appalling lack of faith in the good sense as well as the goodness in mankind, in people, are the causes of the present conflict. While peace on earth is considered by politicians and statesmen to be a far-off objective of starry-eyed dreamers, it will be denied us. When it is seen for what it is, a desperately urgent need within man's grasp today, it will be given us. When we can prevail upon President Johnson, Mr. Wilson, General de Gaulle – in fact, on all the political and religious leaders who pay tribute to ideals – to speak these truths to their people, then the people will demand that their leaders seek and find peace and goodwill on earth.

Chapter 17

THE YOUNG AND THE OLD

THE young, like the old, are always with us. They are beginning a life made partly for them by the old, and in that simple
fact is buried much of the tragedy of our age and civilisation.
The old so often feel that the young are not only ungrateful for,
but reject much of what has been done for them. The young
as often feel that so much of it was done badly, that they have
inherited a legacy of war, hate, poverty, corruption and fear –
all the evils in society. The old feel that the young never realise
how many things are better than they used to be.

Because of these differing points of view there is a deep chasm
between the two groups, sometimes bridged by understanding,
liking and respect; too often never bridged at all.

The middle group, those who are neither old nor young, are
harassed by different problems. They try to and often succeed
in maintaining harmony between the others but they are preoccupied in earning a living, bearing and bringing up families,
running households and businesses. They tend to be impatient
with the young for not having the common sense which can only
be acquired by the years, and exasperated with the old for losing
patience – even for needing attention; or worse, for serving no
purpose in society.

So there is a kind of three-way conflict, with the middle
group often weighed down with problems and burdens, fighting
on both fronts, disgruntled and frustrated because neither the
young nor the old seem to realise how difficult life is until they
in turn lose patience.

In general, too, the young have little patience with their
elders.

So whatever the causes, the effect of this environmental – not
instinctive – conflict is the same on each of the protagonists:
they lose patience with the other two. Very often, they have
plenty of justification at the time. The problem changes in
degree, but never in nature, from generation to generation; but
is always with us.

It may well be worth reflecting on the phrase "environmental, not instinctive, conflict". The implication is that

both young and old are victims of or at least are strongly influenced by the conditions in which they live, and from this environment, acquire certain attitudes. But to me, an "environmental" influence can be, and often is, inherited, and when it is, appears to be instinctive. Thus one's parents or grandparents can be influenced by their environment, become prejudiced by it, pass all such prejudices on, and so affect children and grandchildren by an environmental influence not directly exerted on the children. Class hatred, what we know as racial hatred, attitudes towards religion and sex, virtually every aspect of daily life, arise out of these inherited environmental influences. Man's true instinct, true nature, are buried deep beneath countless layers of such influences, some going so far back that it is not surprising that it is hard to distinguish them from instinctive reactions.

One of the best examples of this is in the conflict between the old and the young.

At the present time the young are suffering the sharpest pangs of impatience and showing it in mass demonstrations against the decisions of authority. The protests in England against nuclear weapons, in America against the war in Vietnam, in Japan against the Government – these and many others stem from a single basic cause: youth's dissatisfaction with things as they are and consequent impatience to "improve" or at least to change them. The old, for the most part, condemn what the young are doing.

The problems and the attitudes of the old and the young consequently appear to be very different. But are they?

Whether we relish the fact or not, there is in the West a growing problem created by the elderly – the parents and grandparents of youth – and this is beginning to preoccupy some countries in the East. In days gone by, the children, when married, accepted responsibility for their parents and often for their grandparents, much as they accepted responsibility for their own children. This is becoming much less common. Whether because of changing attitudes, a faster tempo of life, the lack of servants, the fact that teenage girls who used to do much of the housework now spend much of their time in study or outside the home, there is less patience with, and less tolerance of, the old folk as part of the family. Because this is so evident, the old people become even more querulous and intolerant than the years and their aches and pains might ordinarily make them, so that all the members of the family are too often kept at a stretch of nervous and emotional tension.

Various attempts to solve this problem have been made, some reasonably satisfactory for a minority, some most unsatisfactory.

The most satisfactory appear to be the new towns in America which are built for Senior Citizens only. Except for professional advisers and some craftsmen, the whole community is made up of retired people, most of them elderly and all apparently reasonably content. They have a wide range of amenities for leisure, as well as some duties, and because theirs is usually a well-integrated community they do not appear to be bored or frustrated. Life, even in age, has a purpose; each individual has an objective. There are difficulties, and, of course, misfits; but Senior Citizen townships may yet prove a significant contribution to the solution to the problem of the older generations.

Old people's homes, more common today in Great Britain and Europe, provide some facilities, including a little nursing and help with housework. Experience shows that for as long as the old person can do something for himself, part of the problem is solved. There is, nevertheless, a great deal of resentment among the old, particularly when they have just been compelled – and usually they have to be compelled – to enter a home. They feel neglected and rejected by their children, and the bitterness invoked on both sides *is* one of the saddest features of modern society.

Is there an answer?

While the present conventions hold, no.

It is the restriction on personal freedom, on the *Self*, in all phases and all ages of living which frustrates, oppresses and sometimes enrages us. It can too easily bring us to the point of revolt.

Behind *all* unrest there lies the spectre of enforced self-denial. Individuals and groups are in cages, and it is the cage one hates, because in it one is restricted, cannot express oneself, cannot do what one knows instinctively is best for oneself.

A young man, given the opportunity to play a full part in society, will "find himself" by his exertions and his endeavours; today he is far too often compelled to attempt and achieve far *less* than he can, and so to deny his own belief in his quality and his ability. So, to try to prove it, he attempts those things which he *cannot* do; to do *more* than his best – or more than he is permitted. Or else, bitter and resentful, he attacks some attitude or some bastion of society which he sees as the cause of so much that is wrong.

In fact, what is wrong is the cage into which society forces him, the cage which denies him the opportunity of carrying out responsibilities which are his by natural right, to earn his living *for his own sake*, to play his part in society *because it is the only way to make sure society plays its part by him.*

It is exactly the same with the old people. When it doesn't neglect them, society places them in that comfortable cage of inaction, of purposelessness, of uselessness to the community. They hate that cage because it puts an artificial limit on their capacity, just as a similar cage restricts the young.

Too many, far too many of us, *have* to deny ourselves even the right to carry out responsibilities we are eager to acknowledge and accept.

It is restriction on this particular aspect of personal freedom which corrodes society and creates unhappiness, even despair – a cage of restriction which society has in so many ways made deceptively attractive. Education is a cage; retirement is a cage; marriage is a cage. We need and we *want* education, retirement and marriage, but if there are bars around them, caging us in, revolt or dissatisfaction or unhappiness are absolutely inevitable. The only cage acceptable to man is an open one – like that Jonathon Griffin envisaged his traveller contriving for the tropical birds in his dark, northern forest:

"He contrived for them a room of light;
Above, below, on every side, shade.
Between shade and light no bars, no net,
The bright birds stayed."

The cage of marriage is perhaps the most alluring and at the same time the most confining, for as society and sexual morality exist today it is often impossible for either partner to break out of the cage, agonising though it might be to remain inside it, without causing anguish to the other. It is often said with fervent conviction that one must never hurt another human being – but what if the cage of marriage hurts *oneself* so much? Each individual knows for certain the depth of personal hurt, but no one can be sure whether the *other* partner will suffer *more* or *less* deeply.

It is not marriage but the way we look on marriage which makes it a cage of iron bars. Now, if it were a cage of light . . . (see Chapter 19).

One of the present conventions – or "cages" – is that man and woman become too old to work; or at least to work constructively. So retirement for them is the end of an era, of an epoch – too often, of life. There would be virtually no problem of the old if there were something *useful* for them to do, for only by making themselves useful can they feel wanted or needed; and only when they feel wanted can they believe they are being appreciated. Once they feel appreciated, the self in them blooms and is happy.

It really *is* as simple as that. Too often, the approach of age is regarded with apprehension simply because it will lead to inactivity with its inevitable sense of uselessness. The human being who feels useless to society cannot be happy in it, whether or no he can afford all the creature comforts he may need.

Youth's problem seems, on the surface, to be quite different. The old have passed their time of usefulness to others, the young are still waiting for theirs. Yet basically their problem is the same. They feel that society neither needs nor wants what they have to give it, so they are frustrated and dismayed. Curiously, attempts to solve the problem of youth follow much the same lines as attempts to help the old, for clubs and homes are the usual panacea for both groups. An old people's home and a youth club have exactly the same purpose, to create interests *for* human beings who are bored because they have no purpose and are not allowed to be themselves.

(Youth Clubs do fulfil the need of some young people – or at least, some of the needs – but many of the young derive no help at all from them. As a result, juvenile delinquency is increasing, there are "irresponsible" protest marches and even riots, civil disobedience and, in extreme cases – mostly in the Far East – rebellions. In the forefront of all the riots, the attacks on embassies, the eruptions of nationalistic fervour and outbursts of hatred against other nations, are the more militant – and often the more frustrated – youths, especially students. As often as not they are the instigators.)

Both the old and the young, then, feel they are of little or no use to society, although they are aware of this in different ways. Neither has enough to do, to think about, to plan and work for. At the same time, the middle group feels oppressed by having too much to do and so becomes exasperated with each of the others.

Some people insist that a "properly integrated family" is still the answer, but today there seems little hope of integrating the old into their own families. There seems much more chance of integrating them into communal groups. Here we have another aspect of the grouping problem which exists in industry and commerce; and the answer may well lie in another aspect of alliance.

o

As we have seen in Alliance in Industry, the first essential is for each group (men, management and money) to realise that it cannot exist without the other two. In a Communal or Society Alliance, the same is true but is generally less obvious. In the Self-ist philosophy, no one gets everything he should in industry or in politics until he gives of his best to others; the same is true of a community or nation. The old are too prone to believe that, having given of their best, society (meaning those younger than themselves) owes them a living; the young labour under the illusion that the world owes *them* a living.

Neither is true.

No one owes *anyone* a living; one way or another, all who can must earn it for themselves.

No one doubts that if the young had plenty of constructive work to do, they would be more contented. "The devil," we have been told for generations, "makes work for idle hands to do." No old adage is more true. If the idle are young, the "work" they find is too often criminal or anti-social – what else can explain the fantastically high rate of rape and drug-addiction by youths in many prosperous societies? If the idle are old, the "work" they find is usually to gossip, to interfere or meddle, to criticise and to complain.

Are the young and the old, then, misfits in society as it is today?

They were not misfits in primitive societies, simply because the young began to work much earlier and the old continued to work until they no longer could – or else died, as it were, at their posts. One of the great iniquities of the past was that young and old were given too *much* work in bad conditions and were grossly underpaid or under-rewarded. In a Self-ist society, they would have plenty to do, as much as each could manage within his own capacity, and be well rewarded.

Part-time study and part-time work, considered in an earlier chapter, would be the solution to a great many of the problems of youth and juvenile delinquency. So would greater social activity. Given both of these, today's young would have plenty of constructive work to occupy them – unceasing activity in their communities, in their hobbies and in their studies.

In England a particularly "tough" set of youths, the "ton-up" boys, became a menace to many by racing on the highways at over a hundred miles an hour. Not until a post office strike provided the challenge, was a way found to convert their energy and fearlessness into community service. Asked to run an emergency service of drugs from hospital to hospital they volunteered *en masse*. They saved countless lives – and they still do, for the organisation (the Voluntary Emergency Service) has grown very large.

This has been due simply to finding something genuinely worth while to do, and the pride and satisfaction of knowing the success or failure of that rescue scheme had actually rested on them alone, was sufficient reward. There are other examples which offer hope that in a few generations all the social problems which beset people of all ages could resolve themselves. Today the effects of them, the emotional hurt to human beings, can only be prevented if *all* communities begin to put a kind of Alliance Plan into action. All three age groups have to benefit from this; each has to gain equally from it. Doing good for the community's sake simply does not produce enough motivation; to put all his energy into the task, man needs positive personal, material satisfaction or reward.

The most obvious source of material satisfaction is to earn, to win, or otherwise to make money.

It is one thing to make a special effort for a specific charity, or for some local project such as a new swimming pool, recreation field, theatre, or clubroom – but sooner or later the zest for the project dies. Only a few enthusiasts survive; those who derive their positive pleasure or satisfaction from what has been acquired or created. Church fetes, bazaars, jumble sales and the like, all spark the same short-term enthusiasm, but this also dies in all save a dedicated few.

There have been many community efforts in the past, some of them highly successful: the Pestalozzi Villages for orphaned children, for instance, and the Amish Community in Pennsylvania, where all help one another. Oddly, this *is* a form of unrecognised Self-ism. The Amish do not insure their property, for if it is damaged by fire or flood, the neighbours supply both material and labour to restore it. The same practice holds in a number of isolated communities in divers parts of the world. As far as one can tell without sentimentalising, simple rural communities were happier in the past than the big conurbations are today; and the influence and the "thinking" and habits of the great metropolitan areas have encroached upon and so affected village and rural life.

If each individual, of whatever age, had cause or incentive to be proud of or interested in his community, each would contribute more towards it – in cash or in kind – and so there would be more for all to share, to benefit from and to enjoy.

Whether each member of a community actually made a

profit in money, or saved money by paying lower local rates and taxes, or was helped in his own material problems at home – such as gardening, decorating, building – is unimportant. What matters, is that he simply must derive some direct benefit, if his enthusiasm is to be aroused and sustained. Some would derive sufficient sense of satisfaction from seeing how they have helped in the common good. Others would be satisfied with simple pride in work well done. Others would need reward or payment in kind, perhaps in money. *All* would have to see or feel some benefit to themselves.

Projects could range from major undertakings like building an arts or recreation centre, or a theatre, to minor ones like organised baby-sitting, nursing, helping the aged with gardening, cooking or sewing. Or possibly even some simple scheme like planting flowers in public places, or keeping the surrounds of trees in the streets weeded and tidy.

There is hardly a community in any land which does not need a much more plentiful supply of neighbourliness and neighbourhood self-sufficiency, much more kindness, much more contact between persons and groups, a much greater sense of community interdependence. The source of these things, like the source of all goodness, lies in man. There will be plenty of it – and to spare – once man understands the law of Self-ism. Applied to community life, it means simply that the more he puts into the community, the more he can draw out. Given *sufficient incentive to each individual*, there need be no littered streets, dumped automobiles or neglected cemeteries: none of the hundred and one things which spoil both town and countryside. What is more, upkeep of neighbourhood amenities need not be borne wholly by the local authority.

In such community enterprises, the young and the old could work together with a common objective and mutual gain. Each group would have a purpose. Loneliness, a scourge of our age, could become a thing of the past. The frustrations that the young now feel because so much is done badly or not at all, will vanish, for young people will be doing so much by and for themselves. Working together in this way will surely teach each group to respect the special qualities of the other. The elderly will be surprised by youth's eagerness, adaptability, ingenuity and quickness in learning. The young can hardly fail to respect and even envy the wisdom and patience and skill of the old.

And these principles can be applied to *every* country.

When young men are called to "National service" it is for military purposes, training to kill, *and they are paid for it*. No one would expect them to *give* their services. Most nations have this form of national service, which is generally accepted with only nominal protest.

Examples of a form of such service adapted to peaceful purposes, are the British Voluntary Service Overseas and the American Peace Corps, but the most impressive experiment I have encountered is the one in Persia (Iran) where the Shah has applied his theory that "evolution should come from the top unless there is to be revolution from below". He instigated a flourishing and effective form of limited national service for the youth of both sexes, trained them in a variety of occupations such as farming, simple agricultural and civil engineering, building, schoolteaching and nursing, and sent them off to teach in the remote villages. There seems no good reason why this should not be adapted so that for a day a week, say, or one week in five or six, community work as a form of national service could be paid for by the community – or out of any savings made or profits which arise from the work.

A supreme example of what can be done is shown in the record of New Haven, Connecticut, U.S.A., and I can do no better than quote from *The Slumless City* by Ian M. Ball which appeared in the *Weekend Telegraph*:

"Many British towns still have slums – old tenements over-crowded with poor families. New Haven, Connecticut, had them too. How this city has used government grants – £164 for each citizen – and America's greatest architects to banish slums could be a lesson to our town-planners.

"Americans are no longer joking so heartily about President Johnson's blueprint for the Great Society, a country of blight-free communities, and recently a great deal of attention has been paid to a city that has been moving towards this goal for the past decade. New Haven, Connecticut (population 152,000) is about to realise the American dream of a slumless city.

"Ironically, it has not been a Johnsonian disciple but the man who was President Kennedy's adviser on urban affairs who has done it all – the city's mayor, Richard C. Lee, who after 12 furious years of running his own city is expected soon to pole-vault straight up to national politics.

"Mayor Lee is one of those public figures who believes politics can be fun. The progress his city has made in the past few years has been a vital factor in the passage of legislation by Congress designed to provide low-interest capital for cities eager to improve themselves.

"About a third of New Haven has been rebuilt under Mr. Lee's direction. The total cost will be 500 million dollars (£178,500,000) in public and private investment. By demonstrating that it can spend the money wisely, New Haven has obtained grants from the Federal Government averaging 458 dollars (£163. 10s.) for each resident – a far higher sum than any city in the country.

"New Haven is the home of Yale University, and as such has always been a magnet for international visitors. Today, foreign professional types also come to see the town – camera-draped Japanese, social workers from Britain, architects from Scandinavia.

"New Haven was founded in 1638, when an English merchant, Theophilus Eaton, and a clergyman, John Davenport, bought the land from friendly Indians.

"A university town in New England probably conjures up for most people a trim, picturesque community whose municipal problems are limited to undergraduate rowdiness and the occasional pantie raid in the girl's dorms.

"This was far from true of New Haven. Until the mid-1950s it had a Negro ghetto, slums inhabited by Neapolitan and Sicilian immigrants, a decaying shopping area at the heart of the city, and sooty, gloomy 19th-century factories.

"The renaissance began in the slums, known in America as Skid Row. Today what was New Haven's Skid Row is a prestige area and yet they are the same mid-19th-century buildings that 12 years ago housed the city's derelicts.

"Once before they stood in the choicest part of town. They were the town houses of the city's Wasps (White Anglo-Saxon Protestants), the Yankee businessmen and professional people. When the first wave of Italian immigration swept over New England, a few of the better-off newcomers managed to rent houses in this area. The Wasps promptly buzzed off to the suburbs. A little later the successful Italians followed them and left the area to landlords interested only in squeezing as many immigrant families as possible into the stately old terrace houses. It became New Haven's 'little Italy', and it steadily declined.

"When New Haven began to renovate the old centre of the city, its town planners and municipal architects had already seen what private money in London had achieved in saving old Victorian and Georgian terraces. Private individuals in New Haven simply weren't interested, so the Mayor and his planners wondered whether the job could be done with public funds. They decided to try with Court Street, in the worst part.

"Appropriately, one of the men behind the scheme was a descendant of Italian immigrants, Louis DeLuca, an urbane lawyer-turned-town-planner.

" 'We bought about one-third of the street,' he related to me. 'The houses we purchased were suitably spaced so that whatever we did would have an effect on the whole neighbourhood.

" 'We paid about 10,000 dollars (£3,571. 10s.) for each,' he went on, 'and completely rebuilt them inside with Federal Government money so that each house would accommodate two or three families in apartments. That cost about another 10,000 dollars per house, and we sold the houses for roughly 20,000 dollars (£7,143) to private individuals, with the stipulation that the buyers must live in them. The other apartments were rented out by the new owner. When we were finished, the houses in what had been Skid Row sold in one hour.

" 'Property values began to soar and what we hoped for did in fact happen. The people who owned the remaining two-thirds of the houses started to match what the city had done, expending on the average 6,000 dollars (£2,143) a house. The tenants formed an improvement association. Private owners transformed their houses into fine dwellings. We closed off the street to make it a play area and planted a few trees and flowers.'

"Now the street blooms with flowers and shrubbery. There are window-boxes, gaily painted front doors and shutters. It could be a fashionable street in Hampstead or Chelsea. The last old terrace house sold recently for 30,000 dollars (£10,714. 10s.), with no rehabilitation having been done.

"The successful resuscitation of a Skid Row area was exciting enough. But even more satisfactory was that the character of the area had not changed too radically. It remains very largely an Italo-American area; many of the families living in the refurbished houses once occupied sub-standard places in the same street. While successful young couples have moved in, there are still old women in black to be seen, looking as Italian peasant women have looked for centuries.

"In this and other redevelopment areas, New Haven has managed to mix up people from all social and economic levels. A housing project for low-income families is put in an otherwise middle-class area. Often public housing and privately-built blocks of luxury flats stand cheek-by-jowl.

"I asked one of the city's architects, Harris Stone, how this was accomplished. He had recently toured Britain's new towns and some LCC projects: 'We have certainly been able to mix our income groups more easily than Britain. While our *race* problem is a lot more serious than yours, your *class* problem goes far deeper. We can put up co-operative apartments for low-income families in middle-class areas and things usually work out well.'

"The planning is carried out with a sure touch. 'It's like a dream, everything is done with so much style,' said a member of New York's Community Planning Board after a tour.

"When New Haven began tackling its Negro ghetto, the Dixwell suburb, it worked out a scheme under which the tenants could buy the new flats being built through their monthly rent payments. The project was named after a local Negress, a silver-haired grandmother with the charming name of Florence Virtue, who is a deaconess in the Dixwell Congregational Church.

"The architect John Johansen was called in, and did such a good job designing low-cost flats that the area is no longer an all-Negro neighbourhood. Of those who move into the new flats, about 60% are coloured and 40% are white.

"The flats have been built as two-storey town houses, grouped irregularly around a large landscaped area. The monthly payments for these tenant-owners, central heating and hot water included, range from 91 dollars (£32. 10s.) for a one-bedroom flat to 129 dollars (£46) for a four-bedroomed place. The down-payment required is only 325 dollars (£116). By American standards they are phenomenal value.

"What New Haven wanted to avoid, and has avoided, was creating suburbs that became stigmatised as 'the place where the public housing people live'.

"New Haven's planners and lawyers scrutinise every new Federal Government programme to see how their city might take advantage of it. When the Federal Government developed recently a rent subsidy scheme, Mr. Lee flew to Washington the day the programme was signed into law to submit New Haven's application. 'We don't like to waste time,' he told me.

"We talked amidst the clatter and the dust of a construction site where two elegant skyscrapers are rising in the hub of the city. The 19-storey hotel and 16-storey office building will be in a shopping plaza with green walkways above underground parking space. A few years ago this was an area of shabby bars and run-down billiard halls, where nice New Haven folk never ventured. A British firm, Hammerson Property and Investment Trust of London, is a major partner in the 15 million dollar (£5,357,000) scheme.

"All this renovating has been accompanied by a resurgence of civic pride. Ordinary people now talk knowingly about the architectural great: 'Have you seen Ludwig Mes van der Rohe's model of the new housing development he designed?' 'You know Eero Saarinen did the high school just before he died.'

" 'You shouldn't leave town without seeing Philip Johnson's Gothic skyscraper going up on the Yale campus.' A taxi-driver may offer to turn off the meter to take an interested visitor to see a particular new project.

"Normally such public attitudes are created in America by the local information media. In New Haven, the two daily papers were both loyal to Goldwater, and did not take very kindly to any form of government involved in housing.

"Mayor Lee's belief is that people want results rather than ballyhoo. 'Our renewal programme has ceased to be an issue in local politics,' he says. 'The opposition has moved on to other things. We have probably five years to go to finish re-making our city.'

"Early in this remaking process, New Haven uncovered more social problems. With a grant of 2,500,000 dollars (£892,857 10s.) from the Ford Foundation in 1962, the city established an organisation known as Community Progress Inc. It has helped with the adjustment problems of the 5,200 families who have been relocated, developed youth employment programmes, set up nursery schools and even got into the field of legal aid. To sort out the problems of small businesses displaced by re-development projects and resettled in 'industrial parks' on the outskirts of the city, a Business Relocation Office was created, the first in the country.

"All this urban face-lifting has been carried out by intense young men from Yale or its Massachusetts rival, Harvard. As visionary planners do elsewhere, they work in overcrowded, temporary quarters in old buildings. 'We are among the few people in America working frantically to make themselves redundant,' one of them remarked. 'So why do we need a palace?' "

Only clear vision and determination are needed to make something of this kind practicable in every city, town or village in the world – and everyone who lives in the community, young or old, could make a practical contribution.

It is true that in the West there has been one great obstacle to such schemes, the opposition of organised labour. Under an

Alliance in Industry, however, there would be nothing for organised labour to fear. At one time it had good reason to watch its own interests jealously, but, given a changed outlook, organised labour, far from opposing, would be a major source of help. It might take some time for the attitude to change, and no doubt the change would be gradual. But it *would* come, once political and industrial victimisation were things of the past.

The rewards in the developing lands would at first be simple: more food, perhaps, or an occasional visit from a mobile cinema. Almost any form of gain will be worth working for, well worth the effort. But it must be a gain which is obvious, which the individual can see and understand. It must be, in effect, a case of "because you did 'A', you will receive 'B' ".

The world needs a tremendous effort from all of its people – the old, the young, the white, the coloured, the wise and the ignorant. The manpower is available, although at present much of it is being wasted. The technical knowledge and the materials are available too. All that is needed is a motive to which everyone can respond, and Self-ism can supply it, simply by demonstrating that to serve others truly *is* the best way to serve oneself.

That is the very heart of Self-ism – its doctrine based on mankind's essential interdependence, and which deems the interests of all to be best served by the active self-interest of each.

Chapter 18

THE NEW LEISURE AND THE
PURSUIT OF HAPPINESS

WHEN everyone, from employer to employed, manufacturer to distributor to retailer, doctor to nurse, banker to borrower, accountant to client, private investor to public servant – when everyone, no matter what his daily task, carries it out properly, when trade flows freely and the world is more prosperous because of the improvement in techniques and machines, man will have more leisure than he has ever had before.

He will be able to afford to use it.

He will be educated to use it.

He will be in the best possible health to use it.

He will be housed so as to use it best and most comfortably.

He may worship, play, read, take part in or enjoy the arts, study, eat, travel, do everything he wishes to do. He will at last be free.

Will he be happy?

Certainly he will be happier when he recognises the interdependence of all and the benefit to himself of carrying out all his responsibilities – inevitable as Self-ism becomes more widely practised; that is simply a matter of time. I do not believe it need take very much time; this may be wishful thinking, but that does not necessarily mean that it will be proved wrong.

We have tried to probe the material causes of human unhappiness and to show what will happen when these causes no longer exist. This has been done simply by applying the principles of Self-ism to the most widespread human problems. There can be little if any doubt that as a natural law these principles are right, but – *will* the principles work when they are applied?

A simple test is to apply them within one's own sphere of influence, even within one's family.

Is a hungry child happy? After all, hunger is the first cause of infant misery.

Is a sick child happy? Even trifles like wind and wetness cause howls of protest.

Is an ignorant child happy? Surely the urge to be able to do what an older child can do with ease is one of the first desires of a human being.

Is a poor child happy? If he has a tin can and a piece of string, he may be as happy as a rich child with an electric train, but he *has* to have something which he desires, the possession of which will satisfy him. And as he grows older and more aware, he will need better things, from toys to food and from clothes to housing.

Basically we know that a deprived child, adolescent or adult is *not* happy, and it is reasonable to believe that when he is no longer deprived, that cause of unhappiness will be gone.

But will *all* the material causes be gone? And if they go, will all the effects of them be gone, too? We have to remember that "the sins" (causes of unhappiness if ever there were) "will be visited upon the children" for three or four generations. That is a biological fact. It is also a fact that when one removes the cause of an illness, some of the effects remain. After a serious operation, for instance, the patient remains grievously ill and may be convalescent for a long time. This must surely be true of society – which, remember, is simply a word meaning "groups of people living together". One can improve the educational system so that all children are well educated, but this does not educate their parents, nor does it remedy all the things done as a result of the ignorance of their forefathers. It is possible to eradicate a cause; it is much more difficult to remove all the effects of that cause, and it will take much more time.

Until the cause *has* been eradicated, however, the effects *cannot* be removed. So the basic emotional cause of all social evils, and so of human unhappiness, has first to be found.

It is not easy to distinguish between cause and effect, and one vivid instance of this is in the attitude towards crime. In the past, many social workers and students of human nature believed that crime grew out of poverty and hunger. Put these conditions right, they said, and crime will decrease dramatically.

In certain parts of the world, particularly Great Britain, hunger and want have been conquered (except in a very small number of cases). Crime, on the other hand, has increased. The social workers are acutely disappointed, and the moralists are bitter. Neither need be. As I have shown, hunger and want

were not the *only* causes of crime; they were at most contributory
factors. Failure to recognise and to carry out one's responsibility to oneself as well as to society is a basic cause. And failure
to realise that to be constantly on the run from the police, to live
in a kind of permanent fear, never to know whether a "job"
will yield enough to live on – all of which anxieties make for
unhappiness – is simply failure to carry out one's responsibilities
to oneself.

Criminals no doubt *think* they do well. Do they, in fact?

Unquestionably some do, materially. As undeniably there
are pathological criminals who cannot be cured except by a long
course of treatment. But in the quiet of their minds and their
hearts, do criminals really believe they are doing well for themselves? Even the cleverest, even the most hardened – don't *all*
of them live under a constant shadow, the secret fear of being
caught?

I recall the man who called to see me, offering wryly as intro-
duction the fact that we earned our living from the same thing:
crime. He talked, old-lag fashion, out of the corner of his
mouth.

"I suppose you've come to tell me you want some help in
going straight," I said.

"That's right, Guv'ner," he admitted. "But don't get me
wrong. I don't *want* to go straight. I can't earn a living at it.
I've been in and out of jug for forty years, ever since I was nine.*
I'm not trained for no work, and even if I was, the bloody
coppers would nab me for something I never did. But I got to
give it up, Guv'ner. I *got* to. Want to know why?" His voice
rose in horror. "They want to put us three in a cell, the prisons
are getting so crowded."

"How much time do you spend in prison?" I asked, straight-
faced.

"'Bout six months a year," he answered. "The summer's
not so bad outside but in winter it's perishing cold, so I do a
'job' and get nicked. It's not *so* bad inside, though. You're
not so *lonely* as you are outside."

"Are you happy inside?" I asked.

"Happy?" The word obviously startled him. "I get enough
to eat, that's about all."

I do not believe many criminals *are* happy; but undoubtedly
they do learn to live under that shadow of fear of being caught,
of going to prison. Give society several generations of freedom

---

* He was sent to a Reform School for stealing clothes from a second-
hand barrow in Liverpool, he says, in the depth of winter.

from hunger, want and fear, and there will be good reason to hope that the residual use of prisons may be as schools or training centres.

The chapter "A Little Learning" deals, in passing, with communication. We already have the most remarkable means by which to communicate, but it is inescapably true that, to communicate properly, we need to know precisely how to speak so that the other man will understand us. We also need to know *what it is we want him to understand.* Obviously what we must *all* understand are the causes as well as the results (effects) of social and human problems.

There is no problem – political, social, personal, emotional or physical – which cannot be resolved *at least in part* when the cause has been discovered. But causes – like the emphasis on goodness for *its* own sake instead of for *one's* own sake – are often deeply buried in heart and mind, or are so unpalatable or unpleasant that we shy away from them. Or else they conflict with our emotional or religious beliefs, and so we reject them.

I take a simple view. Social ills persist only because we have not found the cause of them; have not faced up even to those contributory causes we have known for generations.

When we face up to Self-ism, in the form of acceptance and fulfilment of our responsibilities for the sake of our own happiness, not only shall we find happiness more often but it will also be more deeply satisfying happiness. I believe absolutely that only through Self-ism can the social and political evils of the world be conquered.

Even when these are gone, however, others will remain. And the one which will cause most unhappiness will be the relationship between man and woman. For there is no denying that the root cause of emotional dissatisfaction and unrest, emotional unhappiness, lies deep in the relationship between the sexes.

I believe that Self-ism both has and *is* the solution to the problem in this relationship; that is why I have made it a chapter in this book. Before discussing it, however, there are other aspects of happiness and of living, other contributory factors in the quest for human happiness. Most of these are to do with pleasure.

When one has done all one should – met all one's responsibilities – then one can relax with a clear conscience and enjoy oneself because one isn't letting oneself or anyone else down.

But in a world where people are drawing closer and closer to one another, the wonderful world of plenty in all things from the necessities of life to new-found knowledge, leisure will become very much more than spare time in which to relax. Using and enjoying leisure will become as integral a part of our life as carrying out the responsibilities of our work and daily round.

Moreover, there will be nothing like the scope for the public-spirited men and women who now find their deepest pleasure in working for the needy, the hungry, the homeless or the frightened. (It is hard to envisage such a world, but it *is* on the way.)

So – what shall we do with leisure? This question will need and will get varying answers from different people. Some will have no difficulty in using their free time: they will be happy to do nothing, or next to nothing – and if they are happy in that way, it is right for them. But most people will soon grow bored with nothing specific to do. For these will not even be enough to seek and find pleasure, for pleasure is an inconstant mistress; what pleases today does not necessarily please tomorrow.

So – what *will* be the uses of leisure?

The human being is seldom more restless, unhappy, dissatisfied and dangerous (to himself and, especially when in groups, to others) than when he is bored. This surely indicates that the only fully rewarding form of occupation is that which ensures mental and/or physical activity, whether in work or leisure. It must, moreover, be something which the individual desires to do, for his own sake.

If it be a game, a hobby, or some form of service to others undertaken simply to escape boredom, the boredom will return. If it is merely in order to get one's mind off one's problems, it will simply add another problem. But once the individual begins to enthuse over what he is doing, to be eager to do it for the enjoyment it gives, then it will be done well, the individual will be much happier, and such happiness *will* be contagious. If it is a form of "do-gooding", the good will be no less (in fact it will be greater) if it benefits the doer.

The most significant aspect of the new age of leisure, however, is that no one need ever again be a square peg in a round hole *all* the time. When the working week is reduced to little more than twenty hours, every man will be able to earn his living in those hours and do whatever he longs to in the rest of the week.

Many a man is both bored and miserably aware that his job keeps him in a rut. But if, while doing this job, he knows that once it is done and his income is assured he can turn to what he *wants* to do, the unhappiness and the boredom will almost certainly vanish.

Good, God and Man

For man, the essential man, is a dreamer. In youth he dreams of prowess on the fields of sport, or of love; in manhood he dreams of what he would do if only he had time. Certainly before the end of the twentieth century, he *will* have time. And the first thing he will find when he does, is that he will need to learn much more than he yet knows, or supposes, so as to do whatever he has longed to try all his life.

Since more and more is constantly discovered, to achieve his own dreams he will have more and more to learn about the arts, about science, about the world, about people. But since he will be doing what he yearns to do, the learning will be deep pleasure to him. He will know the joy of finding these is always something new left to discover, always a closed door which, when opened, will lead to new wonders of which even he had never dreamed. But the realisation of each dream will bring with it new dreams, new worlds to conquer in his mind or by his skills. Life will become for man what it is so often for a child, a golden voyage from fresh discovery to fresh discovery.

For his anxieties, his fears, his problems, will be behind him – whereas the child's lie, unsuspected, in the days ahead.

Here, then, in the full use of leisure, is the fullness of life for every human being: the very essence of self. All man needs for his material well-being, all he needs from learning, all he needs from society, will be his. He will at last have burst the bars of the cage in which the past has imprisoned him, and his world will be full of light.

. . .

This is the life for which mankind is heading. We cannot live it fully yet, but we know we already have the means to ensure our steady and certain progress towards it.

. . .

As we wait for the law of Self-ism to act like yeast in people, we have to cope with the already changing pattern of Western society. And one of the problems we must solve is how to save unlearned man from the boredom of the leisure he has begun to acquire, but which he had not yet learned to use.

This question is allied to a major aspect of social life, in all societies, even the primitive, which has not yet been broached. It is a matter on which there is a great variety of opinion and often considerable scepticism – the matter of culture and the arts.

Culture, like the arts, has often been regarded as a subject too

224

remote for ordinary mortals. In fact, it is part of the warp and weave of life; an integral theme. Just as plants are cultivated to yield the best flowers, and trees to yield the best fruit, so we humans need cultivation to seek and to find the best that is in us.

All men, all women, all children, have some secret longing, a desire to improve, to cultivate themselves.

"I shall do this," they say, or think, or pray, "when I have time, or the money." They do what they can of it with the brief time and little money they can spare from their daily work and obligations. The little they do makes them long for more; for as we have seen, in most men this is the stuff of dreams. Today, great numbers of people, even in an affluent society, seek a way out of the dull, the dreary, the frightening, the dishonest, the corrupt aspects of the world about them. The ways man has chosen have varied from holidays to hashish, but the satisfaction from all of them has been short-lived. The satisfaction from a world in which the Self is free will last for all time.

It will, of course, be a long time before the Self *is* completely free from all its problems: before, for instance, there is no sickness of any kind in the world. For many years the blind, the deaf, the dumb, the victims of all the "natural" diseases and of accidents, will be with us. So many who, in today's world, find relief in helping those in pain or the sick or infirm, will long be able to continue to give such relief.

There will be another "group" of living creatures who will need care, and we know full well how much these mean to many humans: the domestic animals. More and more people are likely to own and to love them; the dog, the horse, the cat, the budgerigar – these and all the others will play an increasingly important part in human leisure.

There will be time, at last, for the full enjoyment of the hobbies, the sports and the pastimes. Need one list them? Is there a man who likes to fish, who can hope to have all the time he wants for fishing? Or a man who likes to sail, or play golf? Or to climb mountains, or even to cycle through country lanes? The lives of a great number of men and women revolve around such interests. With increased leisure, they will be able to enjoy them more and more, so allowing the Self a greater freedom. Moreover, because they are fulfilling their own desires, they will to do whatever they have to do well.

A happy man *always* works well and happiness *is* contagious. The man who is happy in his work contributes to the general well-being not only of himself and his family but of all those who work with or near him. "Laugh, and the world laughs with you" is simple fact.

There is the strong possibility, too, that in the pursuit of his hobby, a man may discover not only his true self but through that discovery may come to recognise his true purpose in life. The man who loves the sea and takes up under-water swimming as a hobby, may well turn to marine biology as an occupation, perhaps thereby increasing not only his own knowledge but the world's. The man or woman with a predilection, and more time to spare, at last, for some specific sport, may find such a deepening interest in the health and beauty of the body that he or she will turn to the teaching of physical fitness to others.

Men will have time and opportunity for subjects they have hitherto hardly dreamed of pursuing. Even those who are fascinated by – and some certainly do have an almost mystic feeling for – the stars and the heavens, will have ample opportunity to learn all they want, and even to become completely absorbed in their studies; again, to the very possible benefit of *all* mankind. For with the age of leisure will come new observatories and planetariums, as well as new textbooks and the specialised education needed to understand the subjects better. Many men find intense satisfaction with a telescope; as their personal knowledge grows, so will the sum total of human knowledge, *and* their own interest in what they are doing. Many, if not most men, do in fact lose themselves more completely in a hobby than in their everyday work. Each will want to practise his own in the best possible way, taking great pride in it, and equal pride in his knowledge of it. Such pride in oneself, remember, is essential to man.

All the sciences will attract men who will inevitably set out to learn all they can of what is already known in such fields, and forever be seeking to discover even more. Every branch of science will have its amateur enthusiasts, its equivalent of today's "radio hams".

It is likely that the sciences will attract men more than women, but in countless spheres, in all the professions and the arts and business, the new society will create true equality for the sexes, each individual having the right – and opportunity for much of the time, at least – to do what he or she most wants and can do best. Most women will obviously want to make their homes as attractive, comfortable and homely as they can be – and these will be able to give their taste full reign. In *décor*, in fashion, or in cooking – whatever they do, will be done in the happiness born of fulfilling personal desire.

226

The New Leisure and the Pursuit of Happiness

Do-it-yourself activities, already immensely popular if only because they save so much money, will bring out the craftsman in men who as yet have had no time to attempt them. Model-making, furniture-making and the love of beauty, of mechanical perfection and of expert handiwork are all closely allied. Many a man will experience for the first time the joy of creating with his own hands objects of use or ornament in which he can take great pride.

And there are the men and women who dream of gardening, whose green fingers are always aching to plant and to reap. To one, it may be anathema, but to a host of others the growing of flowers and plants, even the perfect trimming of a hedge or a lawn gives almost sensuous pleasure.

Out of these opportunities for experiment and discovery and with the increase in education, and so of knowledge, there will be a gradual improvement in standards and in taste. "Keeping up with the Joneses" will no longer be simply a matter of obtaining more cash or more credit, it will mean acquiring equal taste, *cultivating* one's taste in whatever way holds most appeal. Eventually, the possession of wealth will be valuable only for the arts and for leisure. There will be far less need for the great charitable foundations, and when the day comes when everyone has enough, it will cease to matter that a few may have too much.

Life will no longer be a question of who gets the most, but who gets the most out of whatever he has; no longer a matter of who goes furthest but who enjoys life best.

There will be a tremendous increase in social interests and activities. Dancing, skating, card-playing, parties, home entertainments – all of these will flourish and, having more time and money devoted to them, will be enjoyed much more. Travel will increase almost beyond present conception. Some people will travel for the pleasure it gives; the rest and relaxation. Others, to visit unfamiliar places out of simple interest or curiosity – as many do now – or from specific interest in history or in archaeology, in foreign customs and traditions, in food and drink. Some will travel to learn languages, for one of the most common yearnings of mankind *is* this instinct to communicate, to make oneself comprehensible to one's fellow man.

There is endless scope; absolutely endless.

Many will experience for the first time the joys and pleasures of the simpler hobbies, such as of collecting, and begin to understand the fanaticism of collectors. Collecting doesn't stop at dolls from all countries or stamps, or match-box labels; there is

227

an endless variety of collectors' items, costing from pennies to many thousands of pounds. (I never visit a foreign land without bringing home a walking-stick. My son Martin collects hats.)

Through science and the study of space, there will be a new and fascinating hobby, and one which will perhaps enable us to see into man's future. By this I mean the study and the search for the Fourth Dimension, even begin to probe the possibilities of a Fifth. Einstein, Dunne and Locke have shown us flashes of what the Fourth might be and we can be quite sure that others will have "flashes", too – the more there are looking for answers, the more all are likely to find. That there *is* a Fourth Dimension which man equates with time is as certain as the existence of the force of gravity; we simply do not yet know where or how to find it. But as education and knowledge increase – and wisdom with them – we shall draw closer.

One of the ways will be through mysticism – in a different form, perhaps, than we are familiar with today. Not the mysticism of the occult as such, nor of religion, but more of the Yogi or the Buddhist kind – the concentration of man's mind and intellect on the unknown. For as the level of education rises, so are we likely to get more men of genius: the freaks of nature among ordinary men. Moreover, just as the study of the heavens, the universe, the constellations and the galaxies will develop, so will the attempts to penetrate the mysteries and the meaning of the planetary system; the "science" – and a surprising number believe it to be a true science – of astrology.

And finally, there are the arts.

. . .

Art, creative art, is Self-begotten and can never die. There is some appreciation of it in every human being, and everyone grows to some knowledge of it. Almost without exception, knowledge of the arts, or of one particular form of art, begets a desire for greater knowledge. In no sphere is it more true that "a little learning is the beginning of much knowledge" (see Chapter 10) than it is in the arts.

Why the arts are so much a part of man no one has yet been able to explain. Yet from the cave-man who painted in the dawn of time to the child who daubs today, from admirers of Beethoven to fans of the Beatles, from the poorest to the richest, this love of or fascination with, one form of art or another – this urge for the expression of the Self – has always existed.

It is obviously not simply an intellectual attraction, for people

228

with very ordinary intellects respond warmly to one or the other of the arts. It is as obviously not simply emotional, for many who have a fine artistic appreciation are quite objective in their appraisal. It is not wholly spiritual, for it is very materialistic in many forms. Perhaps it is a combination of all three.

Whatever the cause, art appeals to some instinctive quality in each individual human being. No two people see it in the same way; some do not even see colours the same way. Opinions of artistic merit vary fantastically, whether of paintings, scripture, music, poetry or prose. The term has an enormous range, from the finest masterpieces of rare art treasures fully appreciated only by the connoisseur, to the loudest and brassiest form of "pop art".

It encompasses literature in the form of prose or poetry – which for most can only be fully enjoyed in solitude. It encompasses the literature of drama, which needs an audience to bring out all that is best in the players and so in the play itself. It encompasses music, which can give equal pleasure to the individual in the privacy of his home and to the massed audience in the concert hall.

A painting on the wall of one's home can give deep and constant pleasure to the one or the few who see it daily. The same picture can please the changing multitude who visit a gallery or museum.

There is the art, then, of the private and the public pleasure – of the gallery and the museum, of the theatre and the cinema, of beat and of symphony. It does not greatly matter what form it takes, provided it is in no way spurious. It can be original or imitated, created or performed. It can be traditional, conventional, off-beat and "modern". It has something for us all. And as we have more time to listen or look at or to read, so we shall learn more about it and our appreciation of it will grow – as, inevitably, will its significance in our leisure.

Most art has been created for beauty's sake, or in the search for beauty or expression. Some has been born out of anguish and grief; some, out of pleasure and laughter. It has at times been created and performed under patronage, and it has at times been commercialised to a point of heresy or desecration.

There are few sheer pleasures greater than reading a book which holds one enthralled; or a poem which allows one a glimpse not only of beauty but also of the poet's soul; or studying a picture which holds one in its thrall with a kind of aching fascination. Each art form and each work of art, when utterly absorbing, makes man forget himself – and in forgetting

229

himself, find himself. The appeal is always (even when through radio and television, to millions at the same time) to the individual, to the Self in man.

Thus art – the understanding of it, the appeal of it, the love of it, the utter absorption it can offer – can only do more and more to bring out the best in man. Assuredly it will never bring out the worst.

.   .   .

Yet in another sphere where beauty, and love, and utter absorption can bring out the supremely best in man, it can also bring out the destructive worst.

I mean, of course, the relationship between the two halves of Man, between man and woman.

Chapter 19

MARRIAGE, SEX AND SELF-ISM

THE greatest mystery about human beings, surely, is that love, as the sex relationship between man and woman, can be quite the loveliest and most rewarding of all relationships, yet so often ends in emotional disaster, bitterness, even despair.

Is all of this inevitable?

In considering the question one first has to ask whether, in the West, the situation is as bad as we sometimes think. It is easy to cry "Woe! Woe!" about the high divorce rate, but even easier to overlook the great number of happy marriages. And it is easy to forget that practically all human beings know a little of love's exultant happiness and the sexual ecstasy of its consummation. So we are all quite capable of taking delight in love and sex. True, the oft-heard phrase "That honeymoon was soon over", is a cynical reminder that the joy of the honeymoon is too easily spoiled by the day-to-day problems of marriage. Yet – sometimes it does last a lifetime.

Whenever it does, either two affinities, truly "made for each other", have met and married, or each partner has been able to adjust to the needs of the other, each having learned to put the happiness of the other first – as "affinities" do instinctively.

None of this can blind us to the fact that a very high proportion of marriages are unhappy. In Great Britain, one in nine ends in divorce; in the United States, one in four. It is reasonable to assume that at least as many more are held together, in greater or lesser unhappiness, by the partners' determination to "make it work" – for the children's sake, from religious conviction, or simply for economic reasons. Even an unsatisfactory marriage can be much "cheaper" than the cost of divorce and its consequences.

There is no need to accept all of Freud's doctrines to know that sex – particularly the thwarted desire for it – *is* the cause of much frustration, of emotional and psychotic disturbance, of fear and of untold human misery. But we can hardly get rid of sex, so we might reasonably assume that either human misery is here to stay, or that in order to dispel it, we must change our present attitudes to sex and marriage. There are those other

231

causes of human misery (in the West, as we have seen, now beginning to die out) such as hunger, poverty, ignorance, bad housing, epidemic diseases, social inequality and political injustice. We have also seen that there is no evidence to show that human beings are automatically happy, even where these causes of misery have been overcome. In spite of all the improvement in the West's standard of living, both the divorce rate and crime rate continue to rise.

Self-ism is crystal clear on the subject of marriage. Unless one is happy, one cannot make one's partner happy – and if one makes one's partner unhappy, one cannot be happy oneself. Further: neither partner can be happy unless he or she carries out all justly-imposed responsibilities to the other partner. So in marriage, as in all aspects of the male and female sex relationship, it is essential to find out what one's responsibilities are. Left to itself, mankind – particularly the male – does not seem to find this easy, so Christianity and Judaism and consequently the civil law of most Western countries (but not all communities) have laid down a comprehensive list of do's and don'ts. In their simplest form, the most important of these are:

  (i) You must study (and if a man, pay for) the welfare and maintenance of your husband/wife honestly and decently throughout life.
 (ii) You must not be cruel to your partner. (Cruelty to your children is not yet grounds for divorce.)
(iii) You must remain sexually faithful to your partner throughout his/her life.
 (iv) If a man, you must maintain a matrimonial home for your wife.

If you fail in any of these, you may (at your partner's behest) be divorced. If you are the husband, you will probably have to contribute to your ex-wife's maintenance for the rest of her life – or of yours – and for your children until they are of age. If you ever wish to look for happiness in marriage again, you must maintain two homes. If you cannot afford this, then your sexual life is likely to be either promiscuous or inverted unless the woman who might bring you happiness can also bring a dowry.

A whole edifice has been erected to try to ensure that these laws are kept, and prisons are waiting for any who will not or *cannot* keep them. There are special divorce courts, a specially trained divorce judiciary, lawyers, barristers, private detectives, professional witnesses and professional co-respondents.

There are Marriage Guidance Councils with a host of ardent

workers doing an honest and often successful best to save marriages which are on the point of breaking. There are psychiatric clinics, doctors, nurses and therapists, whose sole task is to help with human problems which arise out of the sex–marriage relationship. The Roman Catholic Church flatly refuses to sanction divorce. Altogether, a great army of human beings is at work, trying to hold marriages together, and the material cost to society is incalculable. Moreover, it puts an intolerable strain on the nation's legal system, one of the more deplorable results being that persons maimed for life by accidents may have to wait two or three years before their cases can be heard.

If all these efforts ensured a truly moral or even happy society, there would be nothing to add. But they do not. We all know that the laws of marriage *will* be broken millions of times in every year; the centuries have proved there is one law which countless human beings simply cannot obey, the law which imposes the one-man–one-woman relationship of monogamy. Every citizen *should* keep and uphold the law, of course; but the Self-ist will ask himself whether *anyone* should be obliged to try to uphold a law which he knows (and the law knows) will inevitably and foreseeably be persistently broken.

Has mankind in Western society been attempting to observe a law which should never have been imposed or else has outlived the purpose for which it was made? Has this law been a major reason why human unhappiness has increased rather than decreased even where material conditions have been created for happiness? If so, has it created in man and woman a basic psychological dissatisfaction with life? And have the other social evils of the age been created, in turn, out of this dissatisfaction?

Certainly something has caused them, and we have still to discover what. As we have already seen, it is not good enough to blame "human nature"; basic human nature has been buried beneath layer upon layer of inherited environmental influences, and what we think as human nature today can be changed radically simply by removing some of the prejudices and habits created by those influences. Only the most cynical pessimist will suggest that evils are inherent in man; the fact is that they are inherent in society.

We may need reminding just what these evils are.

The first is the profusion of crime, everywhere. This is not simply an increase in crime in proportion to the growth of population and the opportunities and rewards of crime. It is

233

an increase despite the vastly improved material conditions which, according to most social theorists, should have brought about a marked decrease. Apart from crimes such as murder, robbery with violence, theft and rape, there are such evils as juvenile delinquency, juvenile sexual promiscuity, exploitation of the demand for drugs to "tranquillise" the distraught and the distressed, and the alarming growth of drug-addiction, particularly grave in some countries – the suicides, the artificially orphaned children, and, at least as bad, the baffled, unhappy children required to live with parents who can barely tolerate each other.

There are, too, as we have seen, the evils which arise out of bitter conflicts between employer and employed, the tolerated near-dishonesty in business practices, the tolerance towards cheating Customs and Income Tax, the many small but significant, even sinister, ways in which we have come to tolerate so much law-breaking provided the perpetrator can get away with it. One sample of this was the degree of undisguised public sentiment in favour of the Great Train Robbers. Another, our tolerance of behaviour on the roads, where the commonplace breaking of what seem trifling laws leads to untold grief, pain, injury and waste.

There can be little doubt that these things are symptomatic of unhappy people in an unsatisfactory society. Is that unhappiness not the probable key to the whole problem? And if it is, can it not be traced – *and eradicated*? Is it not just conceivable that these increasingly-tolerated social ills may in fact be due to widespread frustration at society's intolerance over sex and marriage? Is this at the heart of Freud's prognoses on sex? If society could free the sex-and-marriage relationship from its present tensions, and in place of widespread unhappiness create a vast reservoir of human contentment, would there *be* so many social misfits? Would there *be* so much crime, drug-addiction, alcoholism and sex perversion? Would there *be* such generally low standards of behaviour, such tolerance of obvious wrongs? Or would human beings, freed from the need for striving to be what they are not, discover that the real or "natural" bent of human nature is to try to improve, not simply to live with, society and its problems?

The fundamental importance of this possibility surely requires that we examine the facts of the marriage-and-sex malaise with a truly unprejudiced eye and with the greatest possible thoroughness. Everyone knows that the two major grounds for divorce are adultery and desertion. Everyone accepts (even though it does not show in the statistics) that in desertion there is considerable incidence of undetected, or unadmitted, adultery, so that "desertion" might well be adultery masquerading under another name. Cruelty, which accounts for most of the remaining cases, usually arises out of drunkenness, which itself greatly increases the likelihood of adultery.

Clearly, then, the great majority of broken and unhappy marriages are caused by some form of sexual dissatisfaction, frustration or maladjustment between man and wife; or else by the fact that some partners cannot or will not remain sexually faithful to one person. Then is it the sexual relationship alone – rather than unwillingness to respect, care for and be kind and considerate to one's partner – which is the cause of most of the misery? Is it simply sexual maladjustment between two people which so often leads to cruelty and desertion?

Certainly one is forced to face an ugly fact: that in the West, we have come to accept this dreadful complex of unhappiness as integral and inevitable to society.* This is surely the most shocking thing of all that civilised people are prepared to settle for conditions in daily living, in their homes, which fall drastically short of the best in themselves; to accept misery as part of life.

Must we believe that this is inevitable?

It is worth pondering the situation in most Eastern countries, where marriage is regarded so differently. There, it is extremely unlikely that the most ardent feminist who fights with suffragette ardour for a one-man–one-wife marriage law, would be shocked at or even disapprove of a husband having sexual relations with other women. The idea that this could be repugnant to a wife, or should lead to a divorce, is simply not comprehended. That a man shall sleep with more than one woman is regarded as normal and so natural that most societies and religions of the East make provision for this natural need.

A girl-child in these societies grows up familiar with the fact that men are not expected to be sexually content with one woman in marriage. When the girl becomes a woman, she is not therefore emotionally distressed whenever her husband

* There may be exceptions in certain tightly-knit religious groups and communities in which adultery is seldom practised and yet the community appears to be happy within itself. In these cases religious fears of expulsion from the group may impose the acceptance of monogamy, and other group considerations make it acceptable simply because it is inescapable. Evidence in the West shows that once the religious grip is relaxed – when a member leaves the group – there is a very strong tendency in that member to relax the habit of monogamy.

dallies sexually with another. She is not simply tolerant, either; she takes it as a matter of course. She may well be upset, however, if her husband gives more money or presents or even time to another; she expects to be fairly treated.

The Eastern emancipationists' real complaint is that many men cannot afford to keep more than one wife, and neglect the first if a second is taken; they seek an economic, not a moral revolution. It is the appallingly low standard of living in these countries which leads to crime and there is no evidence of psychological problems in anything like the degree extant in the West.

After considering these inescapable facts, it is thought-provoking to turn back to the West's religious and social objections to sex before marriage, and particularly to extra-marital sex in our monogamous society. The main objections are:

   (i) That pre-marital and extra-marital sex is morally wrong in itself.

  (ii) That if a man has taken on the responsibility of marriage, he seldom has the time and/or money to devote to the proper and necessary needs of his wife, children *and* another woman.

 (iii) That it is emotionally bad for the other partner, often creating deep emotional distress. Conventional teaching *has* made the thought of one's partner sleeping with someone other than oneself physically repugnant to most people in the West.

 (iv) That it inevitably leads to lying and deceit, which in themselves are morally wrong.

  (v) That promiscuous sex can lead to serious diseases which can be passed on to one's wife (and possibly children), thus causing great physical as well as emotional suffering.

Obviously (v) is true, and promiscuous sex is wrong – although it is a telling argument that prostitution would hardly be the oldest known profession if every man could stay faithful to one woman quite naturally. And (iv) is true as the law stands – but what if the basic cause of the lying and deceit is *not* sexual unfaithfulness, *but the law, the social attitude which demands sexual fidelity* and fosters a false belief that infidelity is wrong and repugnant?

.   .   .

I pulled myself up sharply after writing the last few para-graphs. Was I beginning to think in terms of free love? Even of the abolition of marriage?

No more, I decided on reflection, than when in pleading for an All Party Alliance I advocated the abolition of democracy as we know it. The purpose of urging a new perspective on politics was to *improve* democracy; the only conceivable purpose in urging a new perspective towards the sexual relationship between man and woman, is to *strengthen* marriage.

.   .   .

It is simple fact that it is biologically possible for a man to have sexual relations with more than one woman. So it may be emotionally and psychologically harmful, it may even be physically harmful, for a man to impose sexual faithfulness on himself so as to obey the moral law. Against this, there is the fact that it is often emotionally and psychologically harmful *to a wife* to discover that her husband is unfaithful. And all of these things cut two ways; biologically a woman certainly need not be faithful to one man, while the divorce courts as well as the prevalence of prostitution and promiscuity among young people prove that many have no desire for such fidelity.

So the question is not *could* one, but *should* one have extra-marital sexual relationships before and after marriage? A supplementary question is: should there be one law for men and another for women? The instinctive and patently the just answer to the second question is surely "no". Until men and women have the same privileges, including a generally-accepted right to decide for themselves about their own sexual behaviour, there can be no true equality between the sexes and so no true emancipation. This answer again evokes a fundamental condition of Self-ism: in an ideal society, each human being *must* be able to do whatever he thinks best for himself, while knowing that if he harms any other person in the process, he will inevitably harm himself.

The next question to consider is whether the determining factor is the act of sexual infidelity or whether it is the reaction of people to the act. "What the eye doesn't see the heart doesn't grieve over", says the old adage; but in the human relationship of marriage, the heart often grieves and is embittered by a partner's *imagined* infidelities. If a husband or wife is even imagined, for instance, to be over-attentive to another woman or man socially, there can be jealousy, scenes, bitter reproaches. So that even by imposing sexual restraint upon oneself, one cannot be sure of saving the other partner from hurt, or of avoiding quarrels and resentment.

From this, it is only a step to wondering whether the real cause of the hurt is simply in the mind – in our reactions to our attitudes which have arisen out of centuries of those inherited environmental influences, and so to what we have been taught, not what we *feel* is right. Obviously one's attitude towards it may well be influenced by the fact that the word "adultery" is in itself anathema to many women, both married and unmarried – and this in spite of Christ's injunction to those about to stone an adulteress to death: "He that is without sin among you, let him first cast a stone at her." *

Could this reproach possibly be interpreted: "He that has never known the desire for a woman other than his wife, let him cast the first stone"?

If in practice the West could look upon the sex–marriage relationship as the East does, accepting and so approving *the inevitability of pre- and/or extra-marital affairs for men* – and could also accept and approve its inevitability for women, would the divorce rate come tumbling down? If it did, then marriage – freed from the ever-present danger of destruction by divorce – would surely become a far, far happier state.

What would happen if we stopped regarding adultery as grounds for divorce? What would happen if *every* woman could regard a husband's life apart from her as his own? If his sex life, love life, emotional life as well as business life, were *his* concerns alone – provided he carried out all the other conditions of marriage: attended fully to the needs of his family, did not incur expenses and responsibilities he could not afford or carry out, was a good companion, and did not neglect his wife or home? And what would happen if a husband respected his wife's life as *her* own, provided she cared for his daily needs, looked after their children and their home, and did not waste his money?

* Since this chapter was written, two significant reports have been made on the question of sex and marriage. The first, the 1966 Lambeth Conference Committee, recommended (or at least suggested) that adultery should no longer be considered grounds for divorce. The second, *Sex and Morality*, from a Special Committee appointed by the British Council of Churches, said: "No rule can cover all the varied and complex situations in which men and women find themselves." And also: ". . . People should be helped to search for values on which they can decide for themselves the right standard of conduct." This report in particular was severely criticised by some church authorities, but was not rejected *in toto*. These are but two of the indications that hitherto inflexible attitudes towards sex and marriage are beginning to change radically.

All of this could be a form of wishful thinking, no doubt. A man's dream of a sexual Utopia, perhaps, with "equal rights for women" slipped in to quell one's conscience? But if such an attitude *could* be adopted, thus banishing all the social ills arising from emotional stresses due to sex, the conditions for something at least approaching Utopia would be at hand for all man- and woman-kind. Utopia, after all, is the perfect world – without crime, sin or unhappiness. To reach it we must find and overcome the *causes* of evil. If the fundamental cause, or even one fundamental cause, of evil is human unhappiness, and if so much human unhappiness derives from our "accepted" moral code regarding relationships between the sexes, then clearly we must challenge the alleged rightfulness of the moral code.

So perhaps the most important question arising from this discussion is: *Have we been wrong over the centuries in regarding adultery as a sin?*

Adultery, I can only repeat, has always been with us. Almost any Roman Catholic priest will absolve it as a normal weakness of the flesh. Most leaders of other Christian sects take the same view. All of *these* things lead one to ask, perhaps with a sharp sense of shock in the face of accepted beliefs: "*Is adultery a sin at all?*" And next: "Could the real sin be society's age-long endeavour to force human beings into sexual monogamy against all natural impulse?"

Is it conceivably true that when we speak of "adultery", we are in fact condemning simply one basic, instinctive factor in the behaviour-pattern of a *normal* adult? After all, no power in the world, not even a happy marriage, can prevent a man or woman from falling in love. We have to remember, also, that love usually comes without warning: literally "out of the blue". Each time it touches man or woman it is an ineffable, often a sublime experience, wholly genuine even when short-lived. But if either of the lovers is already married, it is spoiled and besmirched by the fear of being found out *and* by the fear of hurting the marriage partner. Very few people expect romantic love to last a lifetime, happy though most would be if it did. Yet romantic love, an instinctive emotion, often shows human nature at its finest. It can change mood, temper and behaviour; even the habits of a lifetime. It can strengthen the weak and turn a strong man into a giant. History shows how often it has spurred a man to heights far above his normal capacity.

If this is true – and it *is* true – does it not seem even more possible that no rule of society, even of marriage, should deny a man or woman a love which might transform a whole human

239

life – perhaps for weeks, perhaps for months, perhaps for ever? Does such denial take joy away *only* from the two people concerned? Or does it not rather lessen the corporate happiness of the whole world and so add to the sum total of the world's unhappiness? A happy person infects others with happiness, a miserable one depresses them. No one knows how far the influence of one man's mood can spread, nor what significant issues are affected by it.

Today, when two human beings are taken by storm to a peak of happiness, both are called upon to renounce that happiness if either is married to another. Or else they are forced to break up a marriage which may be securely based on liking, affection, mutual respect, loyalty, love of one's children and even a different, perhaps less passionate, love between man and woman. Is it really right that such an ineffable experience should simply open the door to divorce? On the other hand, is it either right or necessary that a husband or wife should lose all the things they have happily shared, including their sex life, simply because it is perfectly natural and often absolutely unavoidable for either to know happiness with another *as well*?

Need this mean that one is tired of the other? Is it not much more likely that there are times when – in addition to the love, affection and sexual consummation which both partners give and receive within the marriage – one partner or the other may *need* the companionship, the new outlook, even the physical love of another woman or man? And must a husband or wife constantly suppress all instinctive desire to be loved, admired, caressed, even possessed – never allowing themselves to contemplate, still less experience, the joy of a new and possibly far greater love than they have ever known, for fear of losing wife or husband, home and children?

Before these questions can be fully considered, one must ask another: how many men and how many women can lay their hands upon their hearts and swear that their lives are wholly fulfilled with their chosen marriage partner, and that they never yearn for anything more?

It may be impossible to answer that question, but there is irrefutable evidence that many more women than men find the thought of sex-relations with anyone but their chosen mate hatefully repugnant. To those who feel this way, the thought of their partners having sex-relations with anyone also is equally repugnant. Out of this attitude is born jealousy in its most acute form, and jealousy is a frighteningly powerful emotion. It

240

can, in fact, turn love to hate. It does, in fact, cause terrible human suffering. It can and does drive individuals to drink, drugs, despair and even suicide.

The question which surely must be faced, in view of these facts, is whether such jealousy is a biological and so a pathological condition about which nothing can be done, or whether it is an unnatural illness, fostered by the teachings of a misconceived morality. If it is such an illness, can it be isolated and cured and, as a social attitude, prevented?

There is irrefutable evidence that even in England and America many a marriage goes along comfortably and happily because the husband or the wife does turn a blind eye to the partner's extra-marital alliances. In France, it has long been a tradition that the wife will accept the existence of the "other woman". As we have seen, a Moslem woman is accustomed to accepting other wives with equal rights.* American women of the Mormon faith quickly accustomed themselves to sharing a man with as many as twenty other women; the custom was stopped not by those directly affected but by moralists who were thousands of miles away from the apparently contented Mormon society. All of these things surely serve to prove that it is not necessarily in the nature of *all* women to be jealous; nor is it likely to be instinctive in men.

It must be generally accepted that differences of metabolism and the biological natures will make the contemplation and acceptance of the husband's sexual relationship with another more difficult for some women than for others. There is, however, much to suggest that the root cause of jealousy is more environmental than inherent. And if it is, in fact, acquired environmentally then it can surely *be considered and treated as a sickness.*

There is nothing one can do about any sickness, emotional, nervous or physical, unless one knows the true cause of it. Emotional truths are very hard to discover and even harder to accept. But if the causes of jealousy were clearly understood, would its anguish be so great? Might it not even be touched with shame? For jealousy in a man or in a woman is simply the inner self, saying: "If my wife (or my husband) cannot be happy except with me alone, I deny him (or her) all hope of full happiness for ever."

* In France the man is less tolerant, in Moslem countries not tolerant at all, of a wife's infidelity. But these attitudes are due much more to masculine assumption of ownership fostered by the specific national conventions of each than to jealousy.

I find it impossible to believe this is really what the jealous partner means and wants to say.

There are, of course, contributory causes of jealousy, such as fear of the loss of prestige and position, of security, of companionship, the loss of one's neighbours' respect, even of one's family's. There is injured pride, too, at the thought that another woman or another man can offer something one cannot offer oneself. But the basic cause *is* the sense of loss, of losing someone whom one loves, as well as of losing possessions and comforts, family and friends.

Is it not conceivable that if adultery, instead of leading straight to divorce and so to the loss of so much in the eyes of society, were regarded as a quite normal, quite natural part of everyday living, the other partner would feel a sense of assurance rather than of fear? Would there be understanding and serenity in the knowledge that the beloved was happy – and also pride in the certainty that however far away, he or she would happily return?

The changes of attitude contemplated here might seem impossible – but who would think it really a bad thing if they come about? For what benefits to society as a whole might not follow if married couples, freed from their worst and most secret fears, were happier not only in marriage, but as individuals leading a fuller, more rounded life?

Obviously many lovers, today compelled to live under a sense of guilt and shame no matter how bold a face they put on it, would feel they had a *right* to happiness if freed from all social censure. Clearly, such people would be much happier. So would many a man or woman prevented from marrying by the simple lack of possible partners of the relevant age-group, caused by the fluctuating birth-rate figures for the sexes – a problem that has always been and is likely always to be with us.

These would no longer feel robbed, by society as well as nature, of the raptures and some of the comfort of loving and being loved. If they found love, it would be theirs by right. The professional woman who much prefers a career to home-making, and perhaps as a consequence does as great a service to society, could form a romantic friendship which might last a lifetime yet never threaten to break another's marriage, nor threaten her *with* marriage.

There would obviously be far less fear of broken homes, and consequently fewer unhappy children. And since it is inherent in man to hunger for the forbidden fruit, there would certainly be less risk that he would seek sexual adventure for lust's sake instead of for love's. It might conceivably be the beginning of the end of prostitution as well as of divorce; certainly there appears to be no other way to reduce the incidence of either. Of course, there would still *be* divorces, but only those inevitable because two people found it utterly impossible to live together. Such incompatibility of temperament, regarded by our society as "insufficient grounds", is surely the one and only genuine "moral" ground for divorce.

There would remain the greedy, the spiteful and the malicious of both sexes; the possessive and the all-demanding spouse, the truly cruel and the perverted. But if both husband and wife *were* freed from all sense of resentment and frustration at their married lot, were rid of the gnawing, corrosive doubts about what might have been had they not been "trapped" – as so many *feel* themselves to be – surely spitefulness and malice, cruelty and perversion would themselves begin to wither, starved of the conflict on which they thrive.

I believe there would be many changes for the good of man and for the good of woman. For more and more men and women would come to see and understand the simple truth – that to be happy, one must allow happiness to others; while to deny happiness to others is inevitably to deny a measure to oneself.

. . .

There remains but one relationship to discuss; that between man and his "Maker". Can Self-ism seriously hope to reconcile all the religious differences, be acceptable to the true believer, the sceptic and even to those who scoff?

I believe it can do even these things.

Chapter 20

THE WORSHIP OF GOD – AND SELF-ISM

HARD though one may try, it is difficult to see conflict between Self-ism and any religion; indeed, I believe it to be complementary to each. It is probably inevitable that certain religious leaders will oppose it on grounds of dogma, particularly in the early stages, but I find it hard to believe that any can be actively hostile to its truth. So deep in our emotional and religious life is the concept of good for *its* own sake, however, that at first sight giving priority to good for *one's* own sake might well be regarded as heresy; might be seen as an intensification of selfishness, an attempt to justify the attitude of: "I'm all right, Jack, never mind you." Whereas in fact it says: "I can't be all right, Jack – *unless* you are too."

Some religious leaders and some ascetics may oppose Self-ism because they consider self-denial and personal sacrifice to be essential parts of goodness. No doubt they can be, but I have never been able to find proof that they *must* be.

Obviously some forms of goodness do entail self-denial and personal sacrifice, just as some religions entail asceticism, self-abnegation and even flagellation, but it is self-evident that in order to be good one does not *have* to make sacrifices. A millionaire's gift of a fortune does infinitely more good than a pauper's gift of a penny to the recipient – *but not to the giver.* Millionaire and pauper may derive the same satisfaction for themselves, although probably the pauper's will be the greater, the mite being so much more to the poor widow than the fortune to the rich man.

There are surely no religions, although there may be some sects, which deny the basic human fact that self-interest is the natural and wholly justifiable concern of every individual. Wisely applied, self-interest equips a man to be true to his religious as well as to his social and business obligations. A man who keeps himself in good physical condition is obviously better able to look after himself, and others when necessary, than one who goes soft. Lack of self-interest makes a man morally,

244

mentally and spiritually flabby; and so inevitably his religious conviction becomes flabby, too.

These elementary facts are well enough known, but their true significance is too seldom realised. Is there any doubt that a Jew who practises Self-ism will not only be a better citizen and neighbour but also a better Jew? Surely there is not — and the same is true of Christians, Hindus, Moslems, Buddhists, Shintoists, Taoists, Sikhs, Mormons, Seventh-Day Adventists, Anglicans, Roman Catholics, Quakers, Presbyterians, Methodists and Baptists — the members of all religious groups, divisions and schisms. (It will also make better Humanists, Agnostics, Pagans and Atheists!)

It is also obvious that if an Englishman lives by Self-ism he will be a better Englishman, a Russian a better Russian, an Egyptian a better Egyptian. There are over 150 countries in the world; if they all accept and practise Self-ism among their peoples, can they fail to become better nations? There is no limit to improvement in living standards and in social behaviour, any more than there is a limit to goodness. So Negro and Aryan, Oriental and Caucasian, all will benefit.

I became convinced that there must be a benevolent natural law which could be obeyed by all peoples of all races and all religions, when I realised the significance of the fact that the cause of virtually all social evils was buried in the differences among peoples and nations — differences not only of opinion and outlook but of prosperity, natural advantages, culture, development. All of these lead to greed, jealousy, envy — and eventually to conflict.

If afflictions caused by evil had a common cause, I reasoned, *there must be a common cure.*

To say that "good" was the cure was too glib, and as far as we have known it it had demonstrably failed. The more I pondered, the more I became convinced that the reason for man's almost passionate desire for independence arose out of his sense of being either the victim of injustice or the threatened victim of aggression. Men and nations have always, it seemed to me, cried out for independence from one another; and the more independence they seemed to get the more evident it became that they were in fact all interdependent. Certainly this was true economically. Why should it not be true morally?

It seemed unarguable that goodness must exist in inexhaustible supply — a kind of moral natural gas, simply waiting to be tapped. So, why could we not tap it? We knew where it was — deep in man himself. Why couldn't we get more of it out?

Obviously, we were trying the wrong methods, using the wrong key.

We were using the key of "good for its own" sake and it simply wasn't turning the lock in enough doors.

Here was the clue to the identity of the natural law and although the actual summation of the belief has been written and rewritten time and time again, the basic concept has never altered.

Doing good for oneself is instinctive to man and every act of good swells the sum total of goodness from which all men benefit. Doing harm (evil) to others is not instinctive to man but each harmful act takes away from the total good and so robs all men – including oneself. When this simple fact is understood it will be recognised as a natural law: when observance of this natural law has become the norm, it will be shown as the true source of human happiness.

Such a law, or set of principles, or doctrine, had to be examined searchingly in the light of all existing moral as well as economic laws. It had to be one which, once it was both crystal clear in concept and lucidly defined, would be acceptable to all priests, parsons and prelates – and not only acceptable but welcomed, so that they could without hindrance develop, preach and practise it.

It had to be a code of behaviour by which to live: one which would bring out the spiritual, moral, material and physical best in man without conflicting with any existing dogma or belief.

I believe that the natural law of Self-ism will meet all such demands.

No doubt its doctrine will be charged by some with being a materialistic philosophy, but it is infinitely more than that. Alone of the non-religious philosophies it accepts religion. It does not agree with those philosophies which have condemned religion as being old-fashioned, unrealistic, incapable of proof, a soporific invented by those in political ascendancy to stultify those whose daily life is drab and hopeless.

Self-ism believes that the truth – stated earlier in this book and shown by virtually all available evidence – is that no single religion is satisfying and acceptable to all people, simply because all individuals and all races are so different. Each religion satisfies the spiritual needs of *some* people, and it would be positively evil, the negation of Self-ism, to deny any human being the source of his spiritual balm.

In recent years, there has been an increasing desire on the part of most Christian sects for closer understanding, which is why the Christian ecumenical movement has gained such

The Worship of God – and Self-ism

strength. This clearly reflects the growing realisation among all who believe in God that their particular religion is only one way to Him, and that others have *their* particular way, which they happen to prefer. The ecumenical mood reflects the growing realisation of the need for a philosophy or way of life which is common, natural and available to men of all religions and – it surely follows – of no religion.

The doctrine of Self-ism *is* exactly that. It *can* be accepted by everyone, everywhere, without cutting across any belief in God – or any disbelief.

Any philosophy or movement which threatens the existence of any religion is guilty of a grave and fundamental crime. One may happen not to believe in God; one may be convinced, by argument and logic, that there is no Creator; but one man can no more prove His non-existence than another can prove His existence. An agnostic may doubt and an atheist reject Him; in any free society, each has this right. Freedom to form one's own opinion, to express it and try to convert others to it, peacefully, is a basic human right and need. But agnostic and atheist must also grant to believers in God, be they Christian or Shintoist, Jew or Hindu or any other, equal freedom to doubt and to reject *their* scepticism.

There is much more to religion than the principle of man's freedom to worship or not to worship. There is the part which all religions play in the community in which they thrive or have thrived. It would be wicked to attempt to despoil or destroy the help and the strength which so many Christians obtain from their religion, equally wicked to attempt to spoil or besmear the beauty of the great religious festivals and traditions which combine to give joy, comfort and peace of mind to so many human beings. On occasions the truly religious man, the true believer, almost certainly draws close to happiness, which means to him that he is close to both good and God.

Shall anyone be denied such happiness? Even by those who believe him to be putting his faith in a non-existent Creator?

How can agnostic or humanist question the high purpose and the deep and abiding significance to believer and unbeliever alike, of the great pilgrimages such as to Mecca, to Benares, to Rome and to Lourdes? How can there be any doubt that each pilgrimage comforts, assures, inspires and gives spiritual solace to millions? How can one stand aside and regard them simply as a physical activity of others, believing oneself untouched by them? How does any man *know* he will not be indirectly affected by any religious rite or dogma?

247

Countless millions of non-Christians are directly affected by the material or the commercial aspect of Christmas, for instance, and benefit from other holidays which are in fact religious holy-days. The indirect benefit to all, both spiritually or materially, is incalculable; very few if any are untouched.

For that matter, how can any cynic be sure that the daily behaviour of a man who worships a different God, does not have a positive affect on himself? It was a practising Hindu who first cross-bred tangerine and orange to produce santra, one of the most luscious fruits of the earth. It was Livingstone, driven by his concept of God, who made the early discoveries in Africa and told the world about the Victoria Falls. Many religious laws and customs are dietetic or hygienic in origin. No one can possibly know the full effect of what he or any man does, whether there is a religious motivation or not, but with Self-ism every man will come to see what is so obviously true, that just as his actions inevitably affect others, so the actions of others inevitably affect him.

Can one doubt the enormous influence of the Roman Catholic church on millions of non-Catholics? And can one envisage the utter disaster which would follow if any attempt were made to destroy Mohammedanism or Hinduism? It is so unthinkable that no one would dream of trying. Russian Communism has succeeded in withering but not in killing Christianity within its own borders, but the one inescapable way to war would be for Russia (or for China) to attempt to destroy world Christendom.

Can one conceive of the *destruction* of a religion? Surely it would not die any more than Judaism died at Nazi hands. Some civilisations have died, but their religions have never *wholly* died with them; they can be traced in a succeeding re-ligion, just as the religion of the Incas and the Aztecs are evident in many of the regional practices in Roman Catholicism in South American countries today.

And just as no one should (even if they could) destroy a religion, so no one should attempt to destroy or weaken the faith of any individual in his religion. A truly religious man may be satisfied with worshipping by himself or with his family; another may need to try to convert his neighbours; no one must deny him the right to try, nor the neighbour his right to reject.

Only the individual himself can decide whether to believe or not to believe. Only the self can rule the self, a statement which is clearly supported by the Christian concept of free-will.

The Worship of God – and Self-ism

Only the individual himself can make himself *do* anything at all; no matter what pressure may be brought to bear on him, he *has* to speak, think and act for himself.

This is the essence of Self-ism.

Once the natural law of Self-ism has been recognised and applied, the world's religious problems will surely begin to resolve themselves. And when they do, the religions themselves will become infinitely stronger.

.   .   .

Quite distinct from what has gone before in this chapter, there is another religious aspect of Self-ism, an aspect which is largely social.

One of the main purposes of religion is to reform the individual; to teach a man how to behave not only for the good of his soul in the hereafter but also for his life in this world and in society. Crime has never flourished so much nor been so well-rewarded, and criminals have never been more active than they are today. No one would dare pretend that society's problems of crime and juvenile delinquency will be easy to overcome. And only a fool could believe that *all* men in today's world are going to be persuaded to look for goodness – too many are amoral and will cheat, steal, trick and lie for what they conceive to be their own advantage.

However, the vast majority of criminals lead reasonably good lives with their families. Comparatively few are deliberately cruel. A criminal is, in fact, an ordinary member of the human race, having all the human needs, who breaks certain rules of society. As the world is constituted today, it is often of material advantage to a man to break these rules, so no one is going to reform criminals by threats of spiritual damnation. I once talked to a confirmed criminal who said with deep conviction:

"I'd rather back myself to get to heaven than the bloody copper who pinched me, or the beak who sent me down."

And I have never heard it said that absolution should be denied to a criminal; many instinctively crave for it although few may believe in the effectiveness of repentance. They do get some solace from the act of confessing. Apart from the professional criminal, moreover, the world has more than its fair share of opportunists who seldom think beyond their own immediate and selfish interests, even though they keep to the letter of law, or break it only when they feel sure they won't be caught.

At times, even the most selfish men are unselfish with their

249

own children, their wives, their loved ones. There can hardly be a man living who hasn't a soft spot for someone, a good side to his nature. True, a criminal may be the last to accept and live by the law of Self-ism. But he *will* come to live by them – once all the rest of his community does. This will not be simply because he will be shamed into it but because the people about him will obviously be so much happier than he, and life so much pleasanter for them. As Self-ism is applied to industry, commerce and all spheres of social and community activity, life *will* become so satisfying to everyone that none will need to keep on looking for the main chance. They will benefit so much by a world in which the vast majority carries out its responsibilities that a "life of crime" will die a natural death.

Evil only thrives on evil; it *cannot* in the long term overcome good.

Goodness, as we know, is never in short supply, whereas most people dislike and resent and oppose evil. No one can quell all the good in them all the time, whereas most people do quell the evil *once they recognise it.*

Self-ism will absorb the amoral, because a Self-ist morality will give every man what he knows is best for him. Stanley Holloway, as the ribald old coalman in *My Fair Lady*, sings:

> "They're always chucking goodness at you . . .
> But with a little bit of luck
> A man can duck."

No man can ever duck from himself. No one ever need duck from himself. No religious man need "duck" from Self-ism.

We live – we know that we live – in a world of unparalleled and fabulous promise. Science has already revealed to us more than we can fully understand. The cup of wonder in this space age truly runs over. In the air and through the air, fresh marvels dawn. We possess unprecedented means of travel, exploration, communication – of the means to meet our needs and enjoy our life and use our leisure.

There can be no shadow of doubt that materially, mankind is on the threshold of its greatest age.

And spiritually?

Is there anywhere a man of God who can lay his hand upon his heart and swear he believes that Man is today on the threshold of the greatest spiritual age ever known? Such a claim is very unlikely indeed. Most men of God are fearful that the Moloch of materialism will overthrow the forces of good, or that the Devil of destruction will banish Man from the earth.

The Worship of God – and Self-ism

Hope is instinctive and few can believe the worst will happen – but do many see how it can be avoided?

I believe Self-ism will avoid it, simply because Self-ism can show man the infinite store of goodness within himself.

. . .

Perhaps a personal statement of belief should come here, so that none can misunderstand my own convictions.

I have no difficulty at all in believing in a Creator, but even in childhood I had the utmost difficulty in believing in a *good* Creator. The older I grew, the firmer became my reservations. I began to think, perhaps not very logically or rationally and certainly not very originally, but some factors became self-evident, although their simplicity made it easy to overlook them. A good God might send the rain, but would He really send floods with it? He might give us the good earth, but would He really create the conditions of famine? He might build the wonders of the universe, but it was hardly good to add an earthquake belt. To me, it seemed downright wicked.

The idea that it was the Devil who did all the bad things failed to satisfy me, because this good God of my fathers was all-powerful and could obviously control the Devil if he wished. The argument of free will had a convincing ring at first, but gradually that conviction died away; if the Almighty were as good as my religious mentors claimed, why give us the free will to be bad? To be Hitlers?

It made no sense at all to me, even in adolescence. Yet I knew there must be some explanation of goodness in mankind; there must be a source of the inspiration of men who believed in God. Straightforward humanism was not enough, because too many people found no help in it in times of temptation and of stress. I listened to those who said that if there were a God, then He had given us a will, a brain, capacities for love, hate, compassion, sacrifice, entirely God-like power over animals – enough to wreak on them pain, terror, suffering *or* the love and affection which believers so often expect God to give to them.

This did not satisfy me.

I searched for a simple answer – and quite suddenly came upon one. Obviously I cannot be *sure* that it is right, but certainly it has satisfied me far more than orthodox Christianity ever did. In fact, it enables me to accept everything in Christianity *except* the existence of a wholly good God. It allows for the existence of a Creator who is neither good nor bad but neutral – a Creator of everything who has no moral or ethical

251

influence, nor even awareness. Just as the evolution of the human body and brain was conditioned by physical needs, so it seems to me that morality and ethics were part of the same process of evolution.

Goodness has evolved within man himself.

Now if this goodness itself is God – if *Good* is God – then He has been created out of the great human fount of goodness, out of the kindliness, the generosity, the beneficence of all kinds of people of all religions and of all ages. These qualities have been thrust upon man by the conditions of life. The primitive with his worship of the sun, the Greeks and Romans with their mythical deities, the fanatical Moslem, the philosophic Buddhist, the Hindu with his religious complacency – all have goodness in themselves and sometimes show it, but seldom to one another. They are in conflict. But they can all become rational, reasonable neighbours in a religious concept which accepts *either* that goodness is God, *or* that God is goodness, which accepts that good and God, like idealism and realism, are identical twins. It is the worship of God-the-Creator which makes believers draw the sword, not the worship of Good-or-God – for men see peace as the ultimate good.

Against such simple philosophy, the enormous significance and the supreme importance of goodness becomes vividly apparent. All men can worship Good, whether or not they worship it through God. And good *generates itself*. The good done by one generation adds to and so strengthens the goodness of all previous generations.

Every single act of goodness becomes part of the whole, each single act, part of the Creation and the existence of God. For it is demonstrably true that every human being has some good in him, and if Good is God, then every human being has something of God in him. I could gladly, joyfully, excitedly acclaim Christ as the son of *Good*. Is there anyone, even among the millions who deny God, who could not?

Chapter 21

THE ESSENCE OF SELF

I BELIEVE Self-ism to be the law which men throughout the ages have been seeking. We owe its discovery to all of history's idealists who have striven to right wrongs; to all men who have sought the nature of Good, knowing that it was hidden in man, to all prophets who have told of the Voice of God but not known how to make us listen.

I believe Self-ism to be inherent in the creed of Christ and the creed of Mohammed; in the creed of Buddha and the creed of Confucius; to be inherent in the creed of all religions and so the source of the spiritual power which makes all men work together for good.

I believe Self-ism will bring to us the proud assurance that there is no inherent conflict between man and man; between religion and religion; between nation and nation; there is only the conflict between good and evil.

I believe Self-ism to be the power for good in that age-old conflict, because good is the very essence of Self.

I believe Self-ism to be the law by which all the untapped sources of good in man will be released until its benison spreads over all the earth and the day dawns when there will be no want; no fear; neither hunger nor thirst; when all ignorance will be driven out of the minds of men and replaced by knowledge, when all cruelty and hate and folly will have withered and all men will be wise.

There will be no evil when that day comes; and there will be no night.